WITHDRAWN
UTSA LIBRARIES

The
Royal Navy
and the
Sino-Japanese
Incident

The Royal Navy and the Sino-Japanese Incident
1937-41
Martin H. Brice

LONDON
IAN ALLAN

First published 1973

ISBN 0 7110 0402 1

Dedicated to those British ships and servicemen involved in a shooting war for over two years before the Second World War officially began.

All rights reserved. No part of this book may be reproduced or transmitted in any form or by any means, electronic or mechanical, including photocopying, recording or by any information storage and retrieval system, without permission from the Publisher in writing.

© Martin H. Brice, 1973

Published by Ian Allan Ltd, Shepperton, Surrey, and printed in the United Kingdom by Cox & Wyman Ltd., London, Fakenham and Reading

Contents

Acknowledgements 7

Author's Note 8

Foreword 9

1 The War 11
2 The Beginning 31
3 The Defence of Shanghai 36
4 The *Ladybird* and *Panay* Incidents 56
5 The Shantung Campaign 66
6 The Blockade 74
7 The Capture of Canton and the Defence of Hankow 92
8 The Pearl River Blockade 101
9 The Deterrent 106
10 The Hopeful Year 111
11 The Wuhu Beer Incident 122
12 The Blockade of Tientsin 127
13 The Hitler War 135
14 The Deterrent is Despatched 148
15 The End of an Era 152

Appendices

I The Royal Navy on the China Station, July 1937 – August 1939 153

II The Royal Navy on the China Station, September 1939 **155**

III The Royal Navy on the China Station, October 1939 – November 1941 **157**

IV The Warships of the China Station, December 1941, and Their Immediate Fate **160**

Index **164**

Acknowledgements

Little information is available about this aspect of the Royal Navy's history. I am therefore grateful to the following people who supplied me with details of their experiences or otherwise gave me assistance, advice and encouragement. Any misinterpretation of their facts is mine.
Lieutenant-Commander S. J. Barrow, Captain H. T. T. Bayliss, Vice-Admiral Sir Patrick Bayly, Rear-Admiral F. B. P. Brayne-Nicholls, H. G. C. Brice, Esq., Lieutenant-Commander B. L. Butcher, C. J. M. Carter, Esq., Commander C. B. S. Clitherow, Commander W. Donald, Lieutenant J. Evans, W. H. Hole, Esq., Mrs H. Inglis, Lieutenant-Commander P. K. Kemp, Sir Hughe Knatchbull-Hugessen, J. W. Knell, Esq., H. G. Lowder, Esq., Lieutenant-Commander J. A. McClure, Captain D. G. F. W. Macintyre, V. Oliver, Esq., Commander D. J. Pack-Beresford, V. B. Palmer, Esq., Major J. Perrins, W. E. Purkiss, Esq., Lieutenant R. Record, H. E. J. Regler, Esq., Commander H. F. Robertson-Aikman, Commander H. R. Rycroft, Lieutenant-Commander N. Scott-Elliot, J. A. Smith, Esq., W. A. D. Smith, Esq., Commander J. N. N. Synnott, Lieutenant D. W. Toms, Captain H. S. Upperton, Rear-Admiral C. K. T. Wheen, F. C. Wigby, Esq. and The Yangtse Gunboatmen's Association.

Photographic acknowledgements will be found under the relevant captions.

Author's Note

The English spelling of Chinese and Japanese names has proved extremely difficult as there are a great number of variations, most being officially recognized at some time. Whilst every effort has been made to avoid inconsistency and inaccuracy, I have selected the spelling which seemed most common in 1937 and most expedient at the time of writing.

There is also some debate regarding the correct way of expressing a ship's name; 'HMS *Capetown*', 'the *Capetown*' or just '*Capetown*'. I have preferred the last, partly because it gives the ship more personality and partly because it is used in naval despatches.

Foreword

by Vice-Admiral Sir Patrick Bayly, KBE, CB, DSC

When, early in 1938, as a junior officer I asked, more in hope than in expectation, to be sent to 'a small ship abroad', I did not anticipate finding myself in a China river gunboat, soon to be surrounded by an undeclared but none the less nasty and lethal war. Having spent some leave in Czechoslovakia, war in Europe seemed all too possible, but to be projected into an active war in an obscure corner of China was certainly a surprise. What was even more of a surprise was to observe at first hand the pusillanimous attitude of the Western governments towards the Japanese attack on China. The British Government's failure to take an effective lead or stand of any sort, diplomatic, military or commercial, was a disappointment, to put it mildly, since, of all the foreigners, the British had the greatest interests and the most influence in China and knew from their numerous and widespread officials and merchants exactly what was going on. Abject appeasement in every confrontation, large and small, made entirely reasonable Japan's contemptuous assessment of the Western powers as paper tigers and helped to lead them towards their gigantic miscalculation of December 1941.

Meanwhile one saw the bombing and burning of undefended and densely populated areas, the blockades, the daily passage of headless corpses drifting past on the tide, and the casual shootings, bayonetings and clubbings of defenceless and inoffensive people, while Europe was still at peace. And there was also the self-inflicted misery of the Chinese scorched-earth policy, accompanied as it was by widespread epidemics.

In all this we were bystanders and matters reached the pitch where we were even told not to take photographs from our own ships for fear of offending the Japanese. But we observed and reported and, to those who had been in China, the brutality of the Japanese armies in 1941 and after was no surprise.

Witnesses might be sickened by all this, but all was not horror, and peacetime activities and amusements continued with undiminished zest whenever possible, particularly in Hong Kong. However the frustration felt by those in high diplomatic, military and commercial positions can only be imagined as they were endlessly instructed to give in, to apologize, to withdraw, to avoid taking sides.

Martin Brice has done a service in recording the Royal Navy's involvement in this almost-forgotten collapse of will against an aggressor, during the few years which saw the end of a century of Western power within China. Such power might be thought incongruous today, a generation later, but in their time the Western officials, merchants, missionaries and gunboats did much for China that was good and essential in turning her towards industrial revolution and the realities of the twentieth century.

We can now look back on the details of this incident so minor compared to what followed in Europe and the Far East, with detachment. But although our years of privilege in China had probably served their turn, the forcible elimination of all Western institutions by the Japanese imperial war machine would have resulted in an infinitely more humiliating and barbarous future for China, had not the Japanese themselves been overthrown by the Western alliance within a few years. However, in considering this turbulent era, we might echo the Chinese sage who when asked for his estimate of the effect of the French Revolution on history is supposed to have said: 'Perhaps we are still too close to it to know.'

1
The War

The Second World War began in the Far East on the night of July 7th/8th, 1937. Shots were fired from the Yungting Ho river bank at a company of the 3rd Battalion, 1st Japanese Infantry Regiment exercising near the Marco Polo Bridge at Loukiachao outside Peking. Other companies were soon involved and firing became general, both sides suffering casualties.

The Japanese authorities alleged that the Chinese were responsible for this unprovoked attack. Certainly a Chinese sentry may have felt that the Japanese manœuvres were a little too realistic and opened fire in self-defence. The official Chinese account described how the Japanese tried to force their way into Loukiachao to search for a deserter and were rightly resisted by the Chinese gendarmerie. Whatever the reason, there were further exchanges of fire every night and the Japanese immediately began to reinforce their garrison in northern China. The local commander decided that the only way to protect Japanese nationals and his own lines of communication was to drive Chinese forces from the area. Tokyo approved this decision and full-scale operations were mounted against the Chinese Twenty-Ninth Army on July 28th. Twenty-four hours later the Japanese were in control of north-east Hopeh, including Peking itself.

So far the fighting had been confined to the north and the Japanese Government declared that it was doing everything possible to prevent hostilities spreading to other parts of China. Chiang Kai-Shek, however, did not agree that the matter was a mere local disturbance and refused to compromise. On August 6th the evacuation of all Japanese nationals began from towns along the Yangtse and elsewhere in central China. Once they had picked up their civilians, Japanese warships were ordered to concentrate at Shanghai and it was here that the next incident took place.

There had already been a near-crisis at Shanghai on July 24th when a Japanese sailor was reported missing. It was suggested that he had been kidnapped by Chinese criminals and it was feared that the Japanese would seize this excuse for unleashing war on the Chinese around Shanghai. However, punitive measures were forestalled by the arrest of the errant sailor himself at Chinkiang three days later. There had been no Chinese plot. He had simply deserted.

On the evening of Monday, August 9th, Sub-Lieutenant Oyama, commanding the 1st Company, Shanghai Special Naval Landing Force, was shot near

Hungjao Airfield, along with his driver, Seaman 1st Class Saito. Chinese sentries of the Peace Preservation Corps – one of their number was also killed – claimed that the Japanese had tried to force their way into a restricted area. The Japanese authorities denied that their men had tried to enter the airfield and said that the Chinese gendarmerie had shot one of their own men to cover up wilful murder. The Shanghai Municipal Police, accompanied by Japanese officials, proceeded to the scene of the crime in Monument Road on the south-eastern outskirts of Shanghai. Before any action could be taken on the results of their investigation, units of the Japanese Third Fleet arrived to join the warships already at Shanghai. Besides Vice-Admiral Hasegawa's flagship *Idzumo*, there were about twenty light cruisers and destroyers. Other ships, including battleships, carriers and heavy cruisers, remained on patrol off the mouth of the Yangtse.

The Shanghai force was prevented from advancing upriver towards the Chinese Navy's Kiangnan Arsenal and Dockyard near Lungwha by a formidable barrier across the Whangpoo from Nantao to Pootung. Many of the wrecks were seagoing junks, but there were also larger vessels such as the 2,284-ton steamer *Foo Shing*. The land approaches to Shanghai and Nanking were guarded by the Chinese 87th and 88th Divisions, which moved into the Chapei and Kiangwan suburbs of Shanghai. The Japanese asserted that the military occupation of this area was a violation of the 1932 Peace Agreement. They therefore claimed the right to reinforce their own troops, extra divisions being landed at the mouth of the Whangpoo. Firing had begun on August 13th and both sides quickly built up their forces. Soon a major battle was raging just north of Shanghai.

The Chinese resisted stubbornly, although hit by naval and air bombardment. When forced to give ground they did so slowly, withdrawing through a series of prepared positions, each the scene of bitter fighting. These lines of defence were outflanked by the landing of the Japanese Tenth Army in Hangchow Bay on November 5th. The Chinese troops around Shanghai then retreated towards Nanking which the Japanese attacked on December 10th, occupying the whole of the city by the 13th. Chiang Kai-Shek had already moved, establishing first Hankow and later Chungking as the new capital of Nationalist China.

From 1937 to 1941 neither side declared war. The conflict was legally regarded as an incident, not as an official war. At first the Japanese had not wanted to antagonize world opinion by labelling themselves aggressors. They emphasized that they had no territorial ambitions in China but military action was necessary to ensure the safety of Japanese nationals. Their Chinese adventure was merely a punitive expedition to exterminate undesirable bandits – a transparent fiction which, once assumed, they did not care to lay aside even after Pearl Harbor.

On the other hand, as the Chinese Ambassador in Washington explained in

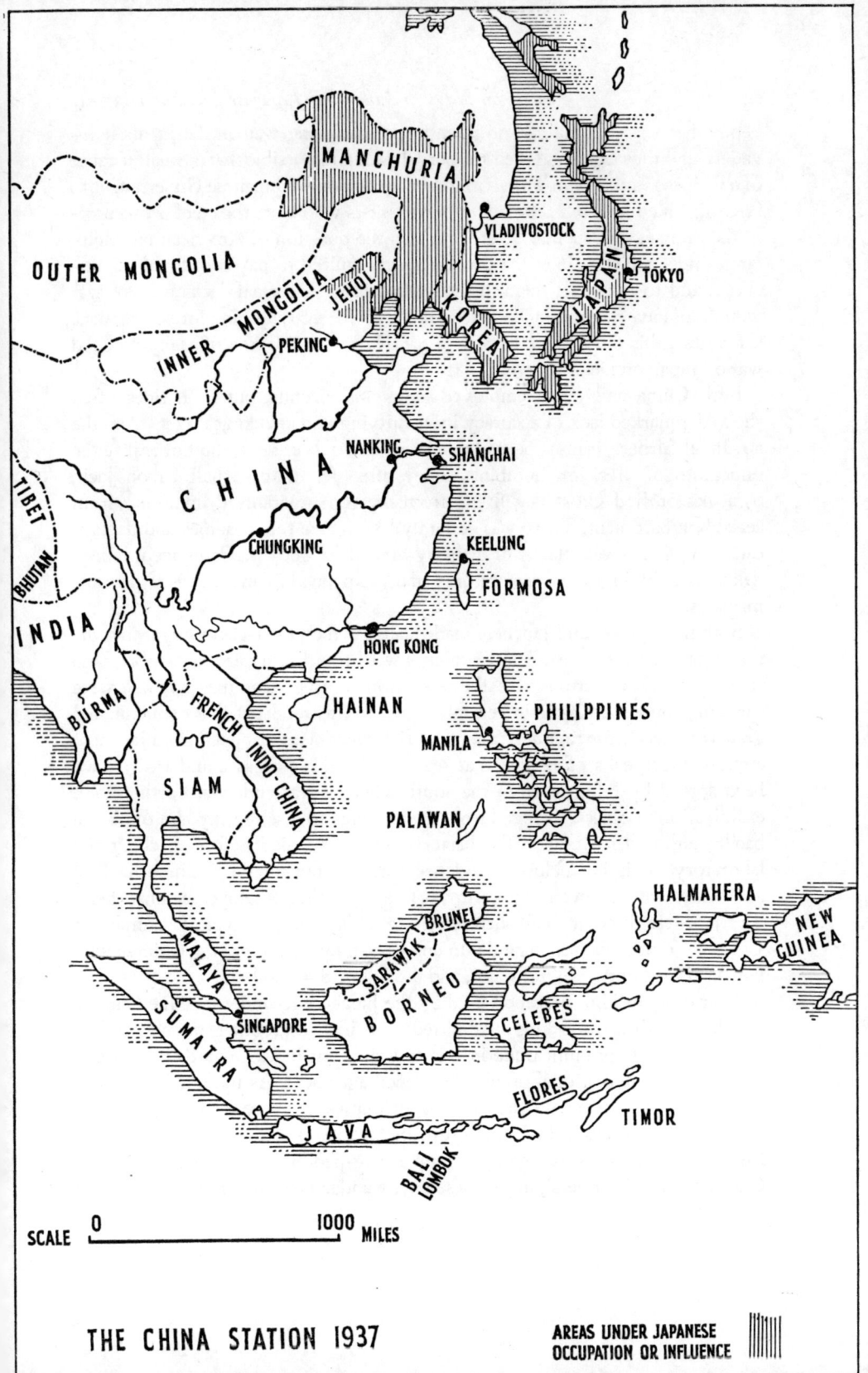

September 1937, China had no intention of declaring war on the Japanese invaders, and thus legalizing their robbery. It was still possible that the maintenance of a Chinese Embassy in Tokyo might yet persuade the Japanese Government to re-establish control over the military extremists who were the chief prosecutors of the campaign in China. There was also the question of American neutrality laws, under which belligerent powers were required to pay cash for their purchases and to transport them in their own ships. A formal declaration of war would not have favoured China, who relied on foreign shipping for her imports. Of course, this did not matter after Pearl Harbor and China officially declared war on Japan on December 9th, 1941.

Both China and Japan employed tanks and aircraft, but both sides often showed a marked lack of accuracy in identifying and attacking targets from the air. In all fairness, it must be said that many neutral residents did not realize the difficulties of precision bombing. They often felt that a small Union Jack, Swastika or Red Cross flag flying from the roof guaranteed immunity from aerial bombardment. There was certainly less excuse for casualties and damage caused by low-level attacks or artillery fire. Many such incidents were indeed deliberate, although the perpetrators usually explained them away as regrettable mistakes.

Both the Chinese and Japanese made claims and counter-claims regarding the use of gas-shells, but insufficient evidence was brought forward to support these statements. More serious was the allegation in 1940 that the Japanese were spreading bubonic plague in central China. It was reported that contaminated grains of rice, cotton rags and other materials were being dropped from Japanese aircraft. Outbreaks of plague that occurred in those areas could easily have been spread by refugees from the south where it was endemic. Furthermore, examination of objects dropped from the air failed to disclose any hint of plague bacilli, although of course the bacteria may have died before reaching the laboratory. This inconclusive evidence was rejected by the Chinese medical authorities who believed that germ warfare was being employed against them. The Japanese discounted all such reports and allegations as typical examples of Chinese Communist propaganda. In any case, they said it was the Chinese who poisoned food and drinking water, and used dum-dum bullets.

A far more insidious weapon used by the Japanese to undermine the Chinese people was drug-trafficking. Admittedly, British and other merchants had profited from the opium trade in earlier years, but it was regarded as an evil business and international opinion hardened against it. As the nineteenth century progressed there were growing opportunities for more secure and less vile cargoes, and the trade died out. From the 1920s onwards, however, Colonel Kenji Doihara, a Japanese agent, built up a drug-peddling ring in Manchuria and China. Chinese 'pushers', in Japanese pay, wandered from fair to fair and from

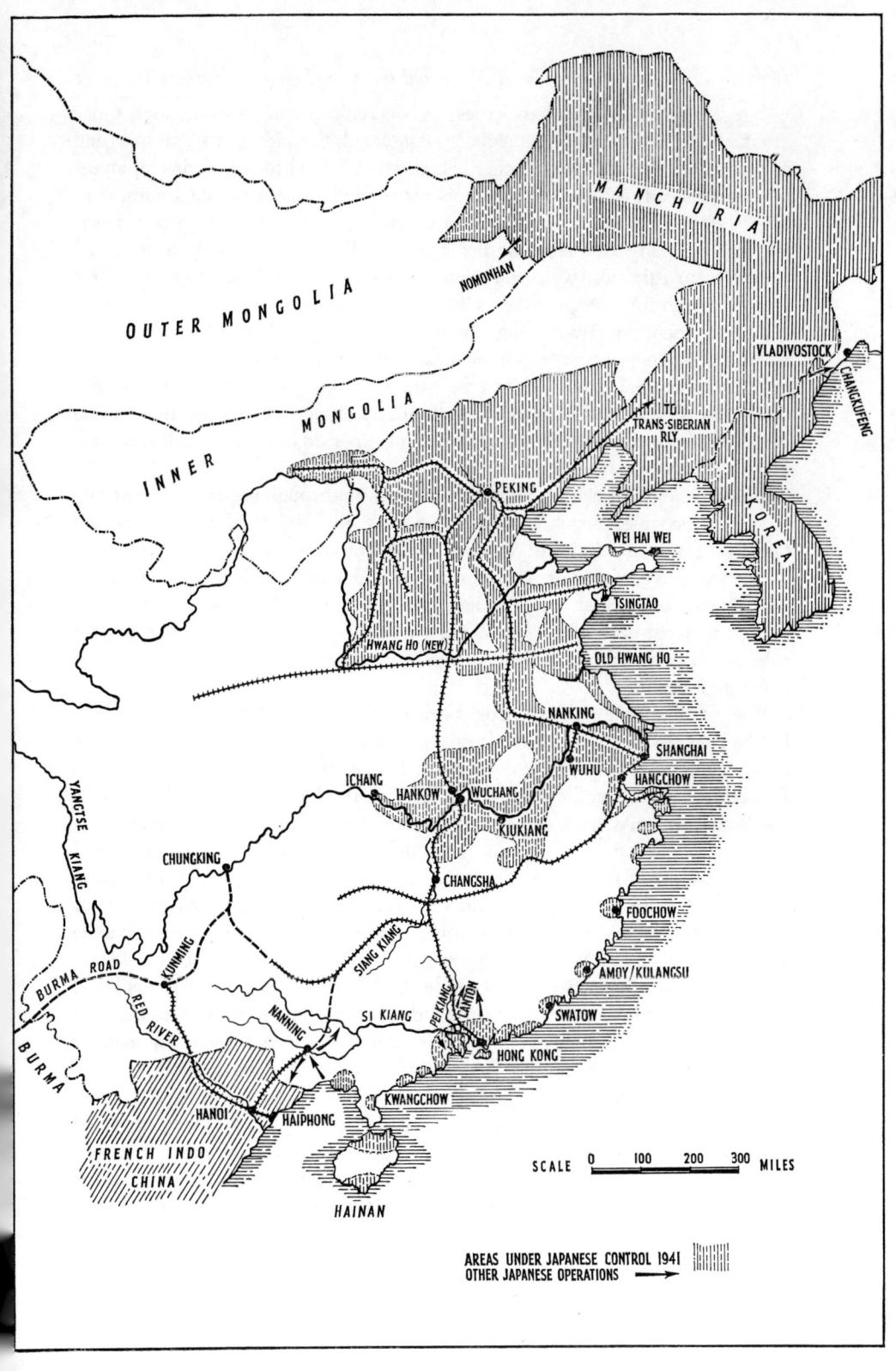

village to village selling patent cures for tuberculosis and other diseases. Once 'hooked' by the opium these medicines contained, the addicts became spies and informers for the Japanese. Richer addicts were forced to pay their employees in drugs instead of cash. Other agents distributed Golden Bat cigarettes, containing small amounts of opium or heroin, thus addicting many more unsuspecting buyers. Many Russians had fled from the Bolsheviks and those who had turned to prostitution were sometimes employed as pedlars, receiving a free pipe of opium for every six they sold to their clients.

The confidence of law-abiding Chinese in their country's currency was shaken when the Japanese began to circulate worthless paper money, issued by such institutions as the Harbin Bank of Territorial Development, which had wound up its affairs in 1916. There were also Reichsmark notes of high denomination which had been printed in Germany during the period of inflation following the First World War.

The Japanese exercised political administration through puppet governments set up in occupied areas. In December 1937 they installed the Provisional Government at Peking, followed early in 1938 by their formation of the Reformed Government of the Republic of China at Nanking. Meanwhile the Municipality of Greater Shanghai had also come under Japanese control. However, it was not until March 30th, 1940, that the Japanese appointed a puppet ruler at Nanking who commanded sufficient respect to rival Chiang Kai-Shek in Chungking.

Wang Ching-Wei had originally been a loyal follower of Chiang Kai-Shek, but he later felt that China had already suffered too much through war and the then unrealized corruption of the Nationalist Government. He therefore fled to French Indo-China and eventually defected to the Japanese who hailed him as the legal ruler of China. Wang Ching-Wei announced that his government would employ reason and diplomacy to establish peace in East Asia. He ordered the liquidation of the Chungking régime and the invalidation of its laws and treaties. All military personnel and civil servants were to return to duty at Nanking where they would be welcomed without recrimination. Some people greeted Wang Ching-Wei as an able realist, strong enough to dominate Chinese politics, control the armed forces and lead China into a new era. Others hated him as a traitor who stole what little industrial profit, agricultural wealth and customs revenue had been graciously left behind by Japanese carpetbaggers. He was denounced by Chiang Kai-Shek and his government was virtually ignored by the whole world except the Japanese.

Those Chinese who could not be drugged by opium, baffled by devalued currency, deceived by collaborators or corrupted by bribes, were to be intimidated by violence. Arson, looting and the murder, rape and torture of civilians and prisoners of war became commonplace as the Japanese armed forces moved

The War

into China. The rumours of such horrors spread out ahead of the advancing Japanese soldiery and served as a warning to anyone who might not co-operate promptly. In their defence, the Japanese argued that such extreme measures were needed to rid occupied areas of disguised terrorists. In any case they contended that even regular Chinese troops were only bandits and should be treated as such.

It is difficult to ascertain responsibility for these atrocities or indeed for most of the incidents of this period. Some cases seem to have been the result of official Japanese policy. Others appear to have been due to an excess of zeal on the part of local commanders who relied on the belated support of their government at home. This support was usually forthcoming, often coupled with apologies to the injured party. The murder of Chang Tso-Lin in 1928, the Mukden Incident of 1931 and the attacks on British and American gunboats in 1937 are typical examples of attempts by extremist field officers to force their government further along the path of Japanese destiny outlined in the Tanaka Memorial, a document which first appeared in 1929. We shall probably never know whether it was written by Baron Tanaka, Prime Minister of Japan in 1927, or whether it was a forgery. It may have been issued by an official Japanese source under Tanaka's name, or it may have been a Chinese statement of what they thought the Japanese were going to do. What is certain is that many Japanese held the same ideas as those expressed in the Tanaka Memorial. The printed words gave visible form to vague musings, while Tanaka's name lent respectability to dangerous ambitions. Now those who desired the expansion of the Japanese Empire, who felt that the home islands were too small for an exploding population, who wished to safeguard the sources of vital raw materials, who wanted to restore the prestige of the Army, or who felt cheated by Western success in China, all could quote the Tanaka Memorial as justification for their actions. The Tanaka Memorial became the Mein Kampf of Nippon.

Two quotations only are adequate examples of the policy proposed in the document:

'In order to conquer China we must first conquer Manchuria and Mongolia. In order to conquer the world we must first conquer China. If we succeed in conquering China, the rest of the Asiatic countries and the South Sea countries will fear us and surrender to us. Then the world will realize that Eastern Asia is ours and will not dare to violate our rights. This is the plan left to us by Emperor Meiji, the success of which is essential to our national existence.'

'The way to gain actual rights in Manchuria and Mongolia is to use this region as a base, and under pretence of trade and commerce penetrate the rest of China. Armed with rights already secured we shall seize the resources all over the country. Having China's entire resources at our disposal, we shall proceed to conquer India, the Archipelago, Asia Minor, Central Asia and even Europe.'

The official publication of such a policy of cynical aggression would only serve to stimulate Chinese resistance to Japanese infiltration and perhaps shock the rest of the world into war against Japan. The Japanese propagandists therefore clothed their grandiose ambition with specious promises to China, negotiations with the West, the declaration of a crusade against Bolshevism and the enunciation of what was described as the Asiatic Monroe Doctrine.

In 1934 the Japanese Foreign Office stated that the maintenance of peace in the Far East was Japan's responsibility. The key to this peace was the stability of China, which could only be achieved by China herself – with Japanese help. Any interference in Chinese affairs by other nations, especially the provision of technical and financial assistance for China's military forces would be opposed by Japan. However, as the greatest threat to stability in the Far East came from Communism, the Chinese Government must co-operate with Japan in eradicating the Red Menace. Only short-sighted, prejudiced Chinese could fail to see the advantages in collaboration with Japan and Manchukuo. United by the single aim of establishing a new order in East Asia, they would realize a relationship of neighbourly amity, common defence against Communism, and economic co-operation. Japanese merchants were not trying to establish a monopoly. They merely wished that China should extend to Japan facilities for the development of China's natural resources. Japan had no territorial claims. She demanded only minimum guarantees for the execution of her function in the establishment of a New Order.

So the foundations of the Greater East Asia Co-Prosperity Sphere would be laid. The nations of the Far East would band together in a grand military and economic union. 'Asia for the Asiatics' would be its theme and the Land of the Rising Sun its divine inspiration. In this Utopia there would be no Europeans, no Communists and no questioning of Japanese guidance. Asia would receive the fruits of Japanese energy and would provide the raw materials necessary for the homeland's expression. This would be the culmination of centuries of discipline and a frenzied industrial revolution. This would be Kodo – the Imperial Way.

The Great East Asia Co-Prosperity Sphere was so skilfully publicized that its propaganda seems to have fooled its own advocates. Certainly the Japanese felt most insulted when fellow Asiatics refused to join their great adventure. Nevertheless Japanese extremists were determined to build an empire in the Far East, with or without co-operation, with or without a cloak of vague ideals. They were continuing the trends of Japan's recent history.

After rejecting Western infiltration for almost two hundred years, Japan suffered the humiliation of being forced to open her land to foreign invaders in the nineteenth century. At first the Japanese watched warily, taking careful note of Western ideas and equipment. Then in the reign of Emperor Meiji (1867–1912), the nation embarked upon an extensive programme of modernization and industrialization. Even before this transition was complete, Japanese eyes were turning towards the mainland of Asia, where an ancient, archaic and inefficient civilization looked with contempt on all foreign barbarians, including fellow Asiatics. Japan, wounded by Chinese condescension, would find an outlet for her exploding population in the unexploited vastnesses of the inner regions of China, Manchuria, Mongolia and Siberia. First came the Ryuku Islands, reaching out south-westwards from Japan towards Formosa and the mainland of Asia, which for generations, had customarily paid tribute to both China and Japan. In 1879 they were officially annexed by Japan.

The histories of Japan and Korea are closely linked, often in war, first one nation and then the other taking the offensive. Now Japan was stronger and gaining in strength, while Korea was the weaker. Japanese infiltration and demands were stepped up, immediately competing with Chinese interests in Korea. On July 25th, 1894, units of the Imperial Japanese Navy sank a Chinese troopship and captured one of her three escorts. Six days later war was declared. By April the following year the Chinese Army had been driven from Korea, their fleet had been defeated off the Yalu River and Japanese troops had occupied the Liaotung Peninsula. After this short war China recognized the independence of Korea (whose monarchy was obliged to accept Japanese advice) and ceded Formosa and the Pescadores Islands to Japan. The Treaty of Shimonoseki also granted the Liaotung Peninsula, but Western pressure forced Japan to give up this prize.

During the Boxer Rebellion in 1900, Japanese soldiers in Peking co-operated with Western troops in the besieged legations, while a larger force formed an important part of the relieving expedition. Although no territorial gains resulted from these military operations, Japan, in common with other leading nations, reserved the right to maintain troops in Peking for the protection of her legation, their lines of communication being further safeguarded by more forces stationed between Peking and Tientsin. These units were maintained and expanded long after the other nations had reduced their legation guards. (The exercises held by this Japanese garrison would eventually cause the Sino-Japanese Incident in 1937.)

Presently the Japanese found themselves competing with the expansionist policies of Tsarist Russia. The result was the Russo-Japanese War of 1904–5. Equipped and trained on modern Western lines particularly by her new ally Great Britain, Japan's Army and Navy won a series of resounding victories. The Russian Fleet was hit by a surprise torpedo attack on its base, Port Arthur, the day before war was declared. Port Arthur itself was captured after a long and bitter siege and the Russian Army was defeated at Mukden. Meanwhile the Russian

Baltic Fleet had sailed half-way round the world – to be destroyed by Admiral Togo at the Battle of Tsushima. This time Japan retained the lease of the Liaotung Peninsula and also gained the southern half of Sakhalin. In addition various agreements with her late enemy enabled Japan to gain commercial footholds in Manchuria and Mongolia. Then in 1910 Japan took advantage of the world situation and her present power to annex Korea which was renamed Chosen – the Land of the Morning Calm.

Japan's intervention in the First World War on the side of the Allies afforded great opportunities, but she almost overreached herself. Early operations were extremely successful and by the beginning of 1915, the German leased territories of Kiaochow and Tsingtao had been overrun, being withheld by the Japanese instead of being returned to China. In addition they presented a note, known from its contents as 'The Twenty-One Demands', to the Chinese Government. Not only did Japan insist on the cession of the territory she had occupied, but she was also to be granted various rights in China and Manchuria. It included the demand that Japanese officials were to advise the Chinese Government on all political, financial and military matters. A number of secret and public diplomatic manœuvres involving Japan, China and the Allies during and after the war virtually confirmed Japanese ascendancy in China, but later negotiations restored Kiaochow and Tsingtao to Chinese sovereignty. In spite of proving that she was now a world power, all Japan had to show for her participation in the First World War was a mandate over a number of former German islands in the Pacific and various concessions and privileges on the mainland of Asia. 'The Twenty-One Demands' accomplished nothing, except to arouse Chinese and Western suspicion of Japanese imperialism. America and Japan were further estranged, while Britain did not renew her treaty with Japan.

Meanwhile Japanese attention had become focused on events much farther north where civil war was raging in Siberia, the aftermath of the Russian Revolution. A Japanese contingent joined the international expedition for the suppression of Bolshevism and the restoration of order in the mineral-rich lands of eastern Russia. The Japanese troops stayed on for an extra two years after all other forces had been withdrawn until the hostility of the Western powers, the Communist defeat of Japan's Cossack protegé, Semenov, and the growing unpopularity of the war, eventually forced the Japanese Government to abandon their Siberian adventure.

During the following decade, Japanese merchants gradually infiltrated the Chinese provinces in Manchuria, leasing land, establishing banks, building railways and making profits. Armed police were employed to protect Japanese interests, as well as regular troops stationed there by treaty-right. Growing Chinese nationalism, exemplified by Chiang Kai-Shek's Northern Expedition of 1926–8 soon clashed with the determination of the Japanese to exploit Manchuria and offset Japan's setbacks during the world slump. A series of riots and incidents culminated in an undeclared war between China and Japan which lasted from September 1931 to May 1933. Military operations were concentrated in northern China although there was also much fighting around Shanghai, especially in the Chinese suburb of Chapei.

Supported by Japanese militarists and politicians, the northern provinces of China declared their independence as the new state of Manchukuo. The spontaneity of this national movement was investigated by the Lytton Commission on behalf of the League of Nations. It reported that Manchukuo was a Japanese puppet state and condemned Japan for unjustifiable aggression. The Japanese delegation, led by Mr Matsuoka, thereupon walked out of the League of Nations, no further action was taken and Japan was left free to exploit the natural resources of Manchuria, rewarding co-operative Chinese with official posts in the government of Manchukuo.

In 1867 Japan had been a backward feudal country. Two generations later she had become a modern, industrialized state, poised ready to embark upon a massive programme of international domination. Yet her leaders had a blind spot. They failed to realize that other nations might have a similar awakening, might have similar national aspirations, might have similar ambition and determination. They misunderstood and underestimated no country more than their intended victim – China.

The Chinese people proudly regard themselves with some justification as the oldest civilisation on earth, their recorded history dating back to the Hsia dynasty of 2000 BC. Art, philosophy, invention and comfort flourished, but the country was so vast and communications so poor that wealth could not be distributed nor administration centralized. Sometimes a strong emperor united the country, but his reign was often followed by chaos when the land was fought over by war-lords and foreign invaders. Usually these latter came riding out of the wastes of Central Asia, but in the nineteenth century Europeans arrived – by sea. They established themselves along the coast and up the rivers, the only sure means of transport in China. They came to trade, exploiting the country and forcing their will upon the disunited Chinese. Yet they also brought new ideas and material benefits, which the Chinese recognized and appreciated – without slavishly worshipping.

Since the beginning of the twentieth century the Chinese people had become more aware of their nationhood. They had been encouraged to look forward to a future of unity by revolutionaries who had received help and education from America, Britain and even Japan. Their aims included the overthrow of the Manchu Emperors, the reform of the government on Western lines and the rejection of foreign economic domination. The Republic of China was formally established on New Year's Day 1912, but no political miracle was wrought overnight. A struggle for power developed between the visionary Dr Sun Yat-Sen, a series of military dictators and a number of regional war-lords. When Sun Yat-Sen died in 1925, the leadership of the Kuomintang or Nationalist Party devolved upon Generalissimo Chiang Kai-Shek. The following year he led his army northwards from Canton, defeating the war-lords and driving the most powerful one, Marshal Chang Tso-Lin who had been backed by the Japanese, into Manchuria. Gradually Chiang Kai-Shek's power and authority increased, radiating outwards from his new capital of Nanking.

Although the Kuomintang was by no means a perfect instrument of government and was itself split into a number of factions, there was no disagreement over the basic aim of unifying China under a Chinese leader. Even Chiang Kai-Shek's most powerful rival, the Communist leader Mao Tse-Tung, had the same long-term goal. The threat of Japanese invasion tended to unite rather than split these various forces in the face of the common enemy. At the beginning of 1937 there were already signs of a reconciliation between Chiang Kai-Shek and Mao Tse-Tung. When the Japanese did attack, the whole Chinese nation was united against the foreign invaders.

This solid front came as a shock to the Japanese who had expected an easy victory, especially after the fall of Nanking. They were compelled to even greater exertions to bring the day of Kodo nearer. In October 1938 another Japanese army went ashore near Canton and further landings were carried out all round the Chinese coast in 1939, 1940 and 1941. By December 1941, some thirty divisions, twenty air squadrons and most of the fleet had served a certain amount of time in China.

Yet each move only further embroiled the Japanese in their Chinese morass. As their armies advanced they suffered heavy casualties from Chinese guerrillas and from regular troops specializing in hit-and-run tactics. Occasionally the Japanese were defeated in full-scale battles such as Taierchwang in the spring of 1938, but more often they found that they only controlled the river valleys, the surrounding hills being held by Chinese troops and bandits. More forces were needed to deal with these attackers, to safeguard communications and to pacify areas that had already been cleared of hostile Chinese many times before.

The Japanese did not believe that the Chinese were capable of such adamant yet elusive resistance on their own. So from 1938 onwards the purpose of the war gradually changed. To put an end to non-co-operation, the Western supply routes to Chiang Kai-Shek must be cut. Nippon herself must first rid Asia of European influence before she could control the Asiatics. Japanese aggressive sentiment was, therefore, directed more and more against the Western democracies. Japanese policy gradually phased from commercial discrimination, through open threats, hostile acts and the occupation of Indo-China, to the attack on Pearl Harbor.

The War

In the midst of this violent storm of warring nations lived the citizens of the neutral powers: Great Britain, France, Italy, Germany, the United States of America, and the rest. They were in China solely for trade and wars were of little consequence provided that business was carried on as usual. They lived in certain parts of certain cities, in concessions and treaty-ports, on islands of their own nationality – surrounded by an ocean of Chinese. They were subject to their own laws, enforced by their own police and administered by their own lawyers. They had their own clubs, their own churches, their own way of life.

This system of extra-territoriality had existed since 1842. Earlier traders and diplomats had found Chinese legal ideas of group responsibility and judicial torture extremely difficult to comprehend. This had been particularly so in cases of murder, when Chinese officials demanded that any foreigner be handed over to them if the real criminal were not immediately available. They had once intimated that they would accept the body of a sailor who had committed suicide as his corpse would be a satisfactory subject for retribution. Not unnaturally foreign officers had refused to surrender any of their nationals – innocent or guilty, living or dead – to these vagaries of Chinese justice.

Such disputes and a number of economic factors besides the odious trade which gave its name to the conflict, led to the Opium War of 1839-42. Britain's victory provided an opportunity for the clarification of the legal issues in the Treaty of Nanking. Hong Kong became British and five treaty-ports were opened to foreign traders. They and their properties were to be accommodated on land leased directly from the Chinese or via the foreigner's own consul.

In all civil and criminal cases, the defendant could only be tried in a court of his own nationality. For example, if an American or a Chinaman sued an Italian or an Englishman, the case would be tried in an Italian or British Consular court. But if a foreigner sued a Chinese, then it would be heard in the local Chinese court.

Presently this incredibly complex system became incomprehensibly complicated. The five original treaty-ports of Canton, Amoy, Foochow, Ningpo and Shanghai were increased in number to over forty. Some foreigners were placed under the protection of more powerful nations. Chinese were admitted to concessions and mixed courts were set up. Municipal authorities were established and public utilities operated in Chinese areas for the benefit of foreign concessions. The concessions themselves became too crowded and foreign residents moved out into Chinese districts, becoming involved in property disputes and local Chinese politics. Foreign loans financed railways, banks and the government of China itself, while without foreign administration the economy of the country would soon have broken down. From 1854 onwards the Chinese Maritime Customs Service was operated by foreigners on behalf of the Chinese Government and until the Sino-Japanese Incident, the Inspector-General was always British. Missionaries of every denomination added their own contribution to the tangled web of Chinese affairs. Truly, this facet of world history was an all-time Chinese puzzle.

But the boisterous, lustful days of extra-territoriality were passing. Guided by modern, enlightened ideas recently expounded by Chinese republicans, China was becoming a responsible state with an important part to play in world affairs. Sun Yat-Sen had envisaged modernizing the political life of China in three stages. Firstly a period of military operations would continue until the whole of China had been unified. Then the Kuomintang would educate the masses in self-government until eventually popular democracy would be introduced. When this position of national responsibility had been attained, foreigners in China would be subject to the laws of their host nation, as in other countries, their protection being the responsibility of the Chinese Government, not the armed forces of a foreign nation. Soon the rising tide of Chinese nationalism would sweep away the antique, ramshackle bastions of extra-territoriality. 'Old China Hands' might regret the passing of their privileges and might protest noisily, but in the end even they would have to accept change and the right of the Chinese to be masters in their own land. The British Government recognized this and in 1937 did not fear a China strengthened by victory over a foreign aggressor.

At the same time, they were not greatly concerned by the possibility of any successful commercial empire-building by Japan – a state of affairs which seemed unlikely in the face of growing intransigence from China's political leaders. Even if Japan won the war, China was so vast a country and her population so enormous that a monopoly of trade was unnecessary and impracticable. Demand swallowed up supply and no merchant need fear the saturation of the market. The potentialities of Chinese trade were staggering. For example, if 482,000,000 Chinese bought just one handkerchief each in 1937, then over £17,000,000 of business would have been done.

All nations were able to share in this latent wealth. Their right had been recognized by China and by the United States of America, Belgium, the British Empire, France, Italy, Japan, the Netherlands and Portugal who had all signed the Nine-Power Treaty in Washington on February 6th, 1922. This agreement was intended to stabilize conditions in the Far East, to safeguard the rights and interests of China and to promote intercourse between China and the other Powers upon the basis of equality of opportunity. Its provisions were serious promises not to be undertaken lightly. They were as follows:

Article 1: The Contracting Powers, other than China, agree:

1 To respect the sovereignty, the independence, and the administrative integrity of China;
2 To provide the fullest and most unembarrassed opportunity to China to develop and maintain for herself an effective and stable government;
3 To use their influence for the purpose of effectually establishing and maintain-

ing the principle of opportunity for the commerce and industry of all nations throughout the territory of China;

4 To refrain from taking advantage of conditions in China in order to seek special rights or privileges which would abridge the rights of subjects or citizens of friendly states and from countenancing action inimical to the security of such states.

Article 2: The contracting powers agree not to enter into any treaty, agreement or understanding, either with one another, or individually or collectively, which would infringe or impair the principles stated in Article 1.

Article 3: With a view to applying more effectively the principles of the Open Door or equality of opportunity in China for the trade and industry of all nations, the Contracting Powers other than China, agree that they will not seek, nor support their respective nationals in seeking:

(*a*) Any arrangement which might purport to establish in favour of their interests any general superiority of rights with respect to commercial or economic development in any designated region of China;

(*b*) Any such monopoly or preference as would deprive the nationals of any other Power of the right of undertaking any legitimate trade or industry in China, or of participating with the Chinese Government or with any local authority in any category of public enterprise, or which by reason of its scope, duration or geographical extent is calculated to frustrate the practical application of the principle of equal opportunity.

It is understood that the foregoing stipulations of this Article are not to be so construed as to prohibit the acquisition of such properties, industrial or financial undertaking, or to the encouragement of invention and research. China undertakes to be guided by the principles stated in the foregoing stipulations of this Article in dealing with applications for economic rights and privileges from governments and nationals of all foreign countries, whether parties to the present Treaty or not.

Article 4: The Contracting Powers agree not to support any agreements by their respective nationals with each other designed to create Spheres of Influence or to provide for the enjoyment of mutually exclusive opportunities in designated parts of Chinese territory.

Article 5 stated that all railways in China should convey goods and passengers without discrimination. *Article 6* emphasized China's neutrality in time of war, while *Articles 7, 8* and *9* dealt with the application and ratification of the Treaty.

The Nine-Power Treaty was the legal basis for the presence of foreign warships. Army personnel guarded concessions and legations, but the maintenance of any country's interests in China was the responsibility of that nation's navy.

From time immemorial, the rivers of China had provided the framework for her internal trade routes. On them had arisen most of her chief cities, and from them radiated, whenever geography allowed, an intricate pattern of canals, creeks and ditches, linking farms, villages and towns. These winding, branching and often tidal waterways were frequently confined between bunds, or artificial banks, themselves enclosing low-lying fields, many reclaimed from the river bed. Farms and villages had been built on the bunds, and so too had old forts, temples and joss-houses, some of which were now ruinous, submerged and dangerous to navigation. The bunds were often thickly lined with mulberry trees providing the basis for the silk industry, groves of bamboo (in a hundred varieties and for which there were a hundred uses), fruit trees and shade trees which gave variety to the densely populated and cultivated scene. Between the banks a ceaseless traffic of sampans and junks was sailed, rowed and poled along, bearing rice, pigs, raw silk, tung oil, and a thousand-odd items, the products of a skilled and industrious peasantry, barely scratched by the Industrial Revolution.

In summer, melting snows from Tibet rolled vast quantities of yellow water towards the sea, shifting sandbanks, breaching the bunds and flooding the neighbouring fields, often to a depth of many feet. The Hwang Ho or Yellow River had done this in 1854 and had completely changed its course so that it entered the sea over 300 miles from its original mouth, drowning so many people *en route* that it was known as China's Sorrow.

Beyond the tidal reaches, the rivers forced their way through mountains and gorges, falling over rapids and twisting round rocks. To all these natural hazards were added human ones. Everywhere semi-respectable war-lords exacted crippling tolls from merchants, riverine and coastal pirates attacked waterborne trade and bandits waylaid travellers even right outside the gates of big cities.

When the Westerners arrived, their commerce followed these natural communications. The enormous Yangtse Kiang – greatest of China's rivers – and its tributaries were obvious trade routes. The Si-Kiang or West River (lesser known but equal in size to the Danube) linked Hong Kong, Macao, the Pearl River Delta and Canton with the south-west provinces. There were many others.

The two great firms of Jardine, Matheson, and Butterfield and Swire, the American oil companies, the other big merchant houses or 'hongs' of many nationalities – all were to be found trading throughout China, their big steamers going upriver many hundreds of miles into the heart of the country. Chinese merchants, too, shared in these modern developments although the traditional junks still plied their business. They were often seen in large 'tows' of twenty junks and many sampans behind a single, small, antiquated tug, the local craft dropping off or joining on as they made their way slowly along the river.

Like the Chinese, the newcomers had to contend with natural and human hazards. European navigators charted and dredged safe channels, established and maintained lighthouses, buoys and other marks, and warned of approaching typhoons. Seagoing warships put down coastal pirates, while for anti-piracy work along the rivers, there were the gunboats, performing a unique role in world history. Primarily intended for the protection of Western commerce, their presence ensured that *all* trade was carried on with the minimum of interference from evildoers. They dealt with all pirates regardless of the nationality of the victim – foreign or Chinese. And the Chinese relied on this protection as much as the foreigners did. The gunboats rarely had to do anything. It was just their presence which deterred piracy; action was too infrequent for their often-bored crews.

Away from 'civilization' – the bright lights and parties of Hong Kong and Shanghai – the gunboats led a very isolated and lonely existence. There were only two officers in each ship (three if a doctor was carried) while the crew varied from thirty to sixty. The ship's company was half British and half Chinese, the latter being recruited in Hong Kong or Shanghai. They provided the cooks, stewards, messboys, boats' crews and some stokers. Some were 'official', that is paid by the Royal Navy, and others, including 'makee-learns', were 'unofficial', being paid by whoever employed them. They and their families were often looked after by the ship's doctor, primarily to safeguard the crew, but with considerable benefit to the Chinese. Every eighteen months, half the British personnel went home, being relieved by new men just beginning their three-year China commission. The Chinese ratings stayed, often in the same ship for the whole of their service life.

The gunboatmen had little contact with the local Chinese and for most of the gunboats' history, learning the Chinese language was positively discouraged. It could lead to all sorts of undesirable relationships and even – it was said – to mental breakdown. Yet such isolation did have one singular advantage. In a society where bribery, corruption and 'squeeze' were a normal part of conducting business, it was certain that the Royal Navy would remain impartial, being so divorced from everything around them.

As one officer wrote: 'the gunboats floated in a dream-like world, uninvolved with local affairs, observing much and understanding little of the teeming life around them, which their presence did much to safeguard for three generations.'

To protect British lives, defend British property, watch over British trade, ensure that British merchants had free access to treaty-ports along ten thousand miles of coastline and navigable waterways, and put down piracy, Admiral Sir Charles Little, Commander-in-Chief of the China Station, had almost a hundred vessels at his disposal. This squadron, impressive enough on paper, included auxiliaries, harbour craft and a number of warships which were by no means suitable for the peculiar duties of the China Station at this period of history – July 1937.

For example, seventeen of those ships made up the 4th Submarine Flotilla, namely the submarines *Odin, Osiris, Olympus, Orpheus, Otus, Oswald, Pandora,*

Parthian, *Perseus*, *Phoenix*, *Proteus*, *Rainbow*, *Regent*, *Regulus* and *Rover*, their depot ship *Medway*, and their attendant destroyer *Westcott*. Each submarine mounted one 4-inch gun, but their primary armament was eight torpedo-tubes. Originally described as 'Overseas Patrolling Submarines', they had been designed for service in the Far East, being stationed there as a counter to Japanese naval expansion. The flotilla was in fact the largest concentration of British submarines outside Home waters, a powerful force in a full-scale naval war, but of restricted use during a period of limited hostilities or for showing the flag in small ports up shallow rivers.

The flotilla seemed to have little to do with the operations of the rest of the China Station, occasionally disappearing on a voyage of its own to Wei-Hai-Wei or Manila or some other place. Most days one of the submarines would slip away from alongside the depot ship and carry out various exercises in a designated area; diving, surfacing, trimming, experimenting with different shades of camouflage paint, firing torpedoes. In wartime torpedoes are set to sink at the end of their run, lest they be recovered and examined by the enemy, but they are too expensive to be thrown away just like that in peacetime. Even in 1937 they cost £2,000 apiece. So, after passing under their target, they stopped, floated and emitted a cloud of smoke which served as a marker to the flotilla's destroyer. If all went well all torpedoes would be recovered and returned to *Medway* by nightfall.

Other specialist ships included the aircraft carrier *Eagle*, the minelayer *Adventure*, the boom defence vessel *Barnet*, the tug *St Breock*, the old escort sloop *Cornflower* (used as a harbour drill ship by the Hong Kong Reserve) and *Tamar*. This last was a veteran of the bombardment of Alexandria in 1882, her new life as a receiving ship at Hong Kong beginning in 1897. Although engineless and covered with deckhouses, she was afloat and boasted a nominal armament of six 6-pounder guns, her name being used as the official title of the Hong Kong base.

The survey ship *Herald* was almost an independent command, usually away on her own surveying the coast of Borneo or some other distant shore. Her crew became familiar with such names as South Balabac Strait, Jesselton, Balambangan Island and Cape Sumpanmangio. Charts had to be checked, soundings taken and bearings read. Theirs was an unspectacular task, demanding painstaking thoroughness and perfect accuracy. Any mistakes they might make would not have immediate consequences, but might remain hidden for years and then prove suddenly fatal.

There were eighteen river gunboats of particular value for the special duties of the China Station. *Falcon* and *Tern* had been designed for service on the Upper Yangtse between Chungking and Ichang, where seasonally-changing whirlpools, rapids and rocks are an ever-present threat. They had a higher speed to cope with the powerful current and deeper draughts to give their keels better grip in the turbulent water. *Gannet* and *Peterel* were longer and were intended for the

Middle Yangtse (the Ichang-Hankow section), while little *Sandpiper* was even more specialized. She was based at Changsha on the Siang-Kiang and although she displaced 185 tons, she could float in 1 foot 10 inches of water, the lowest winter level between Changsha and the Yangtse.

Her hull had been constructed at Woolston, then dismantled, crated up and shipped to China in the liner *Chitral* in 1933. For ease of assembly, port-side items had been painted red and starboard green, the Chinese who re-erected the ship at Shanghai feeling somewhat insulted at what they considered a slur on their intelligence. Although *Sandpiper* could get down the Siang-Kiang, she was expected to spend every winter at Changsha.

The Insect-class (*Bee, Aphis, Cockchafer, Cricket, Gnat, Ladybird, Mantis* and *Scarab*) were much larger and had originally been built to support the Army in Mesopotamia in the First World War. They served on the Lower Yangtse from November to April, but in summer the Upper Yangtse rose considerably – a hundred feet or more. Then the Insects went upriver and relieved the smaller gunboats who came downriver for a change of scenery and a refit. (Grit and sand brought down by the high-level water could do severe damage to propeller shafts, bushes and bearings.) The Insects could even get up the Siang-Kiang in the summer, but they drew 4 feet and *Scarab* had once been trapped at Changsha for the whole winter.

The Yangtse gunboats were often the only representatives of any sort of social stability. Although originally charged with the protection of British lives and property from Chinese rioters and pirates they were often appealed to by Chinese merchants. In more lawless areas even the local Chinese authorities relied upon foreign gunboats for the maintenance of some semblance of law and order, although, of course, they could not admit this officially. The Insects *Tarantula*, *Moth* and *Cicala* together with *Seamew* and *Robin* performed similar services on the Si-Kiang or West River.

Two 6-inch or two 3-inch guns or one 3·7-inch howitzer made up the gunboats' main armament, and they also mounted a number of anti-aircraft weapons, including machine-guns. The short-ranged accurate howitzers were most useful for dealing with rioters or snipers behind riverbanks or up cliffs. The 6-inch guns of the Insects had a flatter trajectory and were not very effective, being designed for firing at large naval targets. There were few of these on China's rivers and a few rounds from a machine-gun usually sufficed for pirate sampans.

For the dual purpose of deterring a would-be aggressor and showing the flag, Admiral Little had the 5th Cruiser Squadron (*Cumberland, Dorsetshire, Capetown, Danae* and *Suffolk*), the 8th Destroyer Flotilla (*Duncan, Delight, Diamond, Diana, Duchess, Decoy, Dainty, Daring* and *Defender*), five escort sloops (*Folkestone, Sandwich, Falmouth, Grimsby* and *Lowestoft*) and the old destroyer *Thracian*.

In the event of a trial of strength between Japan and China, these few warships would have to defend neutral Britain's interests against encroachment by both belligerents. Usually a senior Royal Navy officer contacted the local Japanese and Chinese commanders and handed them a map showing the exact boundaries of the British Concession and the location of all the individual British properties outside those limits. British subjects were advised to leave or get into a safe area. Sometimes armed guards were provided, but the Royal Navy could only open fire if British lives or property were deliberately attacked. Damage or casualties caused by accident or error or by over-zealous local commanders did not count. A definite official hostile act would have to be committed before the Royal Navy could start shooting. Otherwise they must not get involved. Article 950 of King's Regulations and Admiralty Instructions was adamant on this point:

'When powers in amity with His Majesty are in a state of war, or are engaged in hostilities, it is the duty of all His Majesty's officers to observe a strict and impartial neutrality between the contending parties, and to respect unreservedly the just exercise of their respective belligerent rights.'

If just one warship or officer of the Royal Navy once showed official favour or gave official assistance (or what might be interpreted as official favour or assistance) to the armed forces of either of the belligerents, then the other side would be justified in declaring war on Great Britain and attacking her possessions in the Far East. If China took this step, then her navy would have to be reckoned with. It comprised ten cruisers, twenty-three gunboats, nineteen smaller vessels and seven support craft, most of doubtful vintage and effectiveness.

The more ambitious Imperial Japanese Navy was far larger and more efficient, being made up of ten battleships, four aircraft carriers, forty-two cruisers, one hundred and four destroyers, fifty-eight submarines, nine gunboats, forty escorts and twenty-nine support ships. Even in the unlikely event of China inflicting heavy punishment on this mighty array, there would still be plenty left to crush Britain's meagre forces in the Far East – should the Japanese decide that the Royal Navy was helping Chinese military operations. Perhaps in the long run reinforcements from European waters would eventually defeat Japan, but that would be cold comfort to those overwhelmed by the first onset of Japanese aggression. And with other problems nearer home, the British Government had no wish to provoke the Japanese, or even to give them the slightest excuse for unleashing war upon our Far Eastern possessions. If, in spite of all Britain's efforts to keep the peace, in spite of all the Royal Navy's restraint, the Japanese did decide to embark on their full-scale, pre-announced programme of conquest, then....

But all this was supposition. On July 8th, 1937, the Royal Navy, like all British subjects in China, could only wait and see.

2
The Beginning

Sir Hughe Knatchbull-Hugessen, the British Ambassador to China, holidaying with his family at the seaside resort of Pei-Tai-Ho, also decided to wait and see. At that stage it was too early to determine whether Peking or Nanking would be the principal centre of events, so he remained at Pei-Tai-Ho, requesting that a warship be sent to act as a communications centre for Embassy messages. The Navy customarily provided this vital service when normal communications had broken down or were likely to do so. British officials could thus keep in immediate touch with Whitehall during the rapidly developing crises of the Sino-Japanese Incident.

The destroyer *Westcott* arrived on July 10th, 1937, and in response to an urgent appeal from the Chinese Foreign Office, Sir Hughe left Pei-Tai-Ho on the evening of the 12th. Making $24\frac{1}{2}$ knots in the teeth of a gale, *Westcott* hurried him to Wei-Hai-Wei, and by 04.00 hrs, Sir Hughe had conferred with Admiral Little and was on his way again, this time in the cruiser *Danae*. He reached Nanking and was in conference with the Chinese Foreign Minister by 16.00 hrs on the 15th.

Other warships were on the move. Rear-Admiral L. G. E. Crabbe (Senior Naval Officer, Yangtse) had already ordered all gunboats on the river to prepare large Union Jacks for display on awnings. The gunboats were also ordered to conserve fuel oil, as supplies must inevitably dry up if the normal route up the Yangtse were cut. It was even suggested that their boilers be converted to burn coal as well as oil, but this was difficult using local resources and needed dockyard facilities. Most of the cooking on board was already done by Chinese messboys, using their own spirit stoves and charcoal burners. Admiral Crabbe further instructed the gunboats at Hankow to send sections of armed bluejackets ashore to defend Special Administrative District No 3 (the old British Concession), where most British property was situated. As the Japanese evacuated their concession, so the Chinese moved in and it was possible that rioting and looting there would spread to other parts of the city. All British nationals were therefore concentrated in SAD 3 where they were safe, partly because the Chinese expended their violence in the Japanese Concession and partly because the Royal Navy's show of force did dissuade potential rioters.

The Upper Yangtse gunboats had quite enough to do coping with the rampaging river at this time of the year. In many places the Yangtse is constricted by very narrow, towering, twisting gorges, where the water races past at such a rate that a steamer had to go full ahead to get through. When rapids were encountered, maximum speed had to be achieved by a gradual increase in revolutions, rather than by charging the rapids. Even with the engines slamming away at full throttle, the vessel would almost stop dead in the water. The current piled up so violently that the ship's foc'sle could be forced right under the surface, while the Yangtse pilot yawed the ship's head from side to side as though searching for a spot where the powerful current was just a little less swift. Usually the steamboat got through, but sometimes the current was just too strong. When that happened the vessel would drop back, edging inshore until she could be secured to the bank below the rapid. A wire was got ashore and secured upstream above the rapid. The vessel then hauled herself through using her own winch. Of course sailing junks could not get through on their own at all and they had to send a very long, light, bamboo rope ashore to a gang of trackers. A long column of Chinese walking along narrow ledges cut out of the precipitous cliffs then dragged the junk up over the rapid.

When not actually in turbulent water or not making an emergency dash, gunboats and other Royal Navy warships on the Yangtse kept their speed down to about 10 knots lest their wash upset junks and sampans. This rule applied on the whole of the river but the vagaries of the Upper Yangtse current are such that the disturbance of a ship's wake can be dangerous for another twenty or thirty minutes after the steamer had passed. Sometimes too at very high level in particular places: 'the water rises in a dome-shaped mass, then suddenly caves in forming momentarily a deep hole down which the surrounding water rushes with a great commotion and roar. Fortunately these phenomena are rare.'

The current was just one of the problems. There are quicksands, local fogs and violent rainstorms which reduce visibility to nil. Night-time navigation was definitely out on the Upper Yangtse (although quite customary on the lower river) and a suitable anchorage or berth always had to be found before dark.

Although many of the gorges are deep, ledges and sharp pinnacles of rock jut up from the river bed to within a few inches of the surface. They could only be avoided by making sharp turns right across the turbulent current. Each rapid, gorge or other hazard had its own particular route described in Captain S. C. Plant's 'Handbook for the Guidance of Shipmasters on the Ichang-Chungking Section of the Yangtse River', and known by timeless experience to the Chinese river pilots. They brought on board their own quartermasters who steered the ship following the almost imperceptible movement of the pilot's finger. Rarely was a word spoken.

A vessel that did strike a rock might be got off safely, might fill and sink immediately or might get wedged indefinitely. Depending on drought or melting snows in the Tibetan headwaters almost two thousand miles away, the Yangtse

Left: A Chinese junk on the West River. [*Vice-Adm Sir Patrick Bayly*

Below: Tamar at Hong Kong.
[*H. E. J. Regler*

Cicala on the West River. [*Vice-Adm Sir Patrick Bayly*

Sandpiper at anchor, 'like a floating doll's house'. [*Cdr H. R. Rycroft*

On the firing point, Stonecutters' Island, Hong Kong – RN vs USN competition. [*H. E. J. Regler*

Diamond and *St. Breock* exercising off Wei-Hai-Wei. [*H. E. J. Regler*

Capetown's ship's company have thirty minutes' PT after Divisions at Chingwangtao. [*H. G. C. Brice*

Falcon and *Wantung* at Miaoho anchorage on the Upper Yangtse. [*Lt-Cdr J. A. McClure*

Tern at Chungking (summer level). [*Lt-Cdr J. A. McClure*

Tern at Chungking (winter level). [*Lt-Cdr J. A. McClure*

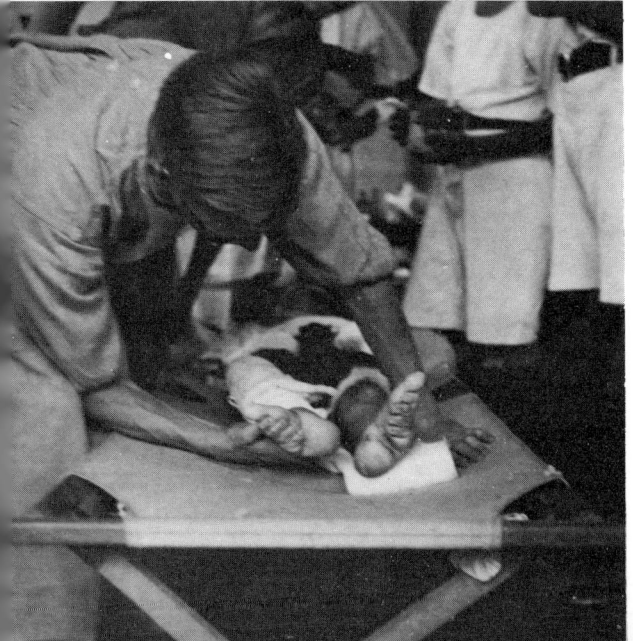

Top: A Japanese armoured motor boat captures a small Chinese gunboat at Tangku in early August 1937.
[*H. E. J. Regler*

Above: Caskets containing the ashes of the first Japanese soldiers killed in the war, begin their journey home from Tangku, August 1937. [*H. E. J. Regler*

Left: Grimsby's medical officer treats a Chinese woman injured by Japanese bombardment at Tangku, August 1937. It is probably the first time her feet have been unbound since she was a baby. [*H. E. J. Regler*

Capetown at Hong Kong. [*H. G. C. Brice*

Capetown's four side-party girls at Hong Kong. [*H. G. C. Brice*

The Kiangyin Boom on the Yangtse. (The original print was folded when personal photographs were sent to the Admiralty for intelligence purposes.)   [*H. G. C. Brice*

Idzumo and *Manadzuru* at Shanghai, August 1937.
                                          [*H. E. J. Regler*

The Beginning

can rise or fall dramatically. Twenty-four hours after getting stuck a vessel might be twenty feet above, or twenty feet under, the surface of the river. If she struck during the high-level freshest season from July to September, she might spend the winter two hundred feet above the lowest water level.

On July 16th, *Gannet* went to help the 955-ton river steamer *Fuh Wo*, stuck on such a rock between Chungking and Wanhsien. All her compartments from bow to engine-room were partially flooded, but her captain got her off and managed to beach her before *Gannet* arrived. Other Jardine, Matheson ships took off her cargo, *Fuh Wo*'s compartments were pumped out and the holes filled with concrete before she could be refloated.

The West River gunboats had their difficulties too. In their area, as throughout China, piracy was a perennial problem. In theory the Chinese Navy normally shared some of the anti-piracy patrols, but they rarely moved away from their moorings. Certainly from now on, such Chinese warships as remained afloat were engaged in more desperate struggles and the Royal Navy carried on alone.

Most Chinese pirates followed a fairly standard *modus operandi*. Mingling with the motley crowd of Chinese passengers, they waited until the ship was at sea before bringing out concealed weapons and taking over. Once in command they robbed passengers and crew indiscriminately and often set fire to the ship before transferring to a waiting junk and escaping to their base at Bias Bay. Occasionally rich passengers were kidnapped and held to ransom. Because this type of crime was so common, special precautions were taken on board the ships trading along the China coast. The bridge and engine room were barricaded off and in some cases protected by sandbags and iron grilles. The officers and trustworthy crew members carried firearms and the radio operator was prepared to send a signal for assistance at any time. Some merchant vessels such as the 398-ton river steamer *Tin Sang* (owned by the Fook On Steamship Co of Hong Kong) also carried a special armed guard for extra protection, which was just as well.

On July 23rd pirates disguised as passengers tried to take over *Tin Sang* when she was on the West River between Shamshui and Chiaoking. They tried to storm the bridge but one of their leaders was killed by the armed guard. Now on the defensive, the pirates were forced below. The gunboat *Cicala*, also on the West River, picked up the call for help and closed *Tin Sang*. As the situation was virtually in hand, there was no likelihood of the gunboat's two 6-inch guns being used, so Lieutenant-Commander J.B. Palmer sent across an armed boarding party to disarm and arrest the pirates. *Cicala* then escorted *Tin Sang* towards the nearest police unit at Chiaoking, but some of the pirates decided to make a break for it. Ignoring threats and rifle-fire they dived overboard and struck out for the shore. One was shot and killed as he was swimming, and two were recaptured by the boats that had set out in pursuit, but the others made good their escape. At Chiaoking the prisoners were handed over to the Chinese police and the bluejackets returned to *Cicala*. The usual fate of such criminals was summary execution without trial by the Chinese, despite strict instructions to all foreign gunboats not to hand over pirates without getting a signed statement promising a proper trial.

So far the Royal Navy had been hardly affected by the outbreak of hostilities. Admittedly the 8th Destroyer Flotilla had broken off their summer exercises at Wei-Hai-Wei and had been dispersed among various Chinese ports to watch over British interests. *Delight* was sent to Tangku where Japanese destroyers had been shelling nearby villages. *Grimsby* was also there and sent a medical team ashore to treat Chinese civilians injured in the bombardment.

The Japanese Army might be capturing Peking, yet it was still a comparatively local incident confined to one province in the north-eastern corner of China. Admiral Little was still able to give an 'At Home' aboard *Cumberland* when the cruiser arrived at Tsingtao from Wei-Hai-Wei. These official parties, together with other social occasions, enabled Royal Navy personnel to meet their opposite numbers in the other services and in civilian life, both British and foreign. Personal relationships might prove all-important when emergencies happened on the far side of the world. There was one awkward moment when Japanese and Chinese naval officers both turned up at this particular function. The Japanese motor boat made fast to the stern of the Chinese launch at the cruiser's boom, but *Cumberland*'s Officer of the Watch smoothed over any unpleasantness.

Even on the Yangtse where the Japanese Navy soon began evacuating their nationals, there was no trouble yet. *Danae* was due to return downriver on August 2nd, but the British Embassy at Nanking was not to be left without the usual cruiser acting as guardship and floating radio station. *Capetown*, destined for this role, had arrived at Hong Kong from Wei-Hai-Wei on July 15th. Her scheduled refit was postponed but she went into dock to have her bottom cleaned and repainted. When she was floated out the ship's side along the waterline was kept free from oil-fuel stains by the usual four side-party girls who came on board. They were paid with food (proper portions, not waste) set aside by the ship's company. The girls ate some of it; the rest they took to sell ashore along with spare pieces of rope and canvas that they had been given. Every warship had her regular group of side-party girls, some of whom built up substantial businesses from this work. *Capetown* left Hong Kong on July 22nd, called at Shanghai and proceeded up the Yangtse to Nanking which was reached on August 1st. *Danae* sailed the next day for Shanghai.

Capetown was now the only large warship up the Yangtse. Her radio would be the British Embassy's link with the outside world as they were soon cut off from the sea when the Chinese mined the Yangtse between Chinkiang and Woosung, and erected booms or barriers across the river. The most substantial obstruction was below Tasha Island near Kiangyin, being made up of fifteen merchantmen, six warships and hundreds of junks, all filled with stones and rocks.

The Beginning

Sandwich relieved *Grimsby* and *Delight* at Tangku on August 4th, arriving about the same time as a strange-looking Japanese vessel. She was big, about 9,000 tons, had a low foc'sle and stern, but a high square superstructure. Heavy cranes and two odd-sized funnels completed her silhouette. Around her buzzed a swarm of small craft.

The sloop's officers studied their reference books and reports of new Japanese construction. Perhaps she was either *Takasaki* or *Tsurugizaki*, but these were reported to be submarine depot ships and there were indications that they were still not complete. In any case they were alleged to have only one funnel. *Akashi*, on the other hand, did have two funnels, but rumours from Japan suggested that she had only been laid down in January and would be completed as a repair ship. In fact, they were looking at *Shinsu Maru*, a ship so secret that she had two other official names, *Ryujo Maru* and *Fuso Maru*. Within her hull she carried twenty landing craft which were launched two at a time through large doors in the stern. Heavy guns, vehicles and stores were unloaded into the landing craft through two more doors in the ship's side. Commander R. A. B. Edwards and his ship's company were probably the first Westerners to see an assault landing ship in action.

Perhaps the Japanese suspected that note had been taken of their latest ship, for they stopped one of *Sandwich*'s launches in Tangku harbour. A Kempetai, or secret police agent, searched the items aboard the boat, including some of Commander Edwards' belongings which he was sending ashore. They did not say what they were looking for, nor did they find anything, and Commander Edwards protested to the Japanese naval authorities. He was told that the people responsible for pulling his luggage about were uncouth reservists who did not know any better.

A month after the first shots had been fired at Loukiachao, the Royal Navy was still undertaking peacetime tasks, unaffected by the Sino-Japanese Incident. Late on August 8th a China National Airways Sikorsky airliner crashed in the sea off Chilang Point near Hong Kong. *Thracian* was sent out to search the area with a Chinese customs cruiser which located the wreckage and picked up eight survivors. They were transferred to *Thracian* at midnight and the destroyer rushed them to Hong Kong for hospital treatment.

Within twenty-four hours of this incident two Japanese servicemen had been shot at Shanghai and the peaceful days of the China Station had gone for good.

3
The Defence of Shanghai

Shanghai would obviously be the next centre of tension and Admiral Little decided that he would be better placed if he went there. *Cumberland* would present too large a target as they passed between Chinese lines and Japanese warships so Admiral Little would transfer to the sloop *Falmouth* at Woosung for the journey up the Whangpoo to Shanghai. He would be accompanied by 155 Royal Navy and Royal Marine officers and men who were to assist in the defence of the International Settlement against possible attack by either the Chinese or the Japanese. Meanwhile *Cumberland* would be joined by *Suffolk* and the two sister-ships would stand by at the Putu Islands.

Italian Savoy Grenadiers, French infantry, United States Marines, were all on their way to reinforce or relieve their compatriots already defending the consulates, concessions and public buildings. On August 14th the 2nd Battalion, Royal Welch Fusiliers arrived off Woosung in the Blue Funnel liner *Maron*, having been rushed round from Hong Kong. *Maron* could go no farther as the Japanese had ordered that only their merchantmen could use the Whangpoo. They claimed that the Chinese might have tried to bring in troops in a merchant vessel wearing another country's flag. Although the Japanese might therefore have fired on neutral merchantmen they recognized that neutral warships were more readily identifiable and could proceed at their own risk. So *Maron* was met by *Duncan* and *Duchess* who then took the Royal Welch Fusiliers upriver. The destroyers moored alongside *Danae* so that the soldiers could be transferred and landed on the French Bund.

Now the Chinese Air Force took a hand. One of their first missions was an air strike against Japanese warships moored in the Whangpoo and bombarding Chinese positions ashore. Curtis Hawk biplane fighter-bombers were to be employed against all the Japanese warships except Vice-Admiral Hasegawa's flagship, *Idzumo*. This old three-funnelled cruiser, a veteran of the Russo-Japanese War of 1904, was the special target of a formation of Northrop 2E attack aircraft. Their crews had been trained in level bombing from a height of 7,500 feet at a fixed air-speed.

Saturday, August 14th was a wet, muggy day. Frustrated by low cloud over Shanghai the Chinese pilots brought their aircraft in at 1,500 feet in a shallow dive. The bomb-aimers, lying flat on the floor and peering between the fixed under-

The Defence of Shanghai

carriage legs suddenly glimpsed *Idzumo* and dropped their bombloads. In their eagerness they forgot to reset their bombsights to the new speed and altitude. The American cruiser *Augusta* was damaged by splinters from a 1,100 lb bomb that fell close alongside, while three more bombs fell in the International Settlement itself, hitting Nanking Road and the Great World Amusement Resort. 1,956 people were killed and another 2,426 injured, most of them Chinese. *Idzumo* was not touched. She continued to attract the attention of Chinese aircraft, artillery and motor boats but remained unscathed.

Off the Yangtse estuary the six Curtis Hawks broke through the overcast to find themselves over a couple of freighters and a three-funnelled cruiser. They immediately peeled off and dived through the rain. The large Union Jacks painted on *Cumberland*'s turrets fore and aft went apparently unnoticed and two bombs exploded fifty yards away on each side of the ship. The British cruiser, between two Japanese ammunition ships, received the same attention as her neighbours and their escorting cruisers and destroyers, which were also nearby and putting up a considerable anti-aircraft barrage. One solitary aircraft was being piloted by Colonel Claire Lee Chennault, an American serving as Inspector of the Chinese Air Force. He had taken off from Nanking to watch his airmen in action, but not knowing that his fighter was unarmed and anticipating more bombs, the ships opened fire on this fresh assailant, scoring several machine-gun hits on its wings. Colonel Chennault believed that *Cumberland* had been one of the ships firing at him. Not always the most placid of personalities, he was particularly irascible when he landed back at Nanking.

Admiral Little's transfer to *Falmouth* was completed without incident, although the Royal Marines' shore-service boots did not do her quarterdeck planking much good. The sloop moved off through the rain and gathering darkness at 20.00 hrs. She passed a Chinese gunboat, a refugee-packed ferryboat and a number of other craft, all darkened and apparently not particular about where they were going. The Asiatic Petroleum Co's Wharf downriver was ablaze, but Shanghai's commercial waterfront was dark, deserted and silent. At 23.00 hrs *Falmouth* berthed alongside *Danae* who provided cocoa and a hot meal for the landing party. They then transhipped to a number of P & O tugs which took them to the French Bund, eventually arriving at the barracks of the 2nd Battalion, Loyal North Lancashire Regiment.

This was to be their home for the next fortnight, but they had very little rest that first night. The Loyals were charged with the defence of five miles of the Concession's perimeter, their single battalion being assisted by two platoons of seamen from *Danae* and the new arrivals from *Cumberland*. They were to hold off an attack by three Chinese divisions through the Chinese suburbs of Shanghai, expected about 02.00 hrs, but instructions were rather vague, although 'fighting to the last man and the last bullet' was mentioned at one time. *Cumberland*'s sailors

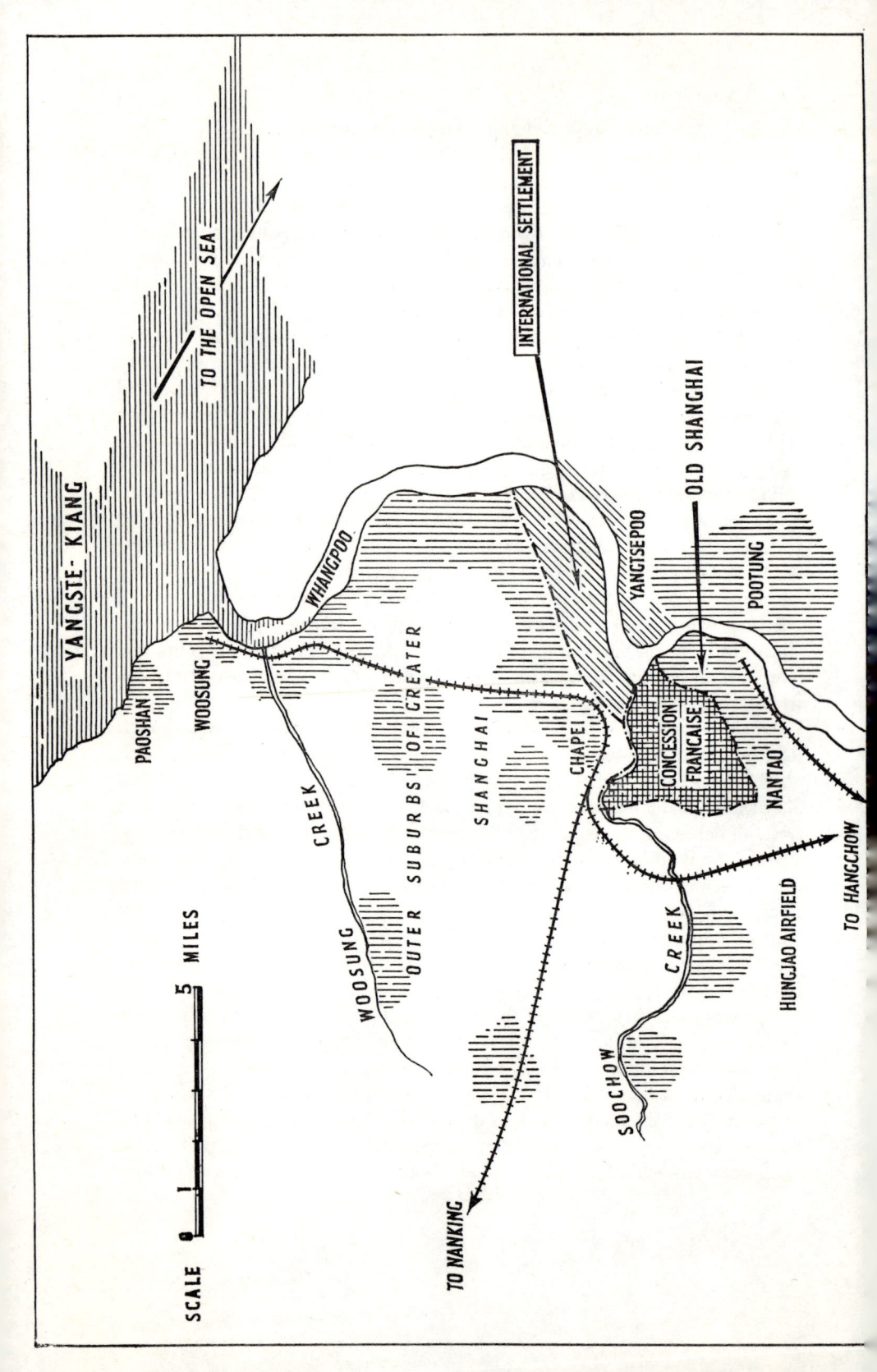

were busy for most of the night filling sandbags with insubstantial ash and rubble, and distributing them along the reserve defence line held by *Danae*'s landing party. After all this the expected Chinese attack did not materialize and all spent a particularly miserable night in pouring rain.

The next morning *Cumberland*'s Royal Marines and bluejackets took over the line between Soochow Creek and the French Concession. Eventually the rain stopped and the men settled down to some sort of routine. The two platoons in the lines were relieved every twenty-four hours by those that had been resting. It took about a week to get their shallow trenches, filled with mud and water and fronted with a sandbagged parapet, into order. They set up barbed-wire entanglements and knife-rests, getting involved in a number of arguments with local Chinese residents in the process. A field of fire had to be cleared around the outposts which meant that all the sugar-cane, trees and hedges had to be levelled for a radius of about a hundred yards. A couple of Chinese who happened to be passing were invited to help and within ten minutes a horde of coolies was bent on clearing most of Shanghai and much of the hinterland, but eventually they were persuaded to take themselves off.

No refugees were allowed into the Settlement thus forestalling any Japanese claims that Chinese were being sheltered there and preventing the population problem getting worse. No food could be taken out whilst ambulances and neutrally-owned vehicles were the only traffic allowed in or out. Double sentries were posted at all times, their equipment including large notices which stated in Chinese: 'If you advance beyond this point you will be shot.' Rations were brought up to the outposts by army lorry and the local European residents made sure that their defenders were well supplied with luxuries like fresh water, iced beer, eggs, vegetables and chickens. Sickness was one of the most unpleasant aspects of their tour of duty. One part of the sector lay close to a Chinese cemetery, overcrowded with unburied corpses, bluebottles from this charnel-house covering the men's food on very hot days so that many personnel suffered from 'Shanghai tummy' and dysentery.

Two more platoons arrived from *Suffolk* plus a pair of 3·7-inch howitzers manned by seamen from both *Cumberland* and *Suffolk*. Every day the two artillery pieces were cleaned and target practice carried out. Once they harnessed up Army mules and set off on a flag-showing tour through the suburbs of Shanghai – a grand cavalcade in the best gunner traditions. During their stay the Naval Howitzer Section did everything possible with their pieces – short of actually firing them at somebody – and were eventually given the task of building reserve posts for the Army. Having plenty of time on their hands they constructed these outposts precisely as laid down in the Army Field Handbook. Their measurements were so exact that the emplacements were regarded as model fieldworks by the Army authorities.

Meanwhile the evacuation of British women and children was being organized by Captain L. E. H. Maund of *Danae*. He set up administrative details of bluejackets to cope with registry, tickets, telephones, lost children, missing luggage and all the various problems that arose. He was also responsible for all the confidential documents from the Consulate and other establishments ashore which were transferred to *Danae* for safekeeping during the emergency. The work was similar to other evacuations of British nationals from other areas of mainland China threatened by the Japanese invasion, but Shanghai was the only large-scale emergency operation. Not only were most Britons congregated there, but in most other places they had some advance warning of what was happening and started to leave for Hong Kong before danger got too close. The families of Royal Navy personnel spending their summer holidays in North China had to be brought back to Hong Kong. They should have travelled by passenger liner, but normal services had been disrupted so special permission was given for civilians to take passage in the depot ship *Medway*.

Some people, evacuated with only a few possessions, found it difficult to make ends meet when they arrived in Hong Kong, so a special fund was set up to alleviate hardship. A number of money-raising schemes were also organised by the ships of the China Station, a typical event being the submarine *Parthian*'s cabaret dance at the China Fleet Club. An immediate mass-evacuation of all British civilians in the Far East was never contemplated by the Government in case the Japanese might regard it as a preparation for warlike activities and promptly launch an attack on our possessions.

The Shanghai piers and waterfront were soon crowded with British women and children. By August 17th over three thousand had been evacuated and many were still waiting. They said good-bye to their husbands and Chinese servants and were ferried out to *Danae* and *Falmouth*. The British authorities gave advance notice of this evacuation to the Japanese, who promised safe-conduct down the Whangpoo, but both ships came under fire for the whole of their sixteen-mile journey to Woosung. Neither was hit, although a shell carried away *Falmouth*'s ensign. Once the evacuees had been transferred to the SS *Rajputana* and she had sailed for Hong Kong, *Danae* and *Falmouth* returned to Shanghai, again running the gauntlet of shellfire. *Delight* and *Duchess* joined in taking further parties down to the liners *Maron*, *Empress of Canada*, *Patroclus*, *Shengking* and *Empress of Asia*. This last had brought the 1st Battalion, Royal Ulster Rifles to Woosung where they were transferred to the D-class destroyers to be taken up to Shanghai. The bombarding Japanese warships they passed, checked fire and saluted.

By now the Whangpoo was crowded with warships of all nations, and the emergency demanded extreme measures. Admiral Yarnell, Commander-in-Chief of the United States Asiatic Fleet, decided to move his flagship *Augusta* farther

The Defence of Shanghai

away from the Japanese cruiser *Idzumo*, thus lessening the risk of being hit by stray Chinese bombs and shells. Already one man had been killed and several injured by splinters. The only spare berth was in front of the Royal Navy buoys, off The Bund, the first trot being occupied by *Danae*, *Falmouth*, *Delight* and *Duchess*. *Augusta*'s stern was secured to this first buoy and she streamed two anchors to keep her bows in place. The 'North China Daily News' recording that this change of berth took place on August 18th, noted with some surprise that a foreign warship was now moored at the head of a line of British warships. The paper remarked that it was 'a move which had never been made by any other vessel'. These were desperate times indeed!

The crew of the *Augusta*, in common with all American personnel serving in China during the Sino-Japanese Incident, were awarded the China Service Medal, sometimes known irreverently as the Woosung Creek Medal. No campaign medal was awarded by the British Government, although a rich well-wisher presented each member of *Cumberland*'s crew with a pair of silk socks!

After their families had gone the men of the British community either joined the Shanghai Volunteer Corps or were concentrated in and around the Consulate, which was supposed to be in a safe zone though really no place in Shanghai could be considered safe. Even the municipal jail had been heavily bombarded by Japanese guns and the Shanghai authorities decided to release several hundred Chinese and European convicts. They arrived at the Royal Marines' outposts in armoured lorries, escorted by armoured cars and motor-cycle outriders. A prize assortment of thieves, rogues and vagabonds was let loose on the surrounding countryside and the naval sentries were told that any male Chinese making a determined effort to get back through the wire was to be shot.

The Japanese-owned Toyoda Cotton Mill just outside the International Concession provided more excitement on August 18th. Chinese mill-girls had been clamouring for their pay which was taken into the factory in a Japanese lorry. Having placated their workers, the Japanese employers now had to face the wrath of a mob of Chinese who had gathered outside. The Royal Marines were therefore ordered to help the Japanese get back into the International Settlement. They drove over in a British truck, concealed the Japanese inside, and then charged out of the factory back to the British lines. The Japanese lorry, empty except for the driver, followed at a slower speed and collected all the pent-up hatred accumulated by the Chinese rioters.

Meanwhile *Lowestoft* had been sent to Gough Island to protect Shanghai's petrol supply while a platoon of armed bluejackets from *Duncan* was entrusted with the defence of the Yangtsepoo Waterworks, a British-owned company. Assisted by a squad of Shanghai riot police, the sailors kept the waterworks intact, in spite of the fighting, looting, murder and rape around them. By arranging a series of truces when the battle became dangerously close, they prevented any damage and were also able to rescue a number of British citizens who had been cut off. They spent ten days at the waterworks until relieved by troops from Hong Kong.

The closing of the Yangtse coincided with the retirement of Captain Pote-Hunt, one of the Admiralty pilots responsible for navigating Royal Navy warships on the Yangtse. He was legendary for his unending stories about life on the river into which he inserted his instructions to the helmsman who had to concentrate on every word. 'I well remember in 'twenty-one or was it 'twenty-two – *starboard fifteen* – we were just coming up to where that – *midships* – junk is now, when a sampan – *keep to port of the next buoy* – crossed our bows and – *steady as you go* – we . . .' and so on for the whole voyage. Admiral Little presented Captain Pote-Hunt with a silver salver inscribed with the names of the 145 different ships he had piloted up and down the Lower Yangtse during his thirty-seven years' service.

Apart from this ceremony, the Commander-in-Chief and his staff were kept busy sending letters of protest to the Japanese who at times seemed to land their shells as close to British property as they could without actually hitting. Their warships had also developed the habit of mooring in such a position that Chinese 'overs' would fall on British-owned buildings. No doubt there were sound military reasons for such manœuvres, but it began to appear as though they were being difficult on purpose. For example, Jardine, Matheson reported that one of their godowns (or warehouses) had been burgled on a number of occasions. There were indications, but no proof, that the breaking and entering was the work of Japanese soldiers. The Royal Navy was therefore asked to provide an armed guard to help the Chinese nightwatchmen by patrolling inside the premises. As soon as the bluejackets took up their positions, the Japanese Army posted sentries outside the walls and gates of Jardine, Matheson's property. They alleged that the warehouse was infested with Chinese snipers so Japanese soldiers were needed to protect British sailors.

The only people who seemed happy in this situation were the nightwatchmen. Time and again Chinese coolies refused to work unless protected by the Royal Navy in the person of an armed sailor. Most had absolute faith in the security afforded by painting a Union Jack on their house or pinning a little flag to their sampan. Such confidence was rather misplaced for flags did not even guarantee the safety of the British Ambassador.

On August 26th Sir Hughe Knatchbull-Hugessen was returning from Nanking to Shanghai by road. A large Union Jack was painted on the roof of his car, but nevertheless it was strafed by Japanese aircraft, and Sir Hughe was badly injured, a bullet narrowly missing his spine. He was rushed to Shanghai, the car being again attacked on the way. He had to spend a month in hospital so the destroyer *Defender* brought Lady Knatchbull-Hugessen direct from Pei-Tai-Ho to be with

The Defence of Shanghai

him. They did not leave Shanghai until October 4th, taking passage in the escort vessel *Falmouth* which was completing a two-year commission. A new crew from England took over the ship when she arrived at Hong Kong four days later. Sir Hughe went on to the Philippines and the Dutch East Indies for convalescence. Although he later came back to Hong Kong, he was advised not to return to duty for some time and accordingly sailed for home.

By now the Army had relieved most of the Royal Navy landing parties at Shanghai. *Cumberland*'s bluejackets and Royal Marines, brought down the Whangpoo in *Defender* and *St Breock*, were all pleased to be back aboard their own ship again, even though it meant receiving ten days' quinine treatment. The cruiser left Woosung on August 30th and was fifty miles off the Yangtse estuary when the American liner *President Hoover* was bombed by Chinese aircraft. *Cumberland* was about a mile away and put a naval surgeon aboard the liner to attend to the seven casualties. The Chinese Government later admitted that their airmen had mistaken the liner for one of two neighbouring Japanese transports.

On September 2nd a typhoon hit Hong Kong. Gusts of 160 mph-plus lashed the harbour, mountainous waves slammed the sea-front, cars were washed into the water and houses blown down. Over six thousand poverty-stricken Chinese fishermen and their families drowned as their fragile sampans, their only homes, disintegrated. The big ships in the harbour began to drag. The liner *Talamba* (8,018 tons) went ashore at Devil's Peak, *Conte Verde*, an Italian liner of 18,765 tons, went aground at Cape Collinson and *Asama Maru* (16,975 tons) drifted broadside into Saiwan Bay, a prohibited area under the guns of the harbour forts. The old escort vessel *Cornflower* also broke adrift and ran aground.

At the height of the storm a Chinese coaster's cable parted and the 1,643-ton *An Lee* slammed into *Suffolk*'s bows. As she crashed past many of her crew leapt to safety on to the cruiser's decks. *An Lee* continued across the harbour, hit the stern of the destroyer *Duchess*, shaved past *Diamond* and ended up on a pier with her stern overhanging the roadway.

Few people witnessed more than their own struggle for survival. The typhoon raged in inky darkness from midnight to daybreak, then passed on leaving a shambles in its wake. Off Formosa the destroyer *Westcott* took a beating from the typhoon as it moved north-eastwards away from Hong Kong.

Westcott already had enough problems. She had spent most of August patrolling the Sea of Japan, being fuelled and stored at sea without entering port. They had come across a capsized junk, probably bombed by the Japanese as target practice, and decided to ram this hazard to navigation, but the Chinese boat-builders had done their work well. The resulting collision started several plates in the forepeak and *Westcott* was soon making water forward. A number of 4-inch shells had to be fired at the wreckage to let trapped air escape before the derelict junk sank. The destroyer then put into Vladivostock so that the ship's diver could inspect the damage and carry out temporary repairs, while the crew enjoyed Russian hospitality.

Returning to Hong Kong via Tsingtao, *Westcott* was hit by the typhoon. Lifelines were rigged, hatches battened down, all loose equipment lashed securely and speed reduced to 'Slow Ahead', but under the terrific buffeting, the temporary repairs gave way and the sea flooded into the asdic compartment. Stanchions between the messdecks were bent and gear broke loose, charging from one side of the ship to the other. Part of the bridge and all the boats were carried away.

But *Westcott* did more than just survive. She increased speed to 'Half Ahead' and went looking for an oil tanker reported to be in distress near by. The search was unsuccessful. The tanker had already gone down with all hands. Another SOS was received, this time from a freighter listing heavily to port after her cargo had shifted. *Westcott* dumped oil on the seas around the stricken ship and they rode out the storm together. In the morning the freighter was escorted into Foochow and *Westcott* made for Hong Kong. Her pumps had been going continuously during this ordeal, and she went straight into dry dock at Kowloon. But there was no rest for her crew who were immediately sent ashore to help with relief work that lasted over a month.

Eventually all the bodies were recovered and the ships refloated. The Hong Kong Government promptly granted permission for work on *Asama Maru* to begin, but she was not refloated until the following March. *Suffolk* had to go into dry dock for repairs to her bow and was therefore not available for transporting troops to Shanghai. This was rather a disappointment as well as a disruption. *Suffolk* like other ships on the China Station, had taken groups of soldiers on summer cruises and familiarization exercises and had acquired a reputation for hospitality in Army circles.

The typhoon had upset many plans, but Japan's invasion of China was unaffected. Within a few days *Thracian* was bustling out of Hong Kong Harbour bound for Swatow to investigate reports of Japanese bombing there. On September 6th the Japanese had announced the institution of a blockade of Chinese shipping from Sanhaikwan on the Manchurian border to Swatow in the south to prevent supplies reaching the Chinese armed forces. Britain and the other foreign powers did not recognize Japan's right to do this because no formal declaration of war had been made. The Japanese claimed that they stopped and boarded Chinese ships only, but several times British merchantmen were investigated by Japanese warships. Although the British Government had diplomatic and political reasons for not objecting to this, they informed the Japanese Government that if a British warship were present on such an occasion her crew would board the merchantman and search for any contraband destined for Chinese forces. Of course the Royal Navy could not be everywhere at once, so masters of British merchant ships were advised to tread warily when dealing with Japanese boarding parties. It was very annoying to be ordered to stop and be searched on the high seas by a foreign warship, and even more so when there was no formal blockade and no legal right of search. No matter how infuriating it might be, it was suggested that Merchant Navy captains co-operate with the Japanese if the latter really insisted on examining the ships' papers. With a warship close alongside, a disgruntled master might not live long enough to appreciate the international incident caused by his obstructive attitude or violent resistance.

In this mounting tension there were some people who were even more on edge than most foreigners – 1,300 White Russian emigrés aboard the passenger steamer *Rosalie Moller* on passage from Tsingtao to Shanghai. Having no home and no rights other than those of the cosmopolitan international concessions of the China coast, these unfortunate people were understandably very nervous. Presently their fears were quieted by the appearance of the sloop *Sandwich* who took up position several miles away and escorted the merchant ship to the mouth of the Yangtse. Lieutenant-General Glebhoff, the emigré leader, expressed his appreciation in a grateful letter to Admiral Little. The Commander-in-Chief was most surprised as the sloop had not been escorting *Rosalie Moller* at all, but quite by chance had been steering a parallel course for most of her voyage.

In some places the Chinese had blocked their own ports to prevent attack by Japanese warships. At Foochow they scuttled several merchant ships and laid two rows of controlled mines to keep the Japanese out but they also kept in a number of neutral merchantmen and their accompanying destroyers, *Delight* and the USS *Barker*. (There was no hardship and the ships' companies made their own amusements. The Americans taught the Royal Navy how to play softball, the British crew becoming the softball addicts of the China Station.) After many arguments they eventually tracked down an elusive Chinese admiral who was apparently the only officer qualified to guide the ships down the Min River and past the boom. They reached Hong Kong safely on September 12th.

Another British warship also reached her destination in September, the gunboat *Sandpiper*. She had completed a docking and refit at Shanghai in June and had been on interrupted passage ever since. Off Woosung a heavy sea almost turned her over, while farther upriver a sudden trick of the current swept her on to *Cricket*'s rudders. *Sandpiper* was holed in the central storeroom, but a collision mat was rigged until she could be docked in a tilting pontoon which enabled one end of the vessel to be repaired while the other end remained afloat. It seemed as though all *Sandpiper*'s doors, bulkheads and decks would be buckled by the strain, but they all returned to normal when the gunboat was refloated.

Sandpiper went right on up to Ichang and spent a month there before returning down the Yangtse to Yochow, where she steamed into the Tung-Ting Hu and up the Siang-Kiang to Changsha. She was now 250 miles from the nearest warship and immediately set about augmenting her anti-aircraft armament. Six extra mountings were built so that all eight Lewis guns could be thus employed. New sights were made and their arcs of fire improved by removing obstructions such as unnecessary stanchions and awnings. The Lewis guns were kept ready for instant action during the hours of daylight and the only problem was caused by the ship's cat who would not stay out of the magazine.

The Chinese boom across the Yangtse had not saved their capital Nanking from attack, but in this case the city was being hit by aerial bombardment. At first the Japanese maintained an official observance of the rights of neutrals and for two months *Capetown*'s crew watched air raids on the centre of Nanking, some distance away. The nearest targets were the power station and the train ferry, both of which were destroyed. Other attacks concentrated on airfields and military installations, but their losses in these day and night raids convinced the Japanese that they could not continue accurate precision bombing and they therefore decided to carry out general attacks over the whole of Nanking, including the foreign concessions.

On September 19th, a very dirty and decrepit boat came alongside *Capetown*'s accommodation ladder and a Japanese admiral came on board. He was bearing a bouquet of chrysanthemums, a gift from another Japanese admiral who had been at Dartmouth Royal Naval College with Captain C. Coppinger. He was also the bearer of a warning. After 08.00 hrs on September 21st, all foreign nationals in Nanking were in danger of being bombed. All warships on the Yangtse were therefore advised to move upriver, otherwise they would be the targets of aerial attack, irrespective of nationality.

The first reaction of British, French and American admirals to these threats was one of refusal, but it was decided to evacuate British civilians from Nanking, just in case. Even without this new development, the blocking of the Yangtse had completely cut the normal supply route so that food and other supplies were getting low. Some stores could be obtained at Hankow via the railway from Canton while electricity for lighting and heating could also be made available farther upriver.

The last of the Embassy staff to be evacuated came on board *Capetown* on the evening of September 20th. It had meant a great deal of hazardous work for the boats' crews who had to steer across the powerful current each time they made the 400-yard journey to or from the ship. Although the landing-stage itself was in calm water, the little dock had a very narrow entrance and an unwary helmsman could be swept against the downstream pier. He would remain pinned there until another boat towed him off. There was no rest even when the boats were moored alongside the ship with their sterns level with the gangway. If the boat's headrope were not secure, the current would gradually force the boat's bow under the

The Defence of Shanghai

steps of the gangway. Any attempt to shove off with a boathook would invariably capsize the boat. The only way out of the predicament was to raise the gangway so that the boat fell astern and righted herself.

On September 21st, a dull overcast day, *Capetown* left Nanking, thus escaping the very heavy air raids which began next day. She anchored for a while at Kiukiang but pushed on upriver after hearing that the Chinese were preparing booms every few miles. Sometimes these obstructions were made up of floating junks secured together by thick ropes and sometimes ships were sunk in the main channel.

Capetown eventually reached Hankow on October 2nd. This was the normal limit for the 4,200-ton cruiser and in fact the Yangtse was already too low to ensure safe navigation downstream, even without man-made obstructions. On September 25th the 2,665-ton *Kut Wo* had run aground at Kiukiang. *Cockchafer* was unable to free the river steamer and even after 200 tons of coal had been taken out of her, it still took three ships all pulling together to get *Kut Wo* off that ledge. Another problem was that the Kowloon-Canton-Hankow railway could not supply the needs of the British Embassy, *Capetown* and the Hankow gunboats for the whole winter. It was therefore decided to evacuate eleven officers and two hundred ratings and Chinese messboys from *Capetown*'s crew by rail. They would be accompanied by seven men, four women and one baby from the British Embassy, and the whole expedition would be under the command of Lieutenant-Commander H. G. Cooke. The Japanese guaranteed the train safe-conduct and also promised the safety of the actual track.

After a certain amount of fuss, the Chinese railway authorities provided a fairly respectable train made up as follows: one baggage van, one 1st class sleeper, one 1st class restaurant car, four 3rd class sleepers (for chiefs and petty officers, Royal Marines, stokers and seamen), one cooking van and one guard's van. The cooking van was absolutely filthy and had to be scrubbed out four times. Even when reasonably hygienic, it was so erratic that it could only be used when the train was stopped. The Chinese authorities could not provide any food, stores or coal for the engine so all this had to be bought or provided by *Capetown*. It was decided to supply provisions and drinking water for four days. The train's water tanks were only suitable for toilet purposes, so the 'Capetowns' collected a host of empty wine bottles, lime juice jars and casks from their own ship and from the gunboats alongside. In all there were about 300 gallons of drinking water, allowing each person three pints a day plus a reserve. A duty officer and petty officer were responsible each day for the issue of provisions and drinking water from the guard's van. They also arranged the sale of beer and minerals, investigated complaints, and made sure that people did not wander off when the train stopped. As the cruiser was moored on the city side of the river all the people and their belongings (a total of 700 kitbags, suitcases, packing cases, baskets of bottles and assorted bundles) had to be ferried across by *Capetown*'s boats to the railway station which was actually at Wuchang. The train was duly christened HMS *Capetown II* and carried boards bearing the ship's motto 'Spes Bona', as well as large Union Jacks. The expedition 'sailed' for Kowloon at 08.30 hrs on October 6th.

Even without an international crisis the journey would have been an eventful one. The single-track line from Kowloon to Hankow had only been completed a few months previously. Through trains were a comparative rarity and there were rumours that some sections of the permanent way were still untested. The Chinese agreed to hold their troop trains in loop-lines so that *Capetown II* could get through. They also agreed to let Lieutenant-Commander Cooke use the post office telephone services to report to Hong Kong. Fortunately these remained intact, so there were few communications difficulties. (There had been instances during other journeys in China when Royal Navy signals had had to be entrusted to carrier pigeon.) Good speed was made to Chenchow which was reached just after twenty-four hours' travelling. A long climb through the mountains was followed by an even more scenic descent from Tengkistang to Lochang.

In spite of their guarantees the Japanese had bombed the next station, Suichow, before the train arrived. No water was available so *Capetown II* went on to Yingtak and awaited developments. They heard that the track had been damaged in six places between Lienkankow Bridge and Canton, including the bridge itself. So they stayed at Yingtak for over fifteen hours while efforts were made to goad the railwaymen into taking action about the damaged track or finding out what was being done about it. Some of the station staff tried to be helpful, but others had either disappeared or were suffering from a form of hysteria officially described as 'air raid paralysis'.

The train hid in a copse along the line when a solitary aircraft flew over and then enquiries were made about taking riverboats down to Canton. This route would probably have been even more difficult as there was a possibility of obstructions across the Pei-Kiang between Yingtak and Canton. It was definitely known that there was a barrier across the Pearl River between Canton and Boca Tigris which had trapped eighteen British merchantmen who were waiting for arrangements to be made for them to be escorted out by *Cicala* on October 9th.

Making the best of *Capetown II*'s situation, a bathing party set off to the river but was immediately recalled when thirteen Japanese aircraft attacked a bridge three miles ahead of the train. The track was slightly damaged but the bridge was untouched. Now began the arguments over repairing the rails which had been cut, but at last Chinese labourers did it and filled in some of the numerous craters close to the line. When that was done there were arguments about getting permission to move, one official being especially obstructive and full of excuses why the train should not move on into the next section. It gradually became apparent that he

Evacuees at Shanghai, August 1937. [*North China Daily News*

Delight berths alongside *Danae* after ferrying troops to Shanghai from Woosung, August 1937. [*H. E. J. Regler*

President Hoover is bombed off the Yangtse Estuary,
30th August 1937.   [*North China Daily News*

An Lee at Hong Kong after the typhoon of 2nd/3rd
September 1937.   [*H. E. J. Regler*

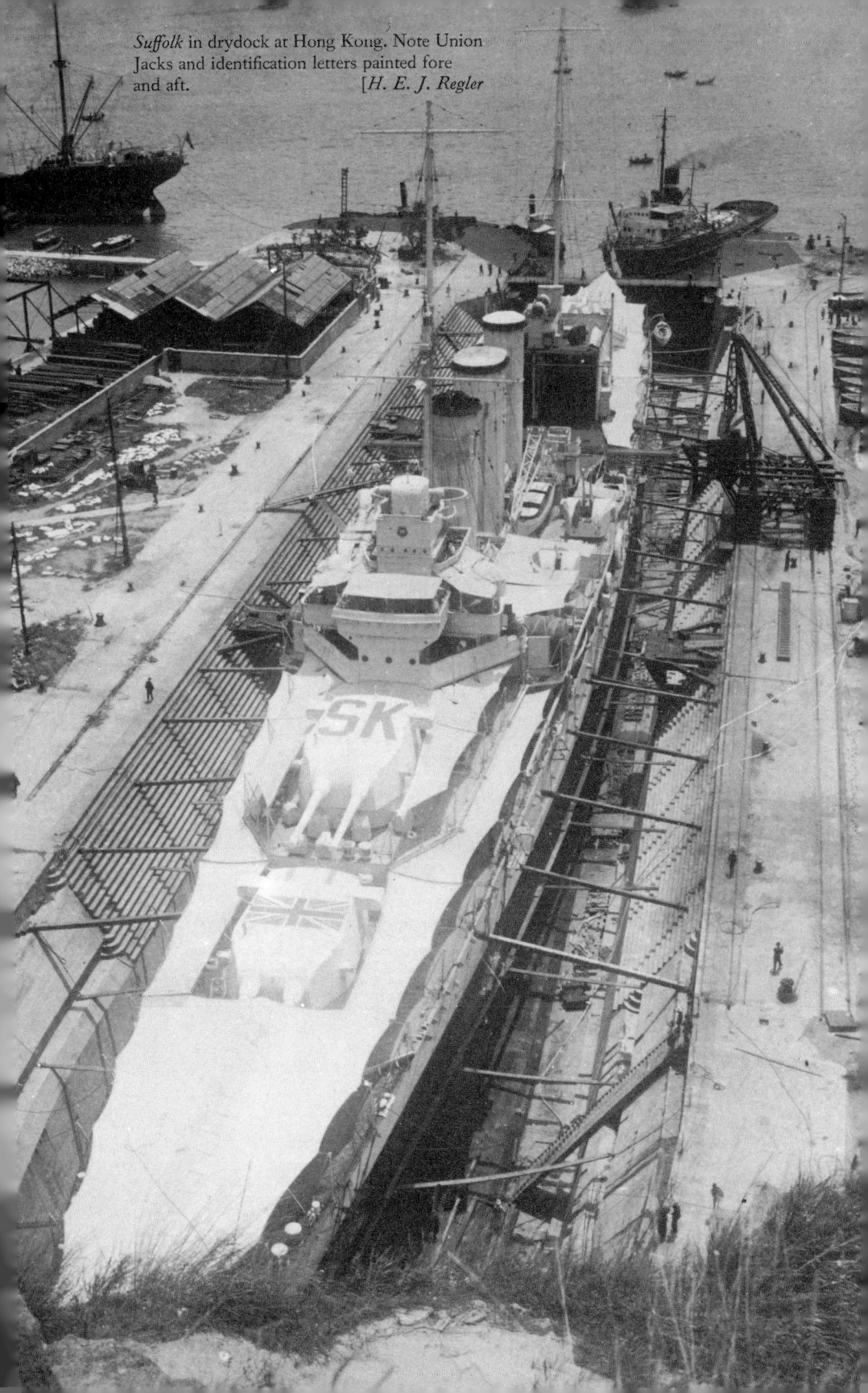

Suffolk in drydock at Hong Kong. Note Union Jacks and identification letters painted fore and aft. [*H. E. J. Regler*]

Above: '*Delight*'s own Babe Ruth.'
  [*H. E. J. Regler*

Left: A rare sight. Chinese guns bring down a Japanese aircraft over Nanking.
  [*W. F. Wilson via H. G. C. Brice*

OPPOSITE PAGE
Top: Entrance to Hsiakwan landing stage, Nanking.   [*H. G. C. Brice*

Left: Filling water tanks aboard *Capetown*'s train before leaving Wuchang. This was not drinking water which was carried separately
  [*H. G. C. Brice*

Right: Capetown's train ready to leave Wuchang on 6th October 1937. The motto translated is 'Good Hope'.
  [*H. G. C. Brice*

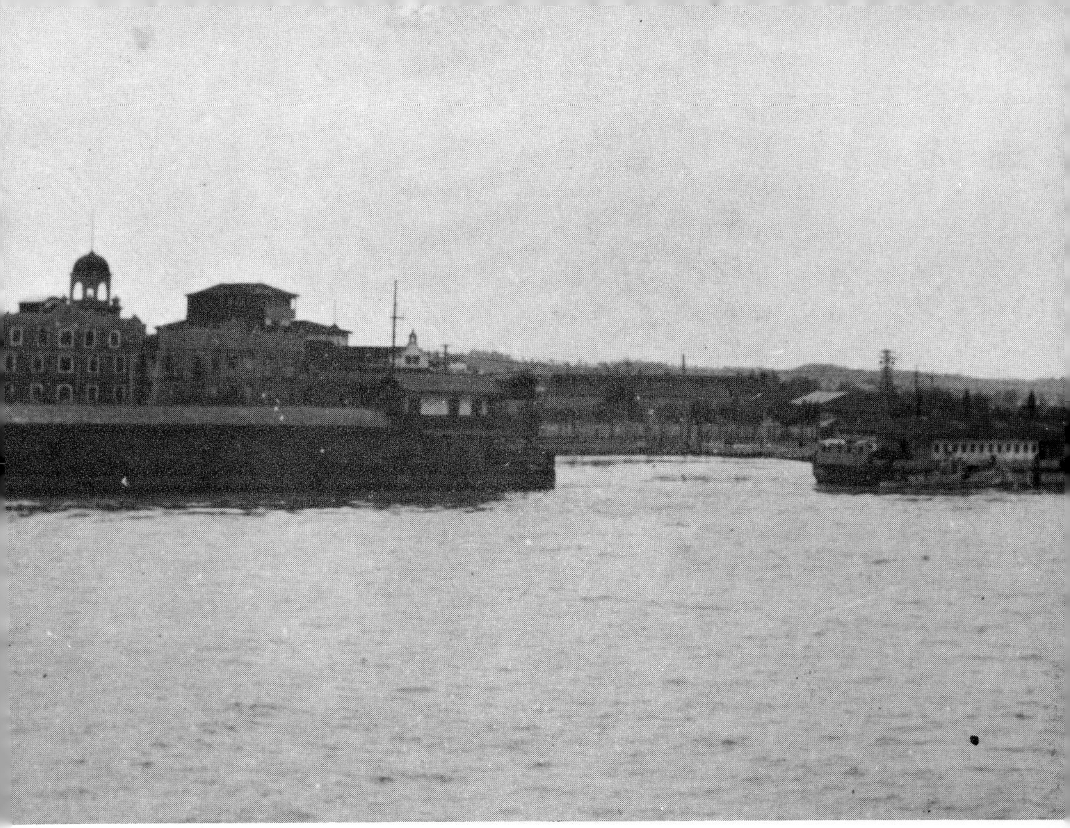

H.M.S
CAPETOWN. II
SPES-BONA.

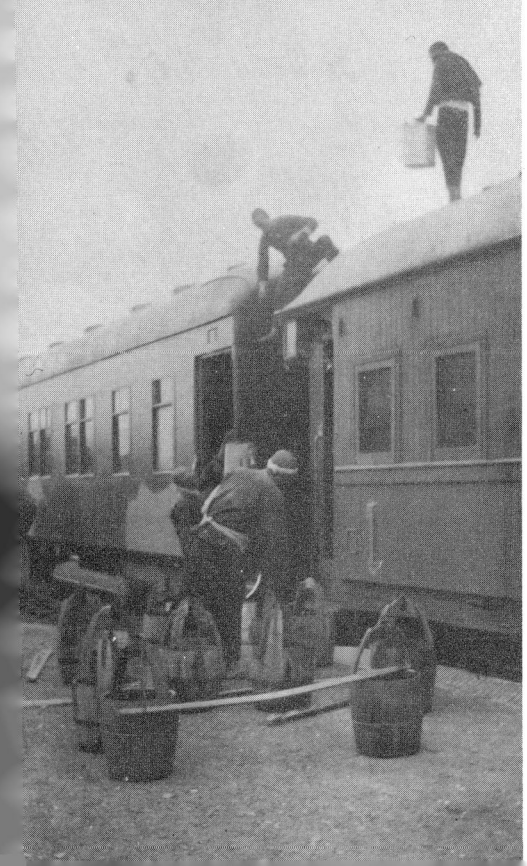

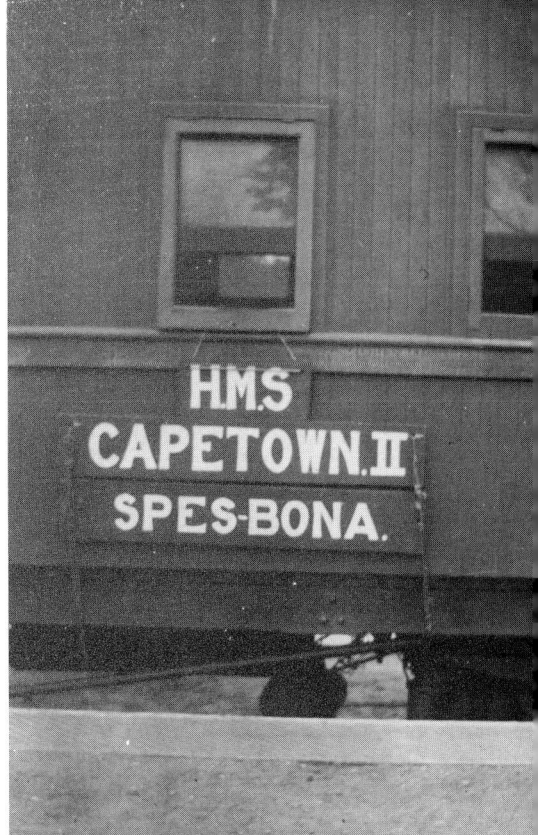

Left: The damaged railway line near Yingtak, 8th October 1937.
[*H. G. C. Brice*

Below: Coolies ferry baggage from *Capetown II* across the Lienkankow Bridge, 9th October 1937.
[*H. G. C. Brice*

OPPOSITE PAGE:
Armistice Day in Shanghai, 1937. *Cumberland* and *Augusta* in the background. [*North China Daily News*

Left: General Matsui, Japanese Commander-in-Chief at Shanghai, arrives aboard *Cumberland*, 10.00 17th November 1937.
 [*North China Daily News*

Below: Bee during an air raid on Nanking, November 1937. Being Yangtse flagship, she has more accommodation than the other gunboats. [*Associated Press*

The Defence of Shanghai

was not anti-British nor was his section inefficient. He was enterprising enough to realize that the presence of *Capetown II* if respected by the Japanese would ensure the safety of his station from aerial attack. When it was pointed out to him that this would constitute an official breach of neutrality and that Japanese retribution on both train and station would be particularly vicious, all difficulties suddenly vanished and the train was given a clear road.

The next halt occurred at Lienkankow. A horde of coolies had rebuilt the bridge with railway sleepers, but the Chinese engine-driver flatly refused to cross the structure. Showing their willingness to tackle any task, as well as fulfil every small boy's dream, a number of ratings stepped forward and volunteered to drive the locomotive and train. They were disappointed as Lieutenant-Commander Cooke considered that the bridge was unsafe and turned down their request. All the passengers, luggage, kitbags, stores and equipment had to be taken across the ramshackle bridge to another train on the other side. This train was very dirty and two of the 3rd class carriages were cattle trucks, their previous occupants having been turned loose in the surrounding fields. However, the dirt and discomfort were bearable now that they were on the last stretch, but there were more infuriating delays before the train was switched on to the new loop-line avoiding Canton.

There were more air raid warnings and more bomb craters were passed at a crawling speed scarcely slower than the train's normal pace. A restaurant car appeared at the Kowloon end of the loop and was attached for the rest of the journey which was completed in another five hours. At 23.45 hrs on October 9th *Capetown II* steamed into Kowloon Station. By 02.30 hrs all personnel and their belongings had been transferred to a ferry boat, crossed the harbour and dispersed to their new ships and establishments. *Capetown II* was no more.

Meanwhile the remainder of *Capetown*'s crew were preparing her for the winter and her eventual breakout to the sea over seven hundred miles away. The cruiser's life went on although at a slower pace. She still had to be kept clean and her machinery in working order, the crew carrying out their care and maintenance duties willingly. Although not exactly living off the fat of the land, they were fortunate in having a Chinese canteen manager who spoke about a dozen Chinese languages and dialects. He out-argued all the sampan-owners who came alongside and made sure that the crew always had adequate supplies of fresh food, although of course it always had to be well-cooked. Besides the Chinese messboys' own little charcoal or paraffin stoves, oil was available for the galley burners, but *Capetown*'s main boilers were not flashed up. This meant that there could be no steam heating so power for lighting, electric fires and motors came from the shore supply via *Laestrygon* hulk. Double sentries (six fully armed bluejackets) were posted around the ship at night in case Chinese looters took advantage of *Capetown*'s reduced complement and tried to get on board. An unpleasant sight early every morning was the execution by shooting or beheading of Chinese Army deserters, opium smugglers and bandits on The Bund. They were usually brought across from Wuchang and tried overnight. Their bodies were left lying in the roadway until sunset when they were carried off in carts. In spite of such scenes, *Capetown* remained a happy ship and some people considered that the worst aspect of their enforced stay was the non-stop Chinese music churned out by the local radio station. Others, more conservative in their eating habits and yearning for roast beef and two veg followed by figgy duff, vowed that once they left the Yangtse they would never again eat rice for the rest of their lives.

Even those accustomed to lengthy service on the Yangtse – the officers and men of the river gunboats – faced acute problems when their relief was arranged. From now on a transfer involved a lengthy and complicated journey overland, although for a while some individuals were still able to travel by China Airways. Soon every form of transport was liable to attack by the Japanese.

In spite of these extra problems, the Royal Navy still had to attend to the routine duties of peacetime. Law and order still had to be maintained lest international trade suffer. On October 6th the freighter *Fausang* arrived at Swatow to load a cargo of sugar, quite a normal, legal and mundane task. Half the cargo had been stowed in the hold when another gang of coolies came along the dockside, boarded the ship and started fighting with the coolies loading the sugar. The original dockers were driven off by the new arrivals, some of whom started to pull the bags of sugar out of the hold and throw them overboard, while the rest brought bananas from a warehouse and packed them aboard *Fausang*. The ship's officers and crew remonstrated with the gang, but were told to shut up or else they would be beaten up. Lieutenant-Commander J. L. Machin in the destroyer *Diana* saw what was happening at the same time as a call for help arrived from *Fausang*'s master. An armed party was sent across to the freighter and all the coolies of both factions were cleared right off the ship and kept off until the whole matter had been sorted out. Apparently the owners of the two strongest waterfront firms in Swatow, exporting sugar and bananas respectively, had chosen *Fausang* as the place for their final showdown. The ship's master, backed by the naval guard, made it clear that there would be no showdown aboard his ship. He had come to load sugar and so sugar was loaded.

A somewhat similar incident occurred aboard the river steamer *Kia Wo* at Ichang on the Yangtse. Two local gangsters, described officially as 'well-known riverside thugs' calmly boarded the ship and started ordering the Chinese crew about. At the captain's request, an armed guard was placed on board and the two characters were soon sent packing. Other merchant ships imprisoned by the Chinese boom farther down the Yangtse at Kiangyin were experiencing discipline problems caused by their enforced boredom. The Chinese crew-members took exception to some order given them by the chief officer of ss *Woosung*, turned on

The Defence of Shanghai

him and threatened to beat him up with broom handles, but an armed guard was sent across from the gunboat *Aphis* to quell what might be regarded as mutiny.

Such incidents emphasized the opinions of some 'Old China Hands' who still considered that Chinese lawlessness was ultimately a greater threat to commerce than Japanese aggression. Some foreigners of extremist views thought that it was a good thing for Chinese troublemakers to be put in their place; the Japanese were only doing what any right-thinking Western government ought to do. Others did not go as far as that, but they saw the war as just another of those natural disasters which afflict China from time to time. They prophesied that when the war was over – and lost by China as it undoubtedly would be – then there would be hordes of demobilized, but still armed, Chinese soldiers wandering about to swell the numbers of bandits and war-lords who preyed on travellers and villagers. The Japanese would obviously be satisfied with their victory and would leave China, so that the task of restoring law and order in the interior of the country would be even more the responsibility of the British gunboats.

Every so often the battle practice targets used by China Station warships for gunnery and torpedo exercises at Wei-Hai-Wei had to be brought back to Hong Kong for overhaul and repairs. With shallow draught hulls made of very solid timbers and surmounted by a light wooden structure, they were unwieldy things even in calm weather, so it was not really surprising when one broke adrift from the oiler *Francol* during an October storm. Her escort *Westcott* could do nothing. If she closed to get a line aboard, the cumbersome thing would probably stave in the destroyer's thin plates. *Cumberland* came to see what could be done but Captain J. C. Leach decided that his cruiser, like the oiler, was not manœuvrable enough to get alongside the target in that weather, although quite capable of towing it once secured. In any case, these ships had other duties to perform and left the area when *Suffolk* arrived on the scene. Captain H. C. Phillips had sailed from Amoy with orders to stand by the target and warn other ships to keep clear. When the weather moderated he secured it and towed it to Hong Kong.

Later in the month *Suffolk* had another emergency call. On October 25th, Captain Phillips sent a medical team across to *Thracian* who immediately slipped in response to an SOS from the *Kaitangata*. This 2,000-ton freighter had caught fire and her crew were abandoning ship. They had tried fighting the blaze, but as she was carrying a cargo of cased petrol, there was little they could do. ss *Nanning* was first on the scene and picked up the survivors. It was just past midnight when *Thracian* transferred the medical personnel to care for those suffering from burns. *Nanning* made for Hong Kong while *Thracian* received orders to sink the burning derelict with gunfire lest she became a hazard to other shipping. By now *Kaitangata* was an inferno. Her decks melted and buckled so that her funnels, mast and bridge collapsed into the hull. Soon afterwards she started going down by the bows and sank without any assistance from *Thracian*.

On October 28th, 1937, the Royal Navy gave an official welcome to Hong Kong's new Governor, Sir Geoffrey Northcote who arrived with Lady Northcote in the P & O liner *Ranchi*. *Thracian*, *Duchess* and two squadrons of aircraft escorted *Ranchi* in as *Tamar* fired a seventeen-gun salute while the other warships in harbour were dressed overall and also sent bands and guards of honour to take part in the official ceremonies ashore.

Shanghai meanwhile had settled down to the strange routine of a city nominally at peace but surrounded by bombing, fire and refugees. To ensure that the combatants respected the neutrality of British properties between the firing lines, the Royal Navy instituted a Whangpoo Patrol. Personnel from the cruiser *Danae* (later relieved by men from *Cumberland*) would be taken by the tug *St Breock* to call at various wharves several times a day. This beat would cover nineteen British properties, boost the owners' morale and encourage the Chinese coolies to stay at work. The tug would also investigate the confiscation of sampans and other small boats by the Japanese. Although such minor craft were operated by Chinese they were usually owned by British companies and *St Breock* would remind the Japanese of this fact so that the boats would be returned.

Whenever possible, the Japanese engaged in bombarding targets ashore were punctilious in observing maritime etiquette, which demands that passing warships salute each other. It seemed rather amusing when gun crews broke off their desperate battle and stood to attention before opening fire again. As this occurred each time *St Breock* passed, these interruptions must have proved very irritating to the Japanese and it might have seemed as though it were being done on purpose. A Japanese Navy spokesman pointed out that *St Breock* was liable to be fired on first and identified later, while making her night rounds, and the same sort of mistake could even happen in daylight.

The idea of a regular patrol was therefore dropped, but the investigation of confiscations continued in areas away from the bombardment. Sometimes small craft had not been requisitioned by the Japanese but had merely been abandoned by their Chinese crews. Three yachts belonging to the Royal Shanghai Yacht Club had been moored up one creek where they were in danger of being hit by stray Japanese shells. *Danae*'s motor boat and *St Breock* towed them to a safer position, while on another occasion they located two badly damaged houseboats at Point Island, downriver from Shanghai. Splinter holes were being patched up and the water bailed out quite capably by four White Russians when a squad of Japanese soldiers arrived and started interfering. They professed ignorance of the English language and tried to drive the Russians away. Lieutenant-Commander M. S. L. Burnett, a qualified interpreter in Japanese, arrived on the scene and pointed out their error – in their own language. The Japanese were apparently so amazed at any Westerner understanding and speaking their language that they cleared off and let the Russians finish the repairs. The houseboats were refloated and towed back to Shanghai. Lieutenant-Commander Burnett then went off to argue with some Japanese troops who had declared their intention of digging a trench right through a section of British property.

In spite of continued representations to the appropriate authorities, Japanese soldiers and sailors did not stop trying to requisition British buildings, nor did they refrain from boarding all sorts of craft belonging to British firms. Their Chinese crews were overawed and the vessels commandeered to clear mines and other obstructions from the Whangpoo. Royal Navy cutters never stopped scouring creeks and wharves for these confiscated boats. In one fortnight alone *Folkestone* restored thirteen of these commandeered vessels to their rightful owners.

Language problems may well have accounted for many of the difficulties in contacts with the Japanese and probably complicated the Keelung Incident of 1936 when two British sailors were arrested after an argument with a Japanese taxi-driver in Formosa. While in custody they were beaten up by the Japanese police who then went on to attack the investigating officer from the destroyer *Bruce*. Diplomatic arguments eventually resulted in the indefinite suspension of all Royal Navy visits to Japan and Japanese territory.

In view of these disagreements and the general trend of world events, many people were no doubt surprised on November 3rd when *Cumberland* dressed ship overall in honour of the Anniversary of the Birthday of the Emperor Meiji. However all foreign ships were similarly adorned as no country except China was at war with Japan, and even that was unofficial. It was – and is – normal procedure for ships of the Royal Navy to dress overall when in company with foreign ships celebrating a special event. Over this period in Shanghai, *Cumberland* was also decorated for the Anniversary of Mussolini's March on Rome, George Washington's Birthday and Armistice Day.

By now destruction at Shanghai was reaching its climax. The Chinese had been outflanked by the Hangchow Bay landing on November 5th and by the 11th they were withdrawing along both banks of the Whangpoo past the International Settlement. Many fires were started, some by the retreating Chinese and some by Japanese shells. The suburb of Chapei was a mass of flames and the Pootung-Nantao boom across the Whangpoo was set on fire. The foreigners' Armistice Day ceremony in front of The Bund War Memorial was interrupted when a blazing junk burned through its mooring and drifted across the river close to the cargo-liner *Taksang*. Royal Navy ratings left their beflagged ships and boarded the junk and a threatened oil lighter to help the fire-float *Poochi* put out the flames. Ashore the British and American Tobacco Company's buildings were ringed by fire, but were saved by another party of men from *Cumberland*. The Armistice Day service was not resumed. One shell exploded near the Cathedral, blowing in some glass, while another shell landed in a blacksmith's forge opposite the Naval Club.

This one, a 12-inch projectile, failed to explode and was promptly employed by the Chinese blacksmith as a very useful anvil.

Then suddenly the fighting was over. The Japanese had won the Battle of Shanghai and were pursuing the Chinese towards Nanking. Shanghailanders could pick up the threads again, return to their damaged homes, revive their sagging profits. They also had to reach some sort of agreement with the Japanese, who had much to arrange. The war for them was not quite over. There was some mopping-up to be done before Nanking fell and Chiang Kai-Shek came to terms. At a conference aboard *Cumberland* on November 17th and at other discussions they insisted that the blockade of Chinese ports must continue, while Shanghai, always attractive to arms dealers from all over the world, must not become a centre for anti-Japanese intrigue. British representatives also took advantage of these talks to complain of the Japanese attitude and behaviour towards Royal Navy warships.

There was a growing number of minor incidents involving the two navies, one such having occurred on November 7th when the destroyer *Decoy* sighted a Japanese convoy on the horizon, on an almost parallel but slightly converging course. No one was in danger as they neared, but a Japanese cruiser escorting the convoy suddenly veered away from the transports and headed towards *Decoy*. The Japanese captain may have thought that the British destroyer was trying to spy on Japanese shipping movements or he may have been deliberately aggressive. Whatever his reasons, the cruiser came in so fast and so close that *Decoy* had to go hard over to avoid a collision.

The Admiralty accordingly warned Royal Navy warships not to carry out any manœuvres which Japanese warships might interpret as hostile. This especially applied to gunnery, torpedo and bombing exercises, although the rule did not apply if the vessel in sight on the horizon were a merchantman. It so happened on November 30th, therefore, that when one of *Eagle*'s aircraft noticed a mercantile tanker in the distance, the crew dismissed it from further consideration and carried out their appointed exercise dropping a series of smoke floats. The aircraft returned to *Eagle* passing over the tanker which promptly opened fire with 3-inch anti-aircraft guns. The merchant ship had turned out to be a Japanese seaplane tender, either *Notoro* or *Kamoi*. Even though the mistake was understandable as both ships had originally been converted from oil tankers, the rule about exercising near other ships, especially Japanese, was re-emphasized. Just to make extra sure that there should be no misunderstandings, Admiral Hasegawa suggested that no salutes be fired when British and Japanese warships met.

As a further safeguard, the Japanese were usually informed in advance of the movement of Royal Navy vessels and personnel in the war zones. But presently the Japanese demanded that this information be given as of right lest regrettable mistakes occur. They also extended their interpretation of war zones to include almost all Chinese rivers and coastal waters under their control, even though the fighting had long since passed on. They explained that this was necessary to prevent the smuggling of goods to Chinese troops and to protect neutral merchantmen from mines, Chinese guerrillas and additional marine hazards caused by the Chinese removal of all navigation marks. This was a purely temporary measure and would be lifted as soon as Nanking was captured and Chiang Kai-Shek came to terms.

Accordingly, at the beginning of December, the Japanese were told that three ratings would be accompanying the British Vice-Consul during his short journey to Tsungming Island in the ferry *Sui-An*. The Vice-Consul was going to search for nine French-Canadian nuns, missing since the occupation of the island three months before. In spite of this advance notice, and in spite of Union Jacks being displayed, machine-guns opened up on *Sui-An* as she approached Tsungming. A Chinese officer in the wheelhouse was mortally wounded and another Chinese member of the crew injured. Bullets were still hitting the bridge as *Sui-An*'s master crawled to the wheel and steered the ship out of danger. The ratings later reported the incident to the appropriate authorities while Mr Boothby went off to look for the nuns. Like so many similar incidents of this time the Navy never learned the result of his quest.

4
The *Ladybird* and *Panay* Incidents

This event seemed of small importance compared with the really grave news which soon came from up the Yangtse. The Japanese, hammering at the walls of Nanking, had no time to be patient. This was to be their last battle, their last victory, and then the war would be over.

The gunboat *Ladybird* had been stationed at Wuhu about eighty miles upriver from Nanking to look after British lives and property. There were about a hundred Europeans in the town, the women and children among them being persuaded to take the first available steamer to Hankow. The properties, however, were too large and scattered to be adequately guarded by *Ladybird*'s small British crew, so they could only be visited from time to time. Meanwhile an endless procession of steamers, junks and sampans was heading upriver as Europeans and Chinese evacuated Nanking before the Japanese invested the city. The various departments of Chinese government, administration and culture were moved to Hankow, Chungking and Changsha, most of the remaining staff at the British Embassy leaving in *Bee* for Hankow on November 24th, 1937. The gunboat flagship had been relieved by *Scarab*, wearing the 'acting broad pennant' of Captain G. E. M. O'Donnell, Rear-Admiral R. V. Holt's Chief of Staff. *Scarab* herself was due to be relieved by *Cricket*.

Soon all foreign warships and merchantmen at Nanking had been concentrated off the upstream end of the city wall – a safe anchorage duly recognized by the Japanese. When final evacuation became necessary, the British and German Consulates would be accommodated in *Scarab*, other foreigners in *Cricket* and friendly Chinese in the ss *Wantung*.

After a few days there came a lull in the stream of river traffic passing Wuhu. The quiet was broken on December 5th when three Japanese aircraft appeared and dropped ten bombs on The Bund and the steamers, lighters, junks and sampans moored close by in an agreed neutral zone. The steamship *Tuck Wo*, owned by Jardine, Matheson, received a direct hit in her boiler-room killing some of the personnel there. The resulting blaze spread to her cargo of cotton and then to the hulk to which she was secured. Captain Hurst, an Admiralty pilot, and Petty Officer Steward Ah Yuen Chang Kaig from *Ladybird* both happened to be on the shore alongside. They quickly collected a scratch crew and took over a damaged launch (*Chengyang*) which was herself in danger of sinking. Captain Hurst jammed *Chengyang* between the old hulk and *Tuck Wo* so that the survivors could jump across and escape the mounting flames. *Tuck Wo*'s master and chief officer had been forced to leap into the water from the foc's'le and they were also picked up by the launch. Bombing was continuing all this time and one man aboard the launch was killed by splinters. *Ladybird*'s motor sampan arrived, but her little push-pull pump had hardly any effect on the flames and she could only help *Chengyang* with the survivors.

Ladybird was raising steam and fusing shell as the aircraft swung round for another pass. This time they approached from dead astern where her 3-inch AA gun could not bear. The first bomb landed ten yards away on the port bow, showering *Ladybird* with splinters, but the rest of the stick fell on The Bund causing many casualties among the Chinese gathered there. The gunboatmen had recently qualified in first aid and they did what they could for the injured, saving many lives. The ship's decks and the pontoon alongside were soon covered with rows of wounded and an ambulance service was organized to take the worst cases to hospital, returning with more medical supplies.

The ss *Tatung* had been holed by a near miss and her engine room was flooding but she managed to reach the shore and was beached. She was about two miles downstream from Wuhu and it was decided that *Ladybird* should anchor near her to deter looters from boarding the damaged vessel during the night. There were no more air raids that day, but all the remaining Europeans, plus the beer in the Royal Navy Canteen, were evacuated and all foreign ships assembled near *Ladybird*. A full report of the day's events was made to the Admiralty and the Japanese were informed of the presence of neutral shipping in what was hoped would be respected as a safe area. Japanese naval representatives called on Captain J. G. L. Dundas of the sloop *Folkestone* (Senior Naval Officer, Shanghai). They accepted responsibility and expressed their regrets and a willingness to consider reparations.

So for the next couple of days the ships were undisturbed although Wuhu continued to be bombed until in ruins, one bomb falling right in the middle of an enormous Union Jack painted on the temporarily abandoned tennis court in the British compound. There still remained at Wuhu five nuns who had not been outside the walls of their convent for many years so *Ladybird*'s motor sampan was ordered to rescue them early one morning. The day's bombing had just begun punctually at 07.30 hrs when the five hooded figures, clasping crucifixes in one hand and a little bundle of belongings in the other jumped into the boat with surprising agility. Even a couple of near misses failed to disturb their composure as the boat sped downriver towards the safe anchorage.

On December 9th advance units of the Japanese Tenth Army arrived at Wuhu as part of their plan to cross the Yangtse and complete the encirclement of Nanking. *Ladybird* was immediately involved in another altercation with the

Japanese. Two Chinese were thrown into the water when their sampan was in collision with a Japanese motor boat. They were then fired on by a second armed launch and one was wounded before being picked up by the British gunboat. The Japanese claimed that this was unwarranted interference but they promised to continue to recognize the safe anchorage being used by the neutral shipping. They also agreed to allow a party from *Ladybird* to check the condition of British properties in Wuhu on the Sunday.

Rear-Admiral Holt at Hankow was now Senior Naval Officer, Yangtse, as Vice-Admiral Crabbe had gone to Hong Kong as Acting Commander-in-Chief, Admiral Little having been taken ill with pleurisy. Lung complaints were common in the China Station's extremes of bitter cold and stifling sodden heat. Over one period of six months ten of the 750 men in the cruiser *Birmingham* were invalided home with tuberculosis. Stokers, working in very high temperatures and humidity, were the chief sufferers.

Admiral Holt decided to come downriver personally to contact local Japanese commanders and discuss the possibility of ensuring the safety of British shipping on the Yangtse. He would be accompanied at the conference by those few British Consulate officials who had stayed at Nanking during the last days of its siege and were now preparing to come upriver. By the time they met Admiral Holt, the Consul (Mr Prideaux-Brune), the Military Attaché (Lieutenant-Colonel W. A. Lovat-Fraser), and Captain O'Donnell would have something else to report.

About 13.30 hrs on December 11th the foreign ships off Nanking came under fire from Japanese positions outside the city and all vessels got under way, the shells following them upriver until out of range. *Cricket* was towing four junks laden with emergency coal for the gunboats while *Scarab* was towing an engine-less Jardine, Matheson steamer, so neither warship could make much speed. The convoy anchored for the night in a rural, almost deserted stretch of the river between Nanking and Hohsien. It did not seem to be near any likely military objectives but *Scarab* handed over her hulk to the ss *Whangpu* to keep her arcs of fire clear. The Americans in the convoy, however, were not happy with this anchorage and so moved on farther upriver to Kaiyuan Pontoon. The US gunboat *Panay* was escorting three Socony oil tankers owned by the Standard Oil Company of New York and mainly crewed by Chinese, but a motley assortment of steamboats, launches, junks and sampans, was also in company. The warships all broadcast their positions which were apparently agreed as safe by Admiral Hasegawa. The British Consulate party also decided to continue upriver, so they transferred to the British Lumber Company's small steamer *Tseang Tah*, arriving at the safe anchorage near Wuhu at 07.30 hrs on the 12th.

Japanese machine-guns ashore opened fire on the tug as her passengers were transferring to *Ladybird*. The ss *Sui Wo* and *Shu Kwang* were also targets and the machine-gunners continued firing at the merchant ships until they were out of range downriver without being damaged. *Ladybird* did not reply, partly because her 6-inch guns would have wrecked British warehouses on The Bund, and partly because the Japanese would then have been given a reason for sinking the gunboat. As soon as Petty Officer Hawkins and another rating, lying flat on their stomachs on the foc'sle, had raised the anchor, *Ladybird* sailed straight for the shore in an effort to dissuade the machine-gunners. She herself then came under fire from field artillery but although over a hundred 6-inch howitzer shells were fired at her she did not answer back and eventually anchored so close to the quayside that the guns could not depress sufficiently to bear on her.

By this time a hit on the forward 6-inch gun had gone on to damage the 3-inch gun and the wheelhouse. One shell had struck the battery deck wrecking the radio aerials and searchlights, and damaging the bridge and officers' bathroom. Another shell had pierced No 2 oil fuel tank, and there were three other hits on or near the waterline, so that a collision mat had to be rigged to check the inrush of water. The pumps were got going and continued working until the ship was drydocked. Sick Berth Attendant Lonergan was killed and Petty Officer Smallwood seriously wounded in the eye. Quartermaster Matthews became a casualty and had to be sent below, whereupon Captain O'Donnell took the wheel, even though one of his fingers had been shot away. Others of the crew were also slightly wounded.

Lieutenant-Colonel Lovat-Fraser and Captain O'Donnell then went ashore to remonstrate with Colonel Hashimoto, the local Japanese commander, first restraining the artillerymen who were still trying to point their pieces at *Ladybird*. A conference began in a nearby office, the two British representatives protesting at this unfriendly act committed by one supposedly friendly nation on another. Their arguments were interrupted by more artillery fire outside, the target apparently being *Bee*, flying the flag of Rear-Admiral Holt and wearing three large White Ensigns. She was just coming round the bend 400 yards away. One shell passed right between her masts, then Colonel Lovat-Fraser was at the gun pulling the artillerymen away by the scruff of the neck. No more rounds were fired and *Bee* berthed safely alongside *Ladybird*. Admiral Holt went ashore and the conference resumed.

Colonel Hashimoto stated that his artillery had orders to fire on all river shipping because the Chinese were using the Yangtse to escape from Nanking. He considered that his men were incapable of distinguishing different foreign flags, and in any case, the Chinese often used the Union Jack as a cover when shooting at Japanese soldiers. Royal Navy sailors also looked like Chinese troops, because although the regular Chinese Army wore khaki, their provincial soldiers were clad in many uniforms. Colonel Hashimoto had thought that the safe anchorage was in fact a Chinese troop convoy, an impression confirmed when one vessel emitted a dense cloud of smoke as though laying a smokescreen to cover offensive action. Finally, and in contradiction, the Japanese stated that the river was shrouded in the thick fog of early morning, a surprising fact not noted by any of the British ships involved. After putting forward such explanations the Japanese apologized and promised to provide representatives at the funeral of Sick Berth Attendant Lonergan. They also agreed to send one officer and six men aboard *Bee* as a guarantee against future attack. These never arrived although three soldiers did go downriver in *Bee*'s sampan with *Ladybird*'s doctor to see if the merchant ships required medical assistance.

By now another bombing incident had occurred, this time involving *Scarab* and *Cricket*, whose captain was now Senior Naval Officer, Nanking. About 13.30 hrs Japanese aircraft had appeared and divebombed them, releasing eight bombs. The two warships, their awnings cut away, opened fire with their Lewis guns, whereupon the aircraft turned their attention to other vessels in the area, including the British steamer *Wantung* with six hundred passengers on board. This attack was also broken up by machine-gun fire from the gunboats. Another section of aircraft then dived on *Cricket* and *Scarab* again who replied with their 3-inch guns as well as their lighter armament. No ship had been damaged, but in the middle of this air raid an American signal arrived asking if the British gunboats were in touch with *Panay* who had broken off an emergency transmission. *Scarab* replied that four columns of smoke could be seen rising from *Panay*'s last approximate position out of sight around the bends of the river.

Cricket and *Scarab* informed Captain Dundas at Shanghai who delivered a further protest to Admiral Hasegawa, asking for guarantees for the safety of British shipping in the areas declared neutral by the Japanese authorities themselves. Such guarantees were not forthcoming immediately, as Japanese airmen claimed they could not tell the difference between stationary and moving ships because the force of the river current created a wake as it rushed past an anchored ship. But Admiral Hasegawa promised to do what he could and instructed Japanese naval aircraft to fly around the British warships to identify them and their anchorage. The gunboats were therefore ordered not to fire at these aircraft unless definitely attacked, the exercise being duly carried out some time later.

Meanwhile nothing further had been heard from *Panay*, a matter of grave concern to Admiral Yarnell in his flagship *Augusta* at Shanghai. It was believed the Japanese were breaking the booms across the Yangtse, but there might be enough obstructions to prevent the 9,050-ton cruiser getting up the river especially as it was at its low winter level. Admiral Yarnell therefore requested Captain Dundas to ask the British forces already upriver to investigate, and a signal to this effect was made to Admiral Holt in *Bee*.

By the morning of December 13th, Admiral Holt was already involved in fresh arguments with the Japanese. Sick Berth Attendant Lonergan was buried, the service being conducted by Acting Bishop Craighill of the China Inland Mission.

Then while *Bee* was preparing to search for *Panay*, Admiral Holt received news of a bombing attack on the US ships. He demanded that the twelve officers and men promised by the Japanese should accompany him but they had still not arrived by the time set for his departure. So he left without them, ignoring the latest Japanese order that no ship must move on the Yangtse. Immediately before sailing, he had learned of American survivors, so *Bee* proceeded at full speed.

About half-way between Wuhu and Nanking a Japanese aircraft circled *Bee* at low altitude and shortly afterwards *Bee* came upon the wrecks of the tankers *Mei Ping* and *Mei Shia*, both burning at Kaiyuan Pontoon near Hohsien. The tanker *Mei An* was aground with her bridge 'crumpled like matchwood', a motor sampan from *Panay* was stuck in the mud on the river bank and various other wrecked or damaged sampans and launches were lying abandoned in the vicinity. A couple of Chinese looters scrambled away from *Mei An*. There was no other sign of life. 'It was like walking into a graveyard.'

Bee arrived about 15.00 hrs and immediately began a search for survivors, soon seeing three people walking along the bank. They were the first *Panay* survivors to tell the story of what had happened. Japanese artillery and naval aircraft had attacked *Panay*'s convoy the previous day. The 450-ton gunboat had tried to put up a defence but had been bombed and sunk, the survivors being machine-gunned by aircraft and launches as they abandoned ship. Captain Carlton of *Mei An*, Signor Sandro Sandri (an Italian war correspondent) and two American ratings had been killed, while over forty officers and men had been wounded. There was no accurate record of Chinese casualties. Certainly two Japanese sentries had been killed by bombing while trying to prevent survivors getting ashore on the Kaiyuan Pontoon. The survivors were found in freezing swamps and icy waters and taken to *Bee* where they received medical attention and were given clothing and other comforts. The search continued after dark, with searchlights illuminating the creeks, islands, mudbanks and reed-beds along the riverbank.

By now Japanese warships had broken through the Chinese booms lower down the Yangtse and the gunboat *Hozu* arrived that night. Next day they were joined by the torpedo-boats *Kasasagi* and *Ootori* and later by the Japanese gunboat flagship *Ataka*, this last firing a salute of thirteen guns. Rear-Admiral Holt was compelled by etiquette to reply but the gunfire alarmed everyone in the vicinity – their nerves were really on edge.

From now on operations were hampered by the presence of Japanese landing parties, whose intervention provoked resistance by local Chinese forces. Armed launches manned by the Japanese Army, claimed to be helping in the search, but in spite of flying a Red Cross flag often opened fire on Chinese soldiers along the creeks. Naturally enough the Chinese replied and also fired on British search parties, mistaking them for Japanese soldiers. Once Admiral Holt and a petty officer went ashore, one waving his cap and the other a Red Cross flag. They were promptly shot at by a Chinese constable. They flung themselves to the ground and the policeman immediately ran forward apologizing profusely. On the whole the Chinese were helpful, but Admiral Holt decided that the Japanese were more of a hindrance and requested their removal. The Japanese authorities agreed but regretted that nothing could be done to implement this request as their landing parties were not equipped with radio. Thereafter the boats from *Bee*, *Ladybird* (who had been relieved at Wuhu by *Scarab*) and the USS *Oahu* (who had also arrived), had to carry a Japanese officer to search for the Japanese soldiers in the area as well as picking up survivors. Eventually all the groups of Japanese were contacted and their landing craft withdrawn.

News came that some survivors had moved inland as far as Hanshan, some twenty miles from Hohsien. It took a long time to locate them, persuade them to come back to the river and then organize their evacuation. It was not until 02.30 hrs on the 15th that the last boatload of survivors reached the ships.

The Japanese offered to take the survivors back to Shanghai but this offer was declined, although some of the wounded, including Captain O'Donnell, later completed their journey in a Japanese flying-boat. The Japanese offer was not in itself exactly reassuring as rumours spread regarding what was happening in Nanking.

The shouts of 'Banzai' at the gates of the city on December 13th had marked the beginning of a four days' crescendo of murder, rape, arson and looting. The Rape of Nanking was the climax of a campaign of frightfulness, acted out in a hundred little villages and towns. Chinese prisoners of war, civilians, men, women, children, the aged, the sick, babies and wounded were killed by pistol, rifle, machine-gun and bayonet. It has been estimated that no less than 200,000 Chinese died.

Meanwhile other Japanese gunboats and torpedo boats had pressed on upriver towards the safe zone at Wuhu. A lone Chinese fisherman in a little sampan just off the first British merchant ship, put his hands up in a token of surrender. A burst of machine-gun fire from the leading warship tumbled his corpse into the river. As each Japanese vessel passed the anchored merchantmen, she trained her guns round, watching for the slightest hint of hostility.

However, the Japanese naval authorities offered to extend what they described as 'all facilities' to naval vessels of any third power wishing to proceed downriver to Shanghai. It was decided that *Ladybird* and the American gunboat *Oahu* should take this opportunity of convoying merchant ships to Shanghai as well as carrying the survivors and the bodies of those who had been killed. *Oahu*, *Ladybird* and ten merchantmen left Hohsien about 13.00 hrs on December 15th. They were accompanied for most of the way by the Japanese gunboats *Ataka* and *Hozu* and the torpedo boats *Kasasagi* and *Ootori*, all their flags at half-mast. *Ladybird* arrived at Shanghai at 16.45 hrs on December 17th. The crew of the cruiser *Augusta* stood to attention and saluted as the gunboat passed in the evening gloom before mooring alongside *Folkestone*. *Oahu* secured alongside *Augusta* and one of the Japanese warships anchored downstream. The freighter *Kung Wo* tied up at Hunt's Wharf while the steamer *Wantung* berthed at the Butterfield and Swire Wharves near the French Bund. The other merchant ships had dropped anchor at the mouth of the Whangpoo earlier in the afternoon. Next day they left the Yangtse estuary in a snowstorm and were at last free to proceed upon their lawful occasions.

The Americans expressed their thanks and appreciation for the services of the British gunboats, rendered 'in a manner most gallant and in keeping with the highest naval traditions'. In recognition of their work, Mr Joseph P. Kennedy, United States Ambassador in London, later presented medals to a number of Royal Navy officers involved, when they returned to England. Other honours were awarded by the British Government. Captain Hurst, the Admiralty pilot, received the DSC while Petty Officer Ah Yuen Chang Kaig was awarded the DSM. Petty Officer Hawkins who had raised *Ladybird*'s anchor under fire and Chief Engine Room Artificer Brook who had raised steam for full speed at such short notice both received the BEM. Lieutenant-Commander P. I. M. Ashby of *Cricket* was awarded the OBE for the moral courage he displayed in opening fire, Captain O'Donnell and Lieutenant-Commander H. D. Barlow of *Ladybird* both received the DSO, while Rear-Admiral Holt was mentioned in despatches.

For a brief while it seemed as though the *Panay* Incident might bring Japan and the United States to the brink of war. The Chamberlain Government in Britain, waiting to see the results of their policy of appeasement, did not take such a hard line. After diplomatic representations the Japanese Government later admitted that Colonel Hashimoto (who had actually hoped to start a war) was responsible for these unprovoked attacks. He was relieved of his command together with those officers felt to have been most involved in the excesses at Nanking. They promised to pay compensation for the death, injury and damage done to British and American nationals and stated that strict instructions had now been given to local commanders to ensure the safety of neutral lives and property. In fact, they were not to open fire on any ship on the Yangtse unless positively certain that the vessel was being used for military purposes. After these announcements the British and American peoples lost their fit of chauvinism and the Sino-Japanese Incident disappeared from the world's headlines.

The Japanese offer of 'all facilities' also included the cruiser *Capetown*, many more miles up the Yangtse at Hankow. Captain Coppinger had good news for the few men left on board who had been expecting a rather lonely Christmas. He addressed the assembled remnant of the ship's company and told them that it had been decided that *Capetown* should try to get downriver. If she did not leave now, the river would definitely be too low for another six months. Not only might there be more obstructions in the river by then, it was also doubtful whether supplies could be guaranteed at Hankow for that length of time. Captain Coppinger had obtained a safe-conduct from the Japanese by radio, but the Chinese had set a time limit on *Capetown*'s move. They were building a fresh boom at Kiukiang, 120 miles downstream from Hankow, and had no intention of delaying its completion to allow British ships to pass. Due to the gravity of the situation, *Capetown* would be carrying twenty-three British women and thirty children, some of them babies. About three hundred British, American, German and other foreign women and children would follow in the steamer *Woosung* to be escorted by the gunboat *Gnat*. Although few people knew of it at the time, *Capetown* would also be carrying $4,000,000 in notes from the American banks in Hankow for deposit in their safer branches in Shanghai. Captain Coppinger then went on to outline the conditions that the Japanese had laid down. All the guns were to be trained fore-and-aft, their breech-blocks removed, the mechanisms sealed up and all armament covered. No sentries were to be posted and nobody must carry sidearms. Only lookouts were allowed topside and all other personnel must remain below. There must be no noise, no singing, no joking, nothing which might possibly arouse the slightest Japanese suspicion or anger. Although the gunboats were accustomed to operating on the river, it was a new thing for a cruiser to attempt the passage at this time of year. There was no question of a Chinese pilot, because of the danger of his capture by the Japanese. *Capetown*'s safety would depend entirely on the knowledge and skill of her crew.

Capetown left Hankow on December 18th, the day after the Japanese had staged their triumphal march through Nanking. The Chinese closed the boom at Kiukiang that night as soon as *Capetown* had passed through, thus forcing the abandonment of the second part of the plan, the evacuation of the three hundred women and children from Hankow. The British authorities therefore revived their original idea of taking them by rail which had at first been dismissed as too dangerous. These refugees eventually arrived safely at Hong Kong on New Year's Day, their train covered with British, French and German flags.

Capetown anchored for the first night just below Kiukiang as navigation was too hazardous for her during the hours of darkness. The Lower Yangtse is notorious for sandbanks which shift and block channels literally overnight. In theory the deepwater channels were marked by bundles of brushwood like inverted besoms, but nobody was on the river to keep the marks up to date and as a result *Capetown* took the ground three times during her journey, much to the chagrin of her coxswain who was at the wheel on each occasion.

The civilian refugees were accompanied by a missionary doctor (Dr McClelland) and a nurse, Mrs Richardson. This was fortunate, for a baby was born to a Chinese woman of British nationality during the voyage downriver. Conditions aboard the fully battened-down cruiser were not of the highest gynaecological standards and many necessities were absent. However, attended by the doctor, the nurse and Petty Officer Sick Berth Attendant Hole, mother and child were soon doing well and the baby had received its first bath – in shaving soap. The historic event was commemorated by a plaque later put up over one of the cots in the sick bay, stating the baby's name and giving the latitude and longitude of its birth.

By now *Capetown*'s crew had heard of the sinking of the *Panay* and the attacks on British gunboats. They knew that there was a very real possibility that *Capetown* might find herself under fire as soon as she encountered the Japanese. Two days after leaving Kiukiang, she was met by the Japanese torpedo-boat *Kasasagi* who flashed a whole series of signals, the general gist of them being that the safe-conduct still held good, provided *Capetown* followed her downriver. Japanese soldiers could be seen on both banks and there were occasional exchanges of fire across the river where pockets of Chinese troops were still holding out. The nauseating shambles of Nanking was repeated at most towns and villages along both sides. The smoke of burning corpses and houses drifted across the river and swollen bodies floated in the water.

Most of the refugees and all the American money was discharged at Woosung where a number of French sailors were embarked for Hong Kong. Then *Capetown* passed through a fleet of Japanese warships waiting ominously at the mouth of the river. They made a polite signal promising further safe-conduct and escorted the British cruiser out of the Yangtse estuary, turning back when the open sea was reached and leaving *Capetown* to proceed independently. She spent a cheerless Christmas Day at sea and arrived at Hong Kong on December 27th. Here the rest of the crew would rejoin and the ship would be refitted, but first there were all the Christmas festivities to catch up on.

Plenty of events had been arranged: Christmas Dinners at the Soldiers' and Sailors' Institute, dances, sporting championships and the revue 'Scandals of 1938' to be performed in *Eagle*'s hangar. Halls, clubs, shops, cafés and recreation grounds were open and the annual inspection of naval landing parties took place. There was even the first of a series of lectures on Hong Kong's air raid precautions, but such serious items seemed out of place now that Nanking had fallen and the war was probably over. At Shanghai, especially, gaiety seemed to develop an even more frantic quality in that artificially international society of crowds, money, the Country Club, the Million Dollar Skyline, neon lights, bustling streets, congested rivers, prostitutes, drug-smugglers, Broadway Mansions, open-air bazaars, sew-sew women, beggars and millionaires. Shanghailanders were determined to ignore death and conquest. For them it was to be 'business as usual'.

5
The Shantung Campaign

Yet it was *not* to be 'business as usual'. It became rather difficult to get on with the Japanese at Shanghai when reprisals were taken against Chinese terrorists, and foreign members of the Shanghai Police Force who arrived on the scene were beaten up. Foreign correspondents had to submit their stories to censorship before using the Japanese-controlled telegraphic services. Some harbour facilities, other public utilities and councils came under Japanese influence. It might almost have seemed as though the Japanese were trying to squeeze out other nationalities were it not for the fact that these measures were ostensibly being taken for the protection of foreigners. For example, the Japanese repeated that they could not risk neutral merchant ships on the Yangtse until all the mines and navigational hazards had been cleared and the roving bands of Chinese guerrillas and river pirates inspired by Chiang Kai-Shek's refusal to sue for peace, had been dealt with. It was a reasonable enough attitude, although it did seem as though they were taking rather a long time to finish the job. It was also surprising that they should embark upon another campaign, before finishing the two they had on their hands already in the north and in the Yangtse valley.

Up to now the Japanese had refrained from attacking or blockading Tsingtao, relying instead on local Chinese collaboration, but on December 18th rioters burned the Japanese-owned cotton mills there. Accordingly the Japanese began their Shantung Campaign, opening with the occupation of Tsingtao and Wei-Hai-Wei. At both these places there were zones or areas of British property and on December 28th, *Dorsetshire* relieved *Suffolk* at Tsingtao to look after British interests there. The weather was bitterly cold. In Captain F. R. Barry's cabin, with all the doors and scuttles closed, two radiators and an electric fire full on, the temperature still only reached 34° F. It seemed impossible that Tsingtao could ever be warm, and unbelievable that next summer the weather would be so hot, and the water so tropical, that sharks would attack and kill a man bathing in the harbour alongside *Folkestone*!

Dorsetshire was secured to a buoy in Tsingtao Harbour and a signalman was landed on the pierhead to keep in touch with the British Consul-General and the Royal Marines who had gone ashore from the cruiser. They cooperated with an International Volunteer Police Force in keeping looters quiet and preventing fires caused by exploding demolition charges as the Chinese blew up their

The Shantung Campaign

important buildings. The Chinese Mayor of Tsingtao withdrew a large sum of money from the bank, bought a brand-new car complete with spares and was seen no more. Captain Barry informed Vice-Admiral Toyoda that Tsingtao was now undefended and the Japanese moved in on January 10th, 1938. They agreed to respect the neutrality of Edgewater Mansions, a large building where all the foreign women and children were gathered, but their first act was to drive *Dorsetshire*'s signalman off the pier at the point of a sword. Captain Barry immediately complained, Admiral Toyoda apologized and the signalman was allowed to return.

Soon Japanese propaganda officers arranged for special balloons to be sent up. They were round with long banners streaming from their anchor-ropes. They bore such slogans as 'Chinese! Japanese are your friends. Shake hands!' and 'Japan and China must work together for Peace in the East'. These appeals were addressed to guerrillas in the surrounding countryside who were known locally as 'Salt Revenue Guards'. The balloons seemed to have little effect.

Meanwhile the Chinese at Wei-Hai-Wei were becoming fearful of the expected Japanese takeover. In such panicky situations violence often breaks out and on January 10th, the British Consul in Port Edward on the mainland asked for help. The Chinese High Commissioner who actually ran the town was not only worried about Japanese soldiers and Chinese bandits, he was also concerned lest he be caught and punished by someone in authority for the misappropriation of funds. Yet, although not entirely honest, he was still the only person with enough influence and power to control the city. If he left, then it was feared that rival gangs and political factions would fight over the port.

In response to the British Consul's appeal the sloop *Sandwich* moved across to the mainland from the island of Liukungtao on January 10th. She arrived about midnight and illuminated the waterfront with searchlights. Everything seemed quiet and this impression of orderliness was confirmed when daylight came. The only thing slightly amiss seemed to be that the streets were *too* orderly, with the Chinese policemen carrying out their duties most efficiently. It soon became obvious that the police, who were paid handsomely by the High Commissioner, had in fact seized and were controlling the road from the town hall to the docks. Suddenly a car raced along this prepared route with three heavily armed guards on each running board. The vehicle stopped alongside the ss *Yochow* and the High Commissioner leapt out and dashed up the gangway. His bodyguard, some waving their broadswords at bystanders, manhandled his luggage (alleged to be the contents of the city treasury) aboard and the steamer cast off. The High Commissioner had left Port Edward open to civil strife, but his policemen remained loyal, even though they had been paid in advance. They stayed to enforce law and order until the Japanese were about to arrive, then made for the hills. Thanks to their devotion to duty and to the presence of *Suffolk* and *Sand-*

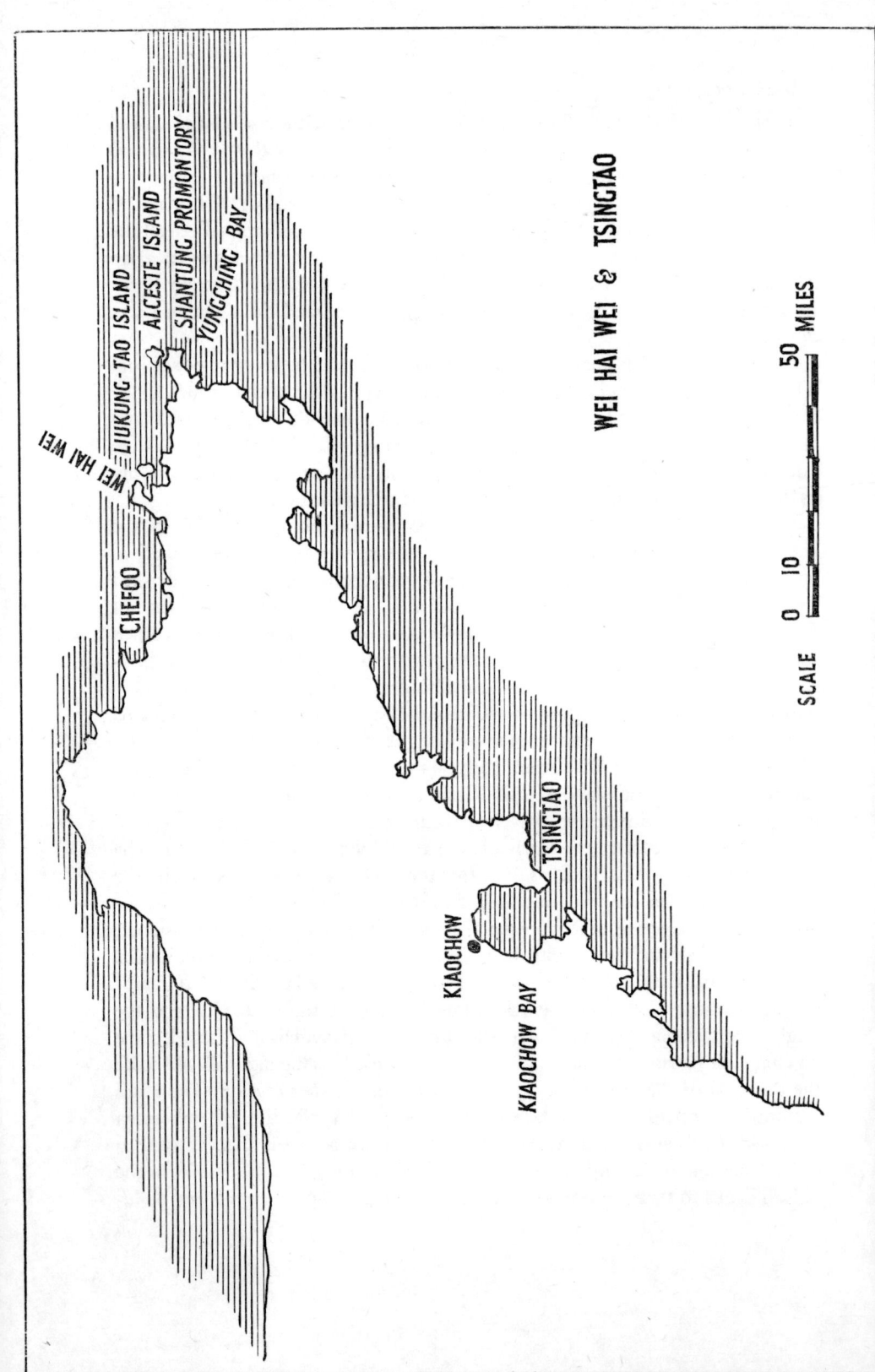

wich, Port Edward remained fairly free from rioting and looting until Japanese forces arrived to establish official law and order. They also erected a triumphal arch.

One could never be quite certain what the Japanese would do when they encountered foreigners, so much depended on the personality of individual officers. For example, on January 24th, *Cumberland* was carrying out post-refit exercises off Hong Kong when the cruiser *Myoko*, Vice-Admiral Toyoda's flagship, hove in sight. Immediately *Myoko* made a querulous signal asking why *Cumberland* had not been polite enough to salute a vice-admiral's flag as was customary naval etiquette. Captain Leach replied that Admiral Hasegawa had announced that salutes should not be fired when British and Japanese warships met, lest the slightest misunderstanding occur. Admiral Toyoda pointed out somewhat abruptly that this only applied to shipping off Woosung where Admiral Hasegawa happened to be at that particular time. Elsewhere salutes should be fired. Captain Leach made an apologetic signal and *Cumberland* fired the salute.

On the Yangtse however, it seemed as though a fresh effort to cultivate friendlier relations with the Japanese had some chance of success. The gunboat *Cricket* had returned upriver from Shanghai to Wuhu where she met British and German diplomatic representatives and took them to Nanking to investigate the state of their respective consulates. Whilst there, Lieutenant-Commander J. A. Agnew arrived to take over as *Cricket*'s new commanding officer and he soon presented two ducks to Rear-Admiral Kondo. They were rowed across in state in a pinnacle and served as 'Duck à l'Empire' at a Japanese Empire Day Dinner on February 11th. The Japanese showed their appreciation by helping to recover a British pontoon damaged in the December bombing. On the whole it was much easier to get on with the Japanese Navy than with the Army, the two services seeming to dislike each other intensely.

Admiral Little was still ill and did not recover sufficiently to travel until March when he returned to England in the liner *Comorin*. His duties as Commander-in-Chief were still being undertaken by Vice-Admiral Crabbe who initiated a defence course for British Merchant Navy Officers at Hong Kong. He was also present at the annual parade of the Hong Kong Volunteer Force, when Sir Geoffrey Northcote, Governor of Hong Kong, congratulated officers and men on the smartness of the drill ship *Cornflower*, now repaired after her mishaps during the previous September's typhoon. Sir Geoffrey later paid an informal visit to the dockyard and the submarine refitting depot.

The new Commander-in-Chief was Vice-Admiral Sir Percy Noble who assumed command on February 5th. One of his first duties was to welcome the new British Ambassador to China, Sir Archibald Clark Kerr, who arrived with Lady Kerr in the P & O liner *Kaiser-i-Hind*. After three days at Hong Kong, the Ambassador's party left again, this time bound for Shanghai in the sloop *Falmouth*. Within a week Admiral Noble had sailed in *Cumberland* on a cruise of inspection around his command area, his first appointment attending the elaborate ceremonies marking the official opening of the great new naval base at Singapore on February 14th.

The Singapore base had been constructed to maintain a fleet capable of depriving Japan of the sea communications she would need should she decide to invade India, Australia or New Zealand. The possibility of such an attack was recognized by some intelligence sources, but there was a stronger belief in London that Japanese maintenance and efficiency were of too low a standard to pose too terrible a threat. Apart from this argument and the problems caused by economic crises, it was felt that stationing a full-sized fleet outside Home and Mediterranean waters would be a departure from historical precedent. Admittedly earlier squadrons had been despatched abroad, but only in pursuit of a similar detachment of enemy forces. It was therefore decided to wait until an emergency arose in the Far East and then send a fleet to Singapore, where it could be operational within three months of the crisis beginning. So, in spite of the brave ceremonial, the battleships did not arrive and the great drydock built to receive them was flooded and used as a swimming pool. Meanwhile secret conversations were opened with the USA, although it seemed unlikely that she would intervene in a war between Britain and Japan unless directly attacked herself.

These affairs of state were hardly known, and the life of Hong Kong continued as it had always done. Slight inconvenience, but no alarm, might be experienced when the colony carried out a blackout-test from 20.00 hrs to 23.00 hrs on March 1st. Ashore, businesses closed early and hotels covered their windows with heavy drapes while ships in the harbour were only allowed to display riding or navigation lights. Royal Air Force aircraft were sent up specially to observe and they reported satisfactory results. But such an event was unusual. A more typical occasion was the Hong Kong Horticultural Society's annual show of flowers and vegetables, music being provided by the Royal Marine band from the cruiser *Suffolk*.

It all seemed far away from Wei-Hai-Wei where the Japanese were beginning to show more interest in the island of Liukungtao, which was shared by the Royal and Chinese Navies. It had been retroceded to China in 1930 after serving as the China Station's summer base for many years. The Chinese had immediately re-leased it to Britain for ten years and had then apparently lost interest in it. Most of the property was owned or leased by the Royal Navy or by the Navy's local contractor Sin Jelly-Belly, and only a small amount retained by China, so that apart from a tiny dockyard the island could be regarded as British. However, the Japanese announced their intention of formally occupying the Chinese dockyard. Perhaps they expected some vast installation to fall into their

The Shantung Campaign

hands. *Capetown* was at Wei-Hai-Wei at this time, so Captain Coppinger accompanied the Japanese landing party, pointing out British property such as moorings, jetties, the canteen and the hospital. The Japanese did not touch these and it was obvious that they were extremely disappointed at the meagreness of their haul, casting envious eyes at the extent of British property.

On March 4th/5th another problem was added to Captain Coppinger's responsibilities. At 01.00 hrs *Sandwich* sighted the 6,380-ton French freighter *Yolande*, bound from Chingwangtao to Shanghai with a cargo of wool, raw cotton and coal, aground in Betty Cove opposite Alceste Island. An officer boarded her and learned that her No 1 hold was flooded, but her master did not require assistance as salvage vessels were on their way from Shanghai and the weather was calm. *Sandwich* continued to Wei-Hai-Wei and reported to Captain Coppinger, who remained in touch with *Yolande* by radio. The weather deteriorated during the next thirty hours, gradually at first and then more violently but *Yolande* still declined assistance until 10.43 hrs on March 6th when she signalled that she had been forced broadside on to the rocks.

A squadron of Japanese warships chose this moment to arrive and Captain Coppinger had to send all *Capetown*'s Royal Marines across to *Sandwich* in case of trouble on Liukungtao. *Capetown* sailed just after 12.00 hrs and after only five minutes the north-westerly gale had stove in one of her boats. Captain Coppinger tried approaching the shipwrecked vessel from seaward, but the seas were too rough, and the temperature had dropped to 38 °F. *Capetown* therefore, went round the Shantung Promontory and anchored in Yung Ching Bay, five miles overland from Betty Cove.

Capetown's motor boat towed her cutter ashore laden with corned beef and biscuits. The rescue party was composed of two officers, twenty men, a Chinese customs official to act as interpreter, and four armed bluejackets as guards against pirates and wreckers reported in the area. All were wrapped up in overcoats and oilskins. They crossed a sandy beach, rough ground and a series of hills. The Shantung Promontory is studded with a number of small huts used as shelters by local fishermen and shepherds. A couple of sailors were left in several of the huts they passed with instructions to get a fire going and have dry blankets and hot drinks ready. The full force of the gale struck them on the crest of the last ridge, looking down on *Yolande*'s shattered wreck. A scramble down the cliff brought them within a hundred yards of the ship, but it was now 17.00 hrs and soon it was getting dark. Waves were sweeping right over *Yolande* and every attempt to pass a line by Schermuly rocket and Coston gun failed. Each time the gale blew the line away from the wreck, or a wave swept it out of the hands of the shipwrecked mariners. It was pitch dark and the temperature went down to 23°F before it was decided to give up for the night. The watchers on the wreck saw the sailors on the cliff-top withdraw, collecting their comrades in the huts as they went and also recovering a semi-conscious Chinese survivor who had swum ashore earlier. It was 02.30 hrs before all the shore-party had returned to their ice-sheathed cruiser.

Next morning an officer and six men set off without any gear to see if *Yolande* was still there. It seemed a waste of time but they reported that although unrecognizable as a ship, the wreck was still there with survivors still clinging to her. The equipment was sent ashore and this time the rocket fell across a stay and was snagged by icicles at the first go. Careful jiggling from the shore end slid the line down into the survivors' hands. Soon they were coming ashore. As each one was helped from the breeches buoy he was taken on a stretcher or otherwise assisted over the ground to the nearest hut. There he was warmed in front of the fire, wrapped in blankets and given a piping-hot drink with a generous tot of rum. Thus fortified he was taken on to the next hut where similar treatment awaited him and so on until he reached the secure warmth of *Capetown* and the medical comforts of her sick-bay. Soon the freezing rain and rough ground began to affect the landing party, so that it became almost impossible to tell which soaked and shivering individual was rescued and which was the rescuer. They persisted and eventually all sixty *Yolande* survivors had been saved, including the captain's daughter and the ship's cat. Nine had been lost earlier. They were all taken back to Wei-Hai-Wei before going on to Shanghai in a British steamer.

While this rescue was underway, Commander Edwards of *Sandwich* accompanied by some of *Capetown*'s Royal Marines, had gone on board the Japanese flagship for a conference. A compromise was reached, whereby the Japanese agreed not to land on the island of Liukungtao provided the British undertook not to send armed parties to Port Edward on the mainland. This was a very reasonable solution, for there was in fact no need for Royal Navy warships to have any direct contact with the mainland. Fresh water for drinking could be obtained from two of the island's wells. Sampan owners brought fresh fruit and vegetables to market on Liukungtao, while 'night-soil' was collected daily by twelve members of the Chinese Sanitary Corps. It was taken to the mainland in barges and sold for fertilizer in paddy fields and market gardens. These barges were known, for obvious reasons, as honey-boats and were a feature of all Chinese ports. They were unwieldy craft, usually propelled by a solitary Chinaman with a single thirty-foot sweep. From time to time one would be upset and when this happened near a British warship, 'Honey-boat capsized' would be piped and everyone rushed to close every scuttle within reach. It was just as well that every Chinaman aboard a honey-boat seemed to be able to swim. There was a notable reluctance on the part of Royal Navy personnel to pick up people paddling unhappily in a spreading slick of evil-smelling filth.

The heavy weather that had wrecked *Yolande* caused more problems as it moved across the China Station. Breaking waves swamped *Lowestoft*'s motor boat while secured alongside the gangway. It was recovered by divers two days later, minor repairs were carried out and the engine stripped down, cleaned and reassembled. Within another few days the motor boat was running perfectly again and some said even better than before! At Hong Kong on March 11th, the 10,421-ton Japanese liner *Haruna Maru* was moving through the central fairway when she touched the destroyer *Duchess* moored in the naval anchorage. Neither ship suffered more than scratched paintwork and there were no political arguments about it, although earlier in the year the Japanese had fined the Shanghai steamer *Marian Moller* 1,500 yen (£80) when stress of weather forced her into a fortified area near Yokohama.

6
The Blockade

Japan's campaign in China had brought neither victory nor reward. Even in the conquered areas the most worthwhile properties and sources of raw materials were either destroyed by fighting or rioters, liable to attack by guerrillas or controlled by foreigners, who also owned most of the merchant shipping so necessary for the exploitation of China. Japan was now almost on a full war economy and she needed those raw materials. There were ways of obtaining them, but to do so Japan alone must trade in China. A trading monopoly would also have the effect of cutting off foreign supplies destined for Chiang Kai-Shek's armies. This latter reason was given for the Japanese announcement that after March 10th, 1938, all ports on the Lower Yangtse would be blockaded until the outcome of the war had been decided. All merchantmen in the area would require permits and would only be allowed to trade at special ports with particular Chinese firms, being liable to be stopped and arrested if carrying contraband of war. Foreign warships would be expected to give advance notice of their movements so that unpleasantness could be avoided.

Very often, therefore, it happened that Royal Navy warships were the only British vessels in Japanese-controlled waters, thus exercising British rights by their very presence. Their work in maintaining these rights became even more difficult to define and carry out, much depending on the political and diplomatic events outside the control of local Naval officers of comparatively lowly rank, who could nevertheless precipitate an international crisis by their actions. Difficulties would be most likely to arise from the establishment of unofficial trading centres in the mouth of the Yangtse. As the Japanese could not be everywhere at once, it became the custom for Chinese who had a cargo but no permit to stand on the bank and wave at British ships passing to and from Shanghai. Once a ship had got the message, it would come alongside the little jetty and load the cargo. The captain might hint that when he passed that way again, he might well have a return cargo to unload. Word got around and this spot on the riverbank soon became a rendezvous for coasting steamers and Chinese merchants. They always had to be ready to disappear at the slightest sign of the Japanese. Even though they were doing nothing illegal, British merchant captains would be arrested and involved in international disputes, while Japanese retribution on Chinese was summary and harsh.

There was no doubt that the Yangtse was vitally important as a supply route for the invading Japanese Army, but it soon became obvious that they were definitely establishing a commercial monopoly. In spite of the alleged perils they allowed their own merchantmen to continue trading in dangerous Chinese waters. A British suggestion that convoys be organized was rejected by the Japanese who said that war material would thus be smuggled to the Chinese in bulk. As far as the Japanese were concerned, the right of navigation on the Yangtse had become Tsing Liang – a meat for the Emperor only. The Nine-Power Treaty was ignored.

There were other ways of gaining control over the resources of China. The sloop *Lowestoft* was despatched from Wei-Hai-Wei and arrived at Chingwangtao on March 31st. Commander Boucher had been instructed to send a party of armed bluejackets by rail to Tungshan, where armed strikers were rioting and attacking the coalmines owned by the Sino-British Kailan Mining Administration. As it happened, he learned that the crisis had been settled by the Japanese occupying forces, who subsequently took advantage of the affair to extend their influence over the company.

Then in April the British Naval Attaché in Tokyo raised the question of Tsingtao, where British shipping was being prevented from using the wharves in the inner harbour, which seemed to be reserved exclusively for Japanese merchantmen. It was pointed out that besides commercial discrimination unnecessary delays had been imposed on British ships during medical inspections. Captain H. B. Rawlings was advised that the matter should be discussed with the Japanese naval authorities on the spot but though this suggestion was carried out the situation did not improve and it was again taken up officially with the Japanese Government. They replied that the exclusion of British ships from the wharves was due to military necessity and to the blocking of the entrance to Kiaochow Bay by the Chinese.

In the same month the 1,337-ton *Tung Wo*, owned by the Indo-China Steam Navigation Company, was seized by the Japanese, who complained that a Chinese passenger had fired on their troops near Haimen. No shots had come from the ship, but she had crossed the line of fire between opposing Japanese forces and Chinese guerrillas and this had probably given the impression of hostility. *Tung Wo* was stopped by military launches and boarded. A Chinese crew-member was bayoneted in the stomach because he would not confess that he had fired the shot and the vessel was taken to the contraband control base at Tsungming Island. Although a thorough search did not reveal any secret arms, the Japanese announced that they were going to hold the steamer indefinitely.

The British authorities hoped that this aggression might be halted by a local display of force, so the gunboat *Cricket* was despatched from Shanghai.

Lieutenant-Commander Agnew had instructions to demand *Tung Wo*'s return and as he was ordered to use force if necessary, *Cricket* arrived at the Tsungming base cleared and ready for action. *Tung Wo* was released. Such an incident might have escalated into war, but diplomatic niceties still had to be observed (perhaps in that way, war itself may be avoided). Civil and service representatives, including Admiral Noble, attended a reception at the Japanese Consul-General's residence in Hong Kong in honour of the Japanese Emperor's birthday. April had brought warm, sunny weather, and a change into white uniforms. It also brought the end of the Hong Kong smallpox epidemic, in which 1,400 people had died. Strict vaccination regulations protected nearly all the men of the China Station, although one naval man did die from the disease. Sports fixtures were played off, the cruiser *Suffolk* doing as well as usual in every event. Her success may have been due to the number of athletes she always seemed to be carrying or to the zeal with which everyone trained. Her ship's company preferred to attribute their success to the good luck brought them by their mascot, Albert the 'Orse. This spotted paper pony was paraded with much pomp during sports meetings and especially after a victory. Whatever the reason, as regards sport, *Suffolk* was the envy of every other ship on the China Station. She also established a reputation among Army personnel. It was the custom for a number of soldiers to join a warship for her summer cruise to see how the Navy did things. They always had an enjoyable time, but those who went to *Suffolk* invariably wrote extra-glowing accounts of their experiences.

The brand-new cruiser *Birmingham* arrived at Hong Kong on April 23rd. Her arrival had been delayed by a number of acts of sabotage. There had been two fires before leaving Portsmouth, one in the starboard hangar doing a considerable amount of damage. The other had started in the wing of a Supermarine Walrus, but the Quartermaster of the Watch spotted it in time and raised the alarm. A Board of Inquiry found that someone had slit a hole in the wing, stuffed in oily cotton waste and set it alight. Then there was another incident in the Indian Ocean when someone threw overboard all the locks of the Mk.XVI 4-inch high-angle guns. They were of a completely new type and until spares were made and sent out from England, the cruiser was virtually without her secondary armament.

A determined search and investigation resulted in the detection of those responsible and established that there was no sinister motive behind the sabotage. The culprits were simply newly joined men who had a grudge against the Royal Navy in general and foreign service in particular and had chosen to endanger their shipmates as a means of expressing their disapproval. They were court-martialled, discharged from the Navy, and sent home to serve prison sentences. The ship's company breathed a sigh of relief. A fortune-teller had forecast that a new British ship would sail for the Far East and be lost with all hands. For a while the acts of sabotage had seemed to indicate that *Birmingham* was going to be that ship.

In due course *Birmingham* moored to a buoy in the naval anchorage at Hong Kong. She was a particularly welcome sight to the crew of the cruiser *Capetown* – their relief had arrived. Three days later *Capetown* steamed out wearing a long paying-off pennant. Other crews manned ship and cheered as she passed. She called at Singapore, Penang, Colombo, Aden, Port Said, Malta and Gibraltar before arriving back at Devonport on June 9th, almost two years after leaving her home port.

There was one more mishap in store for *Birmingham*, when one of her Walruses was blown over by a sudden squall while taxing in the harbour. The aircraft sank, but the pilot and observer were able to scramble out and were picked up unhurt. When the storm abated, divers were sent down to secure a wire round the tail and the aircraft was brought to the surface by the mooring vessel *Moorlake*. *Birmingham* had already sailed for Wei-Hai-Wei on May 3rd, passing through the fringe of a typhoon during her voyage. The heavy seas proved the excellence of *Birmingham*'s bow design as she was able to maintain her speed in spite of a cross swell.

The cruiser *Enterprise* arrived at Hong Kong on May 27th, after a six weeks' voyage bringing out relief drafts from Portsmouth. Those destined for the Lower Yangtse gunboats embarked in *Adventure* and left for Shanghai the following day, while about a hundred, bound for the upper reaches of the river, travelled overland by rail. Their train was twenty-four hours late leaving Kowloon because of a Japanese air raid on Canton. The 'Sailors' Special', with a Union Jack affixed to the roof of each carriage approached Canton soon after a second attack had hit the station. The long train eased on to a loopline to avoid the wrecked platforms and permanent way and was clear of Canton by the evening. The hundred officers and men they relieved at Hankow returned the same way and arrived at Kowloon on June 3rd, having experienced more delays at Canton. They left in *Enterprise* ten days later.

By the summer of 1938 the Japanese armies in northern China had recovered from their April defeat at Taierchwang. In May the Japanese North China Area Army joined up with the Japanese Central China Area Army at Tungshan, but the bulk of the Chinese forces eluded the trap and withdrew westwards cutting the Yellow River dykes behind them. The loss of life among the Japanese soldiers and Chinese peasants was very great as most of the Yellow River found its way to its old mouth south of the Shantung Peninsula.

Although the Japanese in the south had seized the island of Amoy (without occupying the neighbouring international settlement on the island of Kulangsu) their principal effort was now concentrated in the Yangtse valley. The British and American gunboats *Cockchafer* and *Monocacy* were therefore sent to Kiukiang to protect foreign nationals during the coming attack. The two commanding officers established a neutral zone where foreigners could be concentrated and the Japanese agreed to observe it.

A message was also sent to the people at the hilltop resort of Kuling warning them that this was their last opportunity to leave safely. They were not only endangered by the Japanese offensive but also by the retreating Chinese Army and by many small-time Chinese bandits who were only too ready to take advantage of the political vacuum caused by the absence of Chinese authority before the establishment of Japanese control. These thugs believed they were now able to make a name for themselves as great warlords, carve out a chunk of territory and speak on equal terms with the leaders of nations. Such gangsters were usually driven off by the Japanese or were absorbed by a larger band of guerrillas but their activities rarely became known outside their own area, although they were always an extra peril for foreign merchants and missionaries.

The war between China and Japan threatened to dislocate the Royal Navy's usual annual programme. It was the custom every year for China Station warships to quit the stifling heat of Hong Kong in June for the fresher climate of Wei-Hai-Wei, eleven hundred miles to the north. There had been recent rumours that the Wei-Hai-Wei base was now going to be abandoned, but these were scotched by the Commander-in-Chief's announcement that the fleet would sail north as usual. It was considered that such a concentration of Royal Navy warships in Japanese-controlled waters might induce the Japanese to reflect on the latent power still possessed by the British Empire. Another reason for this decision was that this particular June was proving the hottest and driest month at Hong Kong for many years. The King's Official Birthday Parade and March Past of 2,500 officers and men from the Royal Navy, the Army, the Royal Air Force and the Hong Kong Volunteer Defence Corps had to be held in Happy Valley at 08.00 hrs because of the heat. But this was mere inconvenience compared with the water shortages and cholera which were never far away. Only mass inoculation held the epidemic in check. Even the tantalizing waters around the island afforded no relief from the sweltering heat. Bathing was prohibited as the harbour was contaminated by effluent from steamers, junks, sampans and sewers. Shipping companies demanded vaccination and inoculation certificates before accepting passengers even for short trips.

Accordingly most of the China Fleet assembled at Wei-Hai-Wei during the early part of June. *Birmingham* was already there, although she paid a short visit to Chefoo to represent the Royal Navy during the King's Official Birthday celebrations there. *St Breock*, *Medway*, *Westcott*, *Odin*, *Perseus*, *Parthian*, *Otus*, *Grampus*, *Rorqual*, *Phoenix*, *Rainbow* and *Defender* arrived early on to be followed by *Cumberland*, *Suffolk*, *Duncan*, *Delight*, *Duchess*, *Daring* and *Diamond*. *Decoy* and *Eagle* came later, while *Dorsetshire* and *Folkestone* did not

The Blockade

arrive until June 30th. *Dorsetshire*'s exercises off Hong Kong had to be interrupted on June 13th, when an ordinary seaman suddenly fell ill. Acute appendicitis was diagnosed and it was decided that he should be operated on immediately ashore. Doubled up with pain he was strapped into the cruiser's Walrus which was promptly catapulted off. Forewarned by radio, Commodore E. B. C. Dicken ordered searchlights to be played on the dark waters of Hong Kong harbour. The Walrus landed smoothly and within minutes the seaman was on his way to the Royal Naval Hospital. By morning his appendix had been removed and he was well on his way to recovery.

The Japanese made no attempt to prevent the British from using the base at Wei-Hai-Wei, although they invariably kept a warship in the harbour and, contrary to their earlier agreement, regularly sent armed parties around the island of Liukungtao to show their strength. Chinese guerrillas were still operating on the mainland and on one occasion they killed the commanding officer of the local Japanese garrison, while another time they shot up two hundred Japanese in a well-laid ambush. On both occasions the Japanese retaliated with heavy naval and air bombardments of neighbouring villages and they eventually closed the weekly market held by the Chinese on Liukungtao. This was a blow to the British warships as it was the only place where fresh fruit and vegetables could be obtained. Everyone was relieved when a secret market was started on the mainland only to be bombed by a seaplane from the cruiser *Kuma* on two successive weeks, killing over a hundred Chinese peasants and their families.

Occasionally interrupted by approaching typhoons, the China Fleet spent its summer days and nights in target shoots, anti-submarine exercises, musketry courses, amphibious landings, regattas and sports. *Eagle*'s aircraft contributed their share to the round of practices and exercises, and all the Walrus aircraft were catapulted off their cruisers to carry out formation flying, deck landings on *Eagle*, and divebombing experiments. Of course, not all the China Station warships were at Wei-Hai-Wei for the whole summer. Some were still patrolling in case piracy or some other emergency occurred. On June 12th, pirates captured the small Chilean steamer *Don Pedro* in Hangchow Bay and although *Adventure* and *Falmouth* were soon on the scene, the pirates had time to remove part of the cargo before making their escape. They also took away the Chinese owner of the cargo and held him for ransom.

The gunboats also had their usual programme of movements to be carried out wherever Sino-Japanese hostilities permitted. *Sandpiper* had spent the whole winter at Changsha, her captain acting as British Consul with the gunboat's First Lieutenant as Vice-Consul. There was only a handful of Britons there and the gunboat had little to do apart from the usual paperwork and social activities of a consulate. Once they sorted out some irregularity in coal trading and once they encountered a Russian missionary from an obscure sect who wanted a British visa to Persia on his Chinese passport. He did not seem to be all that he claimed and his papers did not bear close scrutiny. He was later investigated by the local Chinese authorities and the last the Royal Navy heard of him was that he had been arrested as a Bolshevik agent. Even the spasmodic air raids of varying intensity that had caused increasing damage since the Japanese threat to obliterate Changsha the previous November left *Sandpiper* untouched. Sometimes it seemed as though the little gunboat was fulfilling no purpose at all.

Yet gradually, in an unassuming and unspectacular way, *Sandpiper* had built up a close relationship with the Chinese, already appreciative of the quantities of war material (which included forty Vickers 6-ton tanks) reaching Chiang Kai-Shek's armies from Hong Kong. It was on this note of satisfaction that *Sandpiper* was relieved in June by *Mantis* for a month's change of scenery at Hankow. All too soon she would be returning to her customary solitary station at Changsha.

Farther down the Yangtse the Japanese were preparing their drive on Hankow and causing more problems for the gunboats. *Scarab* was at Wuhu on June 20th when several Japanese soldiers marched on to Jardine, Matheson's pontoon and boarded a lighter belonging to the same firm. They arrested three of the company's Chinese employees and made it clear that they would detain the barge as well if there were any argument, claiming that these coolies had been stealing wood from Japanese stocks. Protests were made to the appropriate Japanese authority, not about the actual charge, but the manner in which the arrest had been carried out on British property. The Japanese apologized, dropped their charges and released the three men. Nevertheless, *Scarab* was kept busy for the next few days sending armed guards to British vessels threatened with requisition by the Japanese who needed every craft they could lay their hands on to move their army upriver. Her task was eased by an offer of assistance from the American gunboat *Oahu*, her commanding officer being ready to send over an armed guard to help if necessary.

Nor was confiscation confined to the Yangtse. The Chinese Customs Service was run by foreigners, mainly British, and on June 21st, the preventive vessel *Haian* was seized by Japanese naval forces at Tsingtao for use as a naval auxiliary. The foreign, non-Japanese officers were obliged to go ashore and the command of the vessel was entrusted to junior Japanese officers, while the Chinese crew were intimidated into remaining on board. The Japanese Navy explained that the seizure was necessary for preventing arms-smuggling to Chinese bandits. The British Embassy in Tokyo pointed out regularly once a month, that this task should fall on the Japanese armed forces and not on the Chinese Customs Service. No explanation was given regarding the forcible removal of British officers and a similar case then occurred at Chefoo, where the Japanese Navy took over the Chinese Customs launch *Hai Cheng*. Her British

Chinese refugees crossing the river at Changsha in November 1937.   [*Cdr H. R. Rycroft*

12th December 1937. *Panay* goes down four years before Pearl Harbor. A still from the film taken by Mr Norman Alley, a Universal Cameraman.   [*Associated Press*

1645, 17th December 1937. *Ladybird* and *Oahu* arriving at Shanghai with the *Panay* survivors and the bodies of those who had been killed. Note ensign at half-mast and motor sampan amidships. *Idzumo* in background.
[*Associated Press*

Right: Christmas Eve 1937. Captain Coppinger (at right) watches *Capetown*'s baby leave the ship at Woosung.   [*North China Daily News*

Below: A turretless Japanese Type 89-OTSU medium tank which was captured by the Chinese and underwent swim tests at Changsha in December 1937. It sank, but was recovered with assistance from *Sandpiper* (in the background).   [*Cdr H. R. Rycroft*

Above: Ladybird in drydock at Shanghai after being bombarded by Japanese artillery. Shell and splinter holes can be seen in her hull, the officers' bathroom and the 3-inch gun shield. (Not all the gunboats mounted their 3-inch in this position.) Her port funnel seems to have been painted a darker colour than the starboard one (obscured by the bridge in this photograph, but visible in other prints in this series). Note also *Ladybird*'s Royal Coat of Arms, removed from a British Consulate after its destruction by Chinese rioters a decade earlier. *Below:* Another view of *Ladybird*'s shell damage, this time right aft. Note the remarkable length of the Insects' 6-inch guns. [*Lt J. Evans*

Left: Capetown meets rough weather.
[*H. G. C. Brice*

Below: Birmingham arrives at Malta en route for China, 10th February 1938. Having just passed through the Spanish Civil War Zone, 'B' turret still carries red, white and blue neutrality bands.
[*A. & J. Pavia*

Left: Chinese bazaars were opened on board ships when they arrived and when they left the China Station. Here *Capetown*'s ship's company buy their last presents to take home.

[*H. G. C. Brice*

Below: Some ships stayed on the China Station permanently, but exchanging crews. This would be their last view of Hong Kong as the troopship sailed for home. *Falmouth* on the other side of the quay. [*H. E. J. Regler*

Right: Albert the 'Orse and the Cock O' The Fleet on *Suffolk*'s catapult.
[*H. E. J. Regler*

Below: Air raid on Hankow in July 1938. *Gnat* and *Tern* outboard of *Laestrygon* hulk with *Falcon* and *Mantis* inboard.
[*Lt-Cdr J. A. McClure*

Above: A party from *Cicala* helping to salvage a China National Airways DC-2, forced down by Japanese fighters over the Pearl River Delta, August 1938. It was apparently an attempt to assassinate a top Chinese official who changed his plans at the last minute and travelled on another flight. Fourteen people lost their lives. [*Vice-Adm Sir Patrick Bayly*

Below: A creek separating the International Settlement on Shameen Island from the Chinese city of Canton (on the right). It was usually crammed full of sampans and houseboats, which have been cleared out by the Navy to prevent refugees getting into the Concession, to remove any excuse for Japanese bombing the island, and to provide a clear field of fire around the Concession's defences. Note the bamboo structures erected by the Chinese to catch Japanese bombs before they hit the roof. [*Vice-Adm Sir Patrick Bayly*

The Blockade

officers were evicted as well as her Chinese crew being threatened with machine-guns.

In normal times these customs vessels looked after the lights and other navigational aids around the coast of China. So many had been sunk or requisitioned, or otherwise prevented from carrying out their work by the Japanese that the Royal Navy was asked to perform this task, when necessary, in areas outside Japanese control.

So on July 3rd, the destroyer *Diana* arrived off Turnabout Lighthouse near Foochow to investigate reports that the light had gone out for some unknown reason. Everything now seemed normal in daylight, but the European keeper described how five days previously, several Chinese schoolteachers had arrived at the lighthouse, which was situated on shore. They explained that at some future date they wished to bring a party of schoolchildren to tour the lighthouse and see how everything worked. They accepted an offer of tea to discuss the visit further, then suddenly grabbed the European keeper and tied him up, letting in the rest of their pirate band who secured the Chinese keepers and labourers. They stole the lamp, kerosene, cash and clothing and would probably have taken more and done more damage had not a couple of coolies got free and escaped. Believing that they had gone for help, the thieves made off, forcing the keepers to go with them. They had hoped to get plenty of money as ransom, but after journeying for two days the European keeper pretended to be ill. He had put on such a convincing display that the bandits thought he was going to die. As they would only then get a very small amount of ransom money for the Chinese keepers, none for the dead European and would probably face a murder charge as well, they decided to abandon their captives and head for the hills. Left alone, the keepers had made their way back to Turnabout Lighthouse and were endeavouring to get a temporary light going when *Diana* arrived. They seemed to have things in hand but they did need a lamp and some kerosene, and these were sent across before the destroyer departed.

Any hopes that normal trading on the Yangtse might soon be resumed, were dispelled on July 13th when the Japanese announced that only ships under the orders of their Navy or Army could proceed above Kiangyin. They repeated that the river must remain closed to neutral merchantmen because of navigational hazards and military necessity, but it was now obvious that the Japanese needed the sole use of the Yangtse for their own supply ships. This was a direct violation of the Nine-Power Treaty and it became the main argument in most of the Notes exchanged by British and Japanese diplomatic representatives.

Anticipating the extra demands that would be made on the Yangtse gunboats during the expected Japanese offensive, it was decided to reinforce Royal Navy personnel at Hankow with spare men from the rest of the China Station. Accordingly an 'Augmentation Party' of a hundred seamen and stokers were transferred from *Dorsetshire*, *Suffolk*, *Adventure*, *Birmingham* and *Eagle*. They were taken to Hong Kong in *Suffolk* who returned to Wei-Hai-Wei on July 24th while the men continued the journey by rail from Kowloon under Lieutenant-Commander A. A. Tait of *Suffolk*. Their train was probably the last northbound traffic before the Japanese cut the track. On the way they passed the last southbound International Express with over 250 passengers on board. Sir Archibald Clark Kerr was brought back from Canton to Hong Kong by the gunboat *Cicala*, while *Tarantula* paid a short visit to Canton taking Sir Geoffrey Northcote to confer with the British Consul-General there. It might well happen that Canton would be the next target for Japanese assault.

When the Augmentation Party reached Hankow they were organized into three platoons with a company headquarters. They were accommodated in the river steamers *Loong Wo* and *Wulin* and were occasionally sent out on patrol, marching through Special Administrative District No 3 so that they should get to know the area and be recognized by the local population. They had been drawn from the Royal Navy rather than from the Royal Marines or the Army to avoid giving the impression that Britain was creating a garrison for her old concession. It was emphasized to the Japanese that the presence of the Augmentation Party (or Force RF as it was now officially designated) was solely to protect British lives and property during the emergency likely to arise after the breakdown of Chinese rule and before the arrival of Japanese troops. Force RF would be withdrawn by agreement with the Japanese as soon as the necessity for its presence had passed.

It was very important that no misunderstanding occur and that no excuse be given to the Japanese for inflicting upon Hankow the fate that had befallen Nanking. Already Japanese aircraft were striking at targets close to Hankow, including the Chinese suburbs of the city and outlying villages. On August 2nd, six seaplanes attacked the Chinese Customs tender *Chiang Hsing* about thirty miles below Hankow. Her funnels had been painted white and yellow, so that she should not be mistaken for a Chinese naval craft which were usually mud-colour or blue-grey. She was engaged on her regular patrol duty inspecting lights, buoys and other navigational aids. When the attack began she was anchored alongside a light-vessel, but she managed to beach herself on the riverbank just as she was hit by a bomb and caught fire. The survivors were machine-gunned as they struggled ashore and Captain Crawley and two Chinese were killed. The Japanese first claimed that *Chiang Hsing* had been removing beacons, but they then apologized. While the investigation was proceeding *Gnat* was sent downriver to recover Captain Crawley's body for burial. The gunboat was buzzed by Japanese aircraft during this melancholy task but was otherwise unmolested.

This was one of the few journeys undertaken by the gunboats at Hankow as none of them were allowed to move very much. No oil fuel had been brought upriver since the beginning of the war and the British warships had to make do with what was immediately available. There was no question of any vessel actually running out of fuel, but it was decided to conserve the present stocks in case of a real emergency. Rear-Admiral Holt had established his headquarters ashore and so *Bee* was no longer acting as Yangtse flagship. This arrangement saved more fuel and prevented unnecessary wear and tear on *Bee* who was now getting old and was soon to be phased out of service. In the meantime she was sent down to Nanking to finish her days protecting what remained of Britain's interests there.

The Royal Navy at Hankow, together with other foreign forces there, was charged with the defence of those areas where there were foreign residents or properties. Fortunately most of the foreign women had been evacuated earlier and the task of defence was that much easier. Hankow itself is situated on the northern bank of the Yangtse with all the foreign zones located along the river front, usually known as The Bund, although the names varied in different districts. Coming downriver the first area was what had originally been the British Concession which had been handed back to the Chinese in 1927, but was still administered by the British under a special arrangement with the Chinese authorities, its official title being Special Administrative District No 3 (SAD3). Most British property was located here, although there were a number of important business premises in other parts of the city. Next to the British area was SAD2 which had once been Russian but was now run by Chinese. The French Concession was still French territory, but SAD1 (the old German Concession) was under Chinese administration. So too was the last area, SAD4. The Japanese had abandoned their concession in 1937 at the very outset of the war and it had immediately been proclaimed Chinese territory.

A volunteer special police force was formed of 150 men to assist the naval personnel and the Chinese police in maintaining law and order in the Special Administrative Districts. The Municipal Council of SAD3 erected gates to control the mobs of refugees and looters expected to pour into the international areas from the surrounding Chinese city once fighting began. The other Special Administrative Districts soon took similar action. The whole question of refugees was thoroughly debated and it was generally recognized that a safety zone, for noncombatant Chinese and foreigners, would solve the problem. Unfortunately the Chinese and Japanese authorities could not agreed on its location or on the necessary safeguards. It was suggested that SADs 1, 2 and 3, the French Concession and the Chinese area up to the railway line west of the city be regarded as neutral, but conferences about it dragged on for several months.

The delay did not have immediately serious consequences, for the expected

Japanese onslaught did not materialize. This was due to several reasons, one being the fighting between Japan and Russia on the Manchukuo border. Then when the Japanese did resume their advance, the Chinese fought several effective delaying actions, and of course the Japanese were having to deploy more units in anti-guerrilla drives, as well as getting involved in more operations to prevent war material reaching Chiang Kai-Shek. When such measures were taken in areas completely isolated from Chinese forces, it became obvious that their military blockade was more of a commercial monopoly.

On August 2nd, the Japanese naval authorities at Chefoo issued an order enforcing an embargo on a number of exports, such as foodstuffs, to certain ports, including Hong Kong. In accordance with this declaration, they prevented the British steamship *Hupeh* from loading ground-nuts, ground-nut oil and vermicelli for Hong Kong. Five days later the German steamer *Bremerhaven* loaded a cargo of ground-nut oil for Hong Kong. Then the Japanese authorities set up a Lighter Association at Chefoo without consulting the British barge owners there. The Japanese running the association declared that firms who did not join would be unable to obtain labour to work their steamers and lighters. The threat was duly carried out some days later when the stevedores of a British firm were refused admission to the customs compound at the entrance to the port. The matter was brought to the attention of the Japanese Government who replied that the control of ships entering and leaving the harbour was necessary to prevent arms smuggling. It would ultimately be beneficial to all concerned and they denied that threats and force had ever been used. Butterfield and Swire temporarily agreed to put their lighters out of commission for a short time as evidence of their desire to come to a local working agreement, but the Japanese authorities were not prepared to make concessions. Meanwhile the Chefoo Harbour Improvement Commission set up in 1913 by international agreement, dissolved itself under Japanese pressure. Its work and property was handed over to the Chefoo Municipal Council which was then taken over by the Japanese Navy. The British Embassy in Tokyo regarded this transaction as illegal seizure by the Japanese Navy, and refused to recognize it. The Japanese Government made no reply.

On the Yangtse, the task of reporting discrimination against British merchantmen was added to the normal anti-piracy and general duties of the gunboats. *Scarab*'s August patrol below Kiangyin was typical of their work. She first checked that a German trawler *Hai Kong* was trading only at a creek used by British tugs. Next day, the 9th, *Scarab* helped ss *Hansa* clear a lighter's chain cable from her propeller. The German steamer's difficulties were not yet over as a typhoon warning had been broadcast, so *Scarab* towed her to her own sheltered anchorage at San Cha Kwan, where the tug *Christine Moller* arrived. There the ships rode out four hours of 90 mph squalls while the water-level rose from

The Blockade

seven to fifteen fathoms. By the afternoon of the 10th, the swell had moderated sufficiently to allow *Scarab* to go round to Tuan Shan to investigate the condition of the British tug *Victoria*. She had been towing three lighters up the Yangtse under Japanese charter and had run aground on the top of a stone breakwater during the typhoon. The crew were Chinese, but the master was a Dane and seemed on good terms with the three Japanese soldiers on board. *Scarab* signalled *Victoria*'s situation to Shanghai and reported that the Italian vessel *Sandro Sandri* had also run full aground. The receding waters had left her resting amongst some trees thirty feet above river-level and half a mile inland. A channel was eventually dug out to refloat her. Trade was conducted at Hupukow and Haimen, while remnants of the Chinese 84th Division still held out. Somebody opened fire on the gunboat but the Chinese brigade-major later apologized and asked if *Scarab* would like to land libertymen – which was done.

Scarab herself had a narrow escape at Big Tree on the 12th when anchored near the river steamer *Tung Wo*. The tug *Shun Wo* arrived at 23.00 hrs but on making fast alongside *Tung Wo* kept her engines going astern. Within two minutes the 220-ton tug and the 1,337-ton steamer had dragged and were only twenty feet from *Scarab*, who had to shift berth in rather a hurry. Another typhoon warning was broadcast, so *Scarab* spent the next thirty-six hours making sure that all ships in the area were safely out of the way before it struck. This sort of simple task was greatly complicated by the variety of spellings used for the names of ships and places, the inaccuracy of many reported positions, and the habit of some captains of radioing for help, solving the problem themselves and then not cancelling their SOS.

Meanwhile, the big 579-ton salvage and rescue tug *Saucy* had arrived to stand by the smaller *Victoria*, whose master had transferred to the new arrival. Once away from the Japanese he had a serious story to tell as *Scarab* learned in the early hours of the 15th. When *Victoria* had called at Tungchow, a party of Japanese had boarded her, hauled down the Red Ensign, painted out the Union Jacks on her bridge wings and hoisted the Rising Sun. When the master protested, he was promptly kicked unconscious by the Japanese soldiers and locked below while the ship proceeded on her voyage upriver. He had been released when the typhoon overtook them, but too late to prevent *Victoria* running aground. Right now, *Victoria* was being used as a hostel for Japanese soldiers, while a Japanese storeship with more soldiers on board was anchored nearby. Although under Japanese charter, *Victoria* was still a British ship, so the Red Ensign was rehoisted, but technically she was now the property of the Shanghai underwriters that had insured her. There could be serious consequences if this complex and tricky situation was mishandled. *Scarab* was ordered to take possession of *Victoria* if the Japanese abandoned her, but to do nothing while the soldiers remained on board.

There was a brief interlude on the night of the 15th/16th when everyone sheltered from another typhoon. During the storm the *Hansa* dragged her anchor at San Wang Kong and stove in *Tung Wo*'s bow. The latter's anchor smashed through the German ship's stern and the 4,427-ton *Hansa* sank immediately, only thirty people being picked up.

Scarab was not in the vicinity but she had to visit the scene of the tragedy and report on it before returning to *Victoria*. The tug was still hard aground and the Japanese destroyer *Yamakaze* had also arrived, bearing a senior naval officer. He seemed quite reasonable. Under his influence the junior army officers set about controlling their men. He agreed that the ship's owners and insurers should arrange for her salvage and requested that the soldiers guarding the store-laden lighters be allowed to sleep in *Victoria*. For a while the Japanese civilian charterer seemed a law unto himself, threatening people and ordering them about – British subjects and Japanese sailors and soldiers alike. He was persuaded to desist by *Yamakaze* and *Scarab*. He thereupon confiscated Chinese junks and sampans in the area and began unloading *Victoria*'s lighters. The coolies employed on this work would later dig out *Victoria*, and she would eventually pass into Japanese ownership, but this was no longer *Scarab*'s problem. She was relieved by *Aphis* as Below Barrier Guardship on August 20th.

It was about this time that the Royal Navy began to be involved in what the Japanese considered deliberate provocation. All travellers abroad, and especially servicemen, are their country's ambassadors. Although usually aware of their responsibilities, there can be nasty incidents with the local people, either caused by a few persistent troublemakers, by over-enthusiastic appreciation of or participation in local entertainment especially if there is a plentiful supply of cheap beer, or by an otherwise exemplary character who gets drunk, runs off the rails and does something regrettable. Usually a rather tolerant view was taken of these lapses, providing any fracas was confined to the port area. The Japanese were well aware of the weaknesses of human nature. In January a British merchant seaman and a Dutch sailor had been arrested in Nagoya after tearing down a Japanese flag from a doorway where it was being displayed to indicate that a member of the household was on active service. The Japanese court decided that they were being drunk and disorderly rather than intending disrespect to the Japanese flag, and they were punished accordingly.

But in the increasing tension of the Sino-Japanese Incident, any personal acts of drunkenness or bad behaviour began to acquire a political connotation. The Japanese became very quick to seize on insults to themselves or to other Asiatics. They also made sure that their side of any argument was published before the investigating British authorities could issue any statement. Local British officers often had to go to great lengths to ensure that relatively minor incidents were prevented from escalating into possible war.

The Blockade

On August 17th an occurrence at Tsingtao similar to the January incident had more serious results. A stoker from the destroyer *Decoy* got drunk, tore down a Japanese flag, trampled it underfoot, spat on it and then grabbed two Chinese children by the hair and forced them to dance on it. He was arrested and as soon as he sobered up wrote out an apology, but later several petty officers who had nothing to do with the affair were arrested by highly incensed Japanese sentries. The petty officers were held in custody until the arrival of the British Consul in the morning. They were released, but the stoker remained in prison until the Consul had investigated the whole incident. *Decoy* had left Tsingtao by the time the investigation was complete and the stoker's written apology was not acceptable. The Japanese said that if *Decoy*'s captain did not apologize in person, they could not guarantee that Royal Navy libertymen would not be beaten up by Japanese soldiers on leave from the fighting front and exasperated by Britain's support of China. So the destroyer was ordered to return within ten days and Commander W. J. C. Robertson, wearing a frock coat and sword, read a formal apology in the presence of the Japanese Consul-General and a high-ranking Japanese naval officer. He also had to promise the stoker would be suitably punished and only then was the detainee handed over. From now on the British had to carefully avoid arguments with soldiers or sailors, especially at Tsingtao.

The activities of waterfront thugs increased in number and scope throughout the troubled mercantile conditions of the Sino-Japanese Incident. On August 25th, gangsters tried to take over the Butterfield and Swire warehouses at Tangku. The Chinese coolies were cowed into submission while their foreman went into hiding somewhere in the long buildings. Fourteen seamen were sent across to the property from the escort vessel *Grimsby*. They did nothing except march round the compound once or twice, but this had the desired effect. The coolies' foreman came out of hiding and ordered the loafers and thugs off the premises. Work was resumed, but as soon as the landing party was withdrawn, the crooks came back and the foreman went and hid again. It seemed that only the continued presence of the bluejackets could ensure that the gangsters would not eventually dominate Butterfield and Swire's property at Tangku.

Although these villains were vicious cut-throats, they did sometimes show a certain unconscious humour in their outrageous demands. Tug-captains at Taku received the following letter from local bandits:

'Dear Sirs,
Owing to our shortage of provisions we are asking your company to borrow sixteen thousand dollars. This money to be paid in three days. On approaching here blow three blasts. Also two gold chains and four gold rings.'

The presence of a Royal Navy warship dissuaded further communication.

The approaching typhoon season and other natural hazards caused several mishaps in September, the most tragic occurring at Hong Kong where the cruiser *Kent* had just arrived from England. Although the typhoon that brushed the colony did no damage to compare with that caused the previous year, an able seaman was washed overboard from *Kent* and the French liner *Chenonceaux* went aground at the harbour entrance. The destroyer *Thanet* and the dockyard tug *Alliance* went to her help, while other ships lowered boats to search for *Kent*'s able seaman. Searchlight beams illuminated the harbour but they only picked out a turmoil of breaking waves and flying spray. Heavy rain further restricted visibility and the search had to be abandoned. *Chenonceaux* was luckier. Her 250 passengers were taken off by harbour lighters while the warships stood by. The 14,825-ton liner was then towed into Taikoo Dockyard for repairs to her propellers and rudder.

Near Nanking a Japanese tug got into difficulties on the Yangtse. Her tow, a heavy steel lighter, took charge, the hawsers being too long and the current too swift. It veered from side to side, dragging the tug with it until the strain parted the cable. The lighter swept down on *Bee*, whose crew fended it off as it shaved past scraping the gunboat's side, but doing no material damage, and disappeared downstream with the tug in pursuit. After securing it again, the Japanese sent a deputation to *Bee* to apologize for having created a hazard in this way.

Even farther up the Yangtse *Gannet* went to the aid of the Jardine, Matheson, river steamer *Kia Wo* which had struck a submerged rock at the foot of the Kuanyitan Rapid. The master beached his ship and anchored her to the bank with wire hawsers, so that she could not be swept off the ledge and sunk. She was still in this precarious position when *Gannet* arrived and stood by until preparations had begun for her salvage. The gunboat could not wait while the work was carried out – it took too long. Coolies had to cut a slipway in the rocks so that the 1,311-ton steamer could be lowered more than eighteen feet into the river.

The first indications of the most serious international situation so far came on September 11th. *Cumberland*, paying a short visit to Chingwangtao, recalled the sightseeing party that had gone to Peking and sailed hurriedly for Wei-Hai-Wei and Hong Kong. The series of events known as the Munich Crisis had begun. All the China Fleet left Wei-Hai-Wei to take up their war stations and *Adventure* embarked a full load of mines. The Yangtse gunboats at Chungking, Ichang, Kiukiang, Wuhu and Nanking were ordered to move downriver if war with Germany began. If the Japanese objected the gunboats' crews were to burn all confidential material and proceed just the same, forcing their way through if necessary. *Scarab*'s particular orders were for her to be sunk in deep water, after

The Blockade

making contact with the local Chinese Army. With Petty Officer Ah Ching (*Scarab*'s senior Chinese hand) as interpreter, arrangements were made for the 3-inch gun to be landed and mounted on a truck as a primitive armoured car. But before any of this work was begun, five Japanese destroyers arrived and anchored only 1½ cables (300 yards) away. They were so close that Lieutenant-Commander Clitherow realized that their 5-inch guns could not depress sufficiently to hit the gunboat. *Scarab*'s own two 6-inch guns were already loaded and could easily bear on the Japanese destroyers. In fact they could not miss and just one 6-inch shell would not do the vitals of a destroyer much good. So, if war came, and Japan came in on Germany's side, *Scarab*'s 'A' and 'Y' guns would traverse inwards along the line, one shell for each destroyer and a race to get the middle one first.

At the same time as the gunboats were preparing to do-or-die, the Germans in the International Settlement at Shanghai were promising to protect British women if the Japanese invaded. Meanwhile an officer in *Raimondo Montecuccoli* sent an officer in a British gunboat his best wishes as an indication of Italy's sympathies, not knowing that *Dorsetshire* had been stationed off the Yangtse estuary to look out for the Italian cruiser. In fact, *Raimondo Montecuccoli* had already reached a Japanese port so *Dorsetshire* was ordered to Amoy to watch the Japanese cruiser *Myoko*. One of *Dorsetshire*'s officers went on board and was received most pleasantly. Altogether it was a funny sort of beginning for a war.

The oiler *Appleleaf* was ordered to embark Royal Navy wives stranded at Wei-Hai-Wei and take them to Hong Kong. While the civilians were going aboard, the Japanese cruiser *Kuma* arrived and trained her broadside of six 5·5-inch guns on *Appleleaf*'s escort, *Birmingham*. Not to be outdone in such matters of etiquette, Captain E. J. P. Brind ordered his twelve 6-inch guns to be pointed at the hostile warship, which presently departed.

Half-way to Hong Kong *Birmingham* handed *Appleleaf* over to *Suffolk* and put into Tsingtao so that there would be at least one major warship in northern Chinese waters to defend British interests there. Two minor incidents occurred, fortunately without any fuss resulting, although it was quite likely that Japan might take advantage of Britain's preoccupation in Europe. *Duncan*'s postman, who had gone ashore to deliver and collect mail before the destroyer sailed, was returning to the harbour area when he had to pass a group of six Japanese soldiers, one of them an armed sentry. They saw him coming and one barged straight into him, knocking him off the pavement. This situation had the makings of another diplomatic incident. If the postman had lost his temper he could have been arrested by the sentry and another apology could have been extracted from the Royal Navy. Although a burly physical training instructor, the leading seaman ignored the Japanese and walked straight on as though they did not exist. For this restraint he was later commended by his commanding officer.

On another occasion a petty officer from *Folkestone* was quietly having a beer in a Tsingtao café when a Japanese army officer came in already drunk. His long sword clanking on the floor, he went over to the only other occupants of the bar, two American sailors. He asked them in halting English who they were and their reply seemed to satisfy him, so he came across to the petty officer. On learning that he was from the British sloop in the bay, the officer struck him across the face with the flat of his hand. The petty officer pushed away his beer, got up and walked out. With obvious disappointment, the Japanese officer eased his sword back into its scabbard, glared round and stalked off.

It was soon decided that *Birmingham*'s presence was not required at Tsingtao and she was ordered to proceed to Shanghai immediately where she embarked the 1st Battalion, the Seaforth Highlanders. She left Woosung on the morning of September 26th with 700 soldiers crammed aboard, arriving at Hong Kong next day. Her average speed was 28·5 knots, a new China Fleet record for the passage. She was then ordered to proceed to Singapore, while other ships including most of the 4th Submarine Flotilla were also on their way westwards.

Even at this crucial time the Yangtse gunboats had to attend to the most mundane tasks. Due to the Japanese embargo on foreign shipping, there was an acute coal shortage at Nanking. Thanks to their enjoyment of a shipping monopoly the Japanese were the only nationals to accumulate large reserves of coal. If other enterprising merchants wanted coal, they stole it from the Japanese, but they had to be very careful as the dumps were always well guarded. About 20.00 hrs on September 28th the watches on the gunboats *Bee* and *Cricket* noticed a junk full of Chinese quietly secure inside the Hogee Pontoon. This was British property, but as it was empty they could not be doing any harm. Presently it became apparent that some sort of work was in progress, so two searchlights were trained on the sound. The Chinese had made a hole in the wall separating the British and Japanese compounds and were busily removing Japanese coal. They were undismayed by the glare of light and continued working, apparently grateful for the illumination. They did not continue for long as a party of bluejackets was sent ashore and the thieves were immediately arrested. Their junk, by now half full of coal, was sunk as a warning to other miscreants, and especially those who might get Britain involved in yet another international incident.

Meanwhile Admiral Noble had hurriedly transferred his flag to *Kent*. *Cumberland* reverted to the status of a private ship and sailed for England to reinforce the Home Fleet in the anticipated trial of strength with Nazi Germany. Soon after leaving Hong Kong the cruiser ran through the edge of a small typhoon but kept up her speed of 20–22½ knots. Many of her crew lost interest in current affairs and felt that the world would be a happier place if only the weather would improve. The day she arrived at Singapore, Neville Chamberlain reached an agreement with Adolf Hitler and *Cumberland* was able to proceed at a more civilized speed of 14 knots. She arrived at Chatham on November 2nd to the tune of 'D'ye Ken John Peel'. Her crew considered that the Munich Crisis was probably a good thing. It had brought them home three weeks earlier than expected. Most of the other westbound ships were recalled from wherever they had got to and returned to their China bases.

As soon as the news of the Munich Agreement had become known, the plan for the Yangtse gunboats' breakout was called off, but due to difficulties in communications it was not possible to relay the signal to *Cockchafer* at Kiukiang. Admiral Holt and his staff waited anxiously for the first news that the gunboat was underway and was being fired on by the Japanese because she had not got their permission. It turned out that their fears were groundless. The signal had been taken in, *Cockchafer* stayed where she was and nothing untoward occurred.

Now that the threat of full-scale war had been averted, people could relax again and the Navy ostensibly reverted to peacetime routine. But the Munich Crisis had served as a test of battle efficiency and many captains determined that when the next emergency arose their ships would be at an even higher standard of readiness. They instituted an arduous series of practical exercises, training their crews to cope with every possible contingency – as well as a few that might be thought impossible. Many of these manœuvres were decidedly unpopular, especially when they occurred in the middle watch, but they proved their worth twelve months later when a crisis of six years' duration began.

7
The Capture of Canton and the Defence of Hankow

Ever since the beginning of the war the Japanese had been considering the capture of Canton. It had originally been planned in December 1937, but the Japanese Government feared that Britain might get involved if a landing took place at Bias Bay so close to Hong Kong. The operation was called off but reactivated in the summer of 1938. They hoped to cut off 80 per cent of the supplies reaching Chiang Kai-Shek and they also believed that Canton was a hotbed of anti-Japanese intrigue. The area had been bombed since the beginning of the war and this air assault was stepped up, mainly with aircraft from the carrier *Kaga*. The blockade had been extended to include South Chinese ports and invasion convoys assembled in the Pescadores Islands. At the same time some Chinese troops were being withdrawn from the Canton area to reinforce the Hankow sector. Finally, Britain's apparent surrender at Munich indicated that there was nothing to be feared from that quarter even if Hong Kong were involved. The Japanese South China Area Army went ashore from a powerful invasion fleet in Bias Bay on October 12th.

They followed up their assault with a further landing at the head of the Pearl River Delta. Within ten days Canton had been captured and all traffic on the Pearl River, Si-Kiang and Pei-Kiang stopped because of Chinese obstructions and Japanese orders. The speed of the advance caught the Chinese by surprise and all those who decided to leave did so at the same time. There were thousands of small boats on the river, all moving very slowly, but so tightly packed that it was almost impossible to see any water between them. Behind this waterborne multitude rose columns of smoke as the Chinese Army blew up ammunition dumps. Buildings caught fire on the island of Shameen where the British and other concessions were situated. Landing parties from the gunboats *Moth* and *Tarantula* had to fight the nearest fires as well as keeping retreating Chinese and advancing Japanese out of the British Concession. They were helped in the former task by a volunteer German fire brigade who belonged to a firm selling fire engines.

These landings brought the Japanese on to a common frontier with the British at Hong Kong and the Portuguese at Macao. The colonies were virtually invested by the Japanese who were now able to impose the same controls on the Pearl and West Rivers as they had imposed on the Yangtse. Suddenly the war which had seemed so far away, was on Hong Kong's doorstep.

The Capture of Canton and the Defence of Hankow

Meanwhile the Chinese Government had continued implementing their declared intention of defending Hankow stubbornly. They erected machine-gun posts, barricades, barbed-wire entanglements and other fortifications all over Hankow except in SAD3 which Admiral Holt insisted should be regarded as neutral by both sides. As proof of his determination to protect British property and as a token of his good faith, all British shipping on this stretch of the Yangtse would be concentrated at SAD3. Their position was known to both Chinese and Japanese and it was expected that their neutrality would be respected. In any case it was unlikely that any one spot on the river would be safer than any other. The Chinese had built defence works up and down the river banks and their artillery fire, Japanese counter-bombardment and bombing, and Chinese mines made most of the Yangtse near Hankow dangerous. So foreign ships stayed off SAD3, which was just as well, as it would probably have taken about ten days to move all the ships and the thousand foreign nationals somewhere else and it was hardly likely that the Japanese would give ten days' notice of their attack.

In spite of their proclaimed defence of Hankow, the evacuation of the city began, at first civilian refugees and then the military and civil authorities. It became obvious that Hankow would not be the capital of China for very much longer, and as the Chinese Government was now being concentrated at Chungking, the British Diplomatic Mission decided to move to that city, over six hundred miles farther up the Yangtse. In future when Sir Archibald Clark Kerr, the British Ambassador, wished to visit the Chinese capital from Shanghai, he would have to travel to Hong Kong in a liner, then sail to Haiphong in French Indo-China in a destroyer, and finally fly via Kunming to Chungking.

On October 20th the British Diplomatic Mission boarded *Tern* and steamed upriver. Presently the gunboat came up with *Falcon* who had left two days earlier on passage to Chungking to act as winter guardship. Lieutenant-Commander R. S. Abram had received orders to anchor and wait to take over *Tern's* passengers. This done, *Falcon* proceeded to her destination while *Tern* retraced her course to Hankow. This operation was in fact part of the normal seasonal movement of gunboats. *Gannet* was relieved by *Falcon* and sailed for Ichang, whence *Peterel* moved to Hankow. She and *Tern* both secured alongside the old hulk *Laestrygon*.

These were probably the last normal seasonal moves on the Middle and Upper Yangtse. Certainly 21st October was the last day before civilian river steamers were forced to shut down passenger services. Hordes of panic-stricken refugees, fleeing from the horrors of the Japanese advance, swarmed over the steamers *Siangtan*, *Shasi* and *Kut Wo*. The small crews carried by these vessels just could not cope with these masses of people. They were swept aside and within minutes each riverboat was a floating multitude; Chinese packing the decks and cabins, clambering down into the engine and boiler rooms, standing shoulder to shoulder

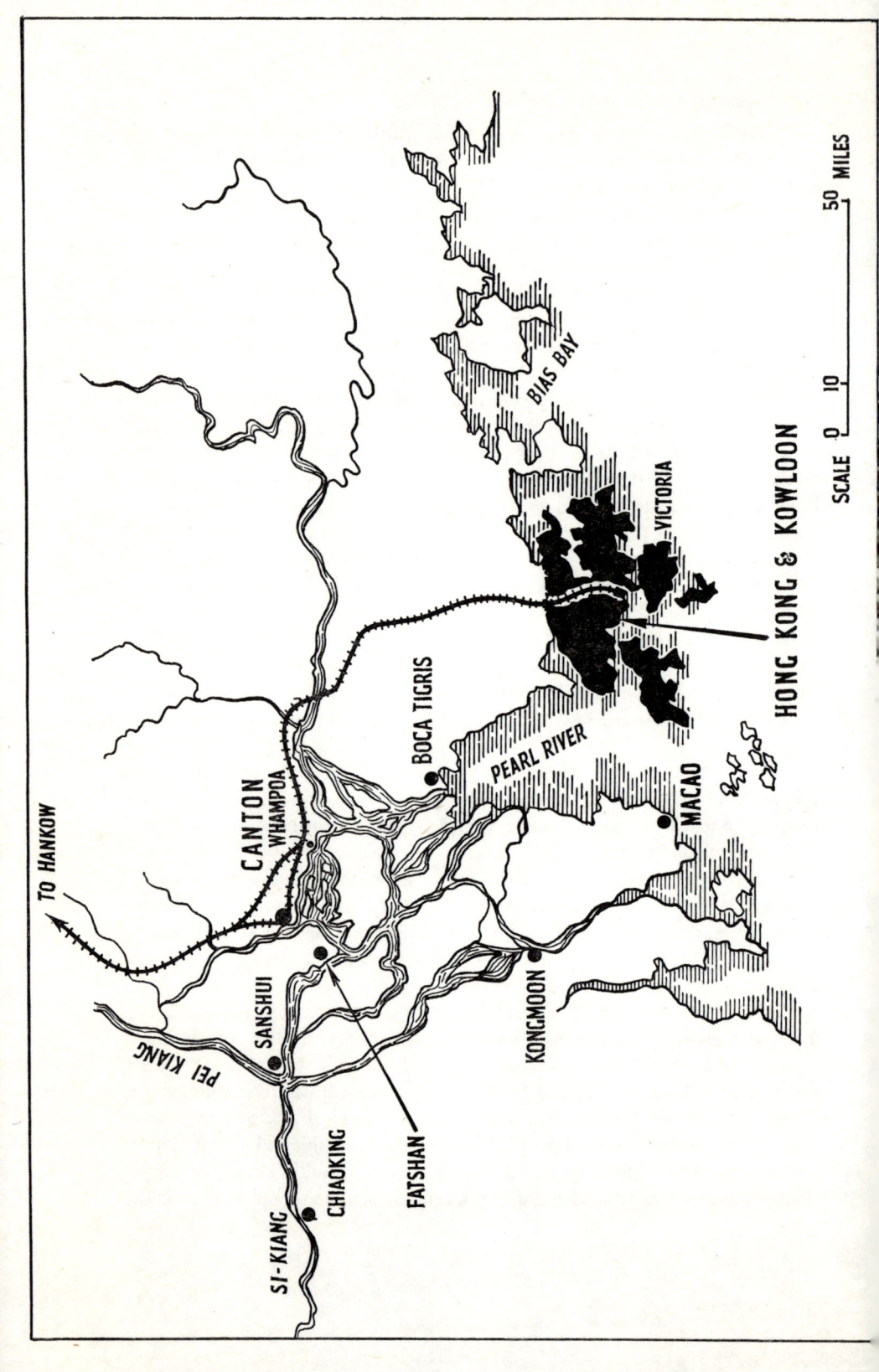

The Capture of Canton and the Defence of Hankow

on the bridge and clinging to every rail. For some to be saved, many had to be cleared off the ship, otherwise the crew could not work her and she might even capsize through sheer weight of humanity on her decks. So armed bluejackets were sent across from the gunboats to get the ships as clear as possible; at least to empty the engine and boiler rooms of refugees and give the captain and his men a little elbow-room on the bridge. With rifles and riot sticks the ships were cleared, but not without danger. Every time a party was sent across there was always the possibility that a fear-crazed Chinese would lash out with a knife or bottle and a sailor be killed or maimed. Yet each time the riverboats were eventually cleared and a few more hundred refugees carried to safety.

There had been occasional air raids throughout the summer but now the Japanese broadcast their intention of bombing all ships, boats and craft trying to cross the river. Admiral Holt refused to move British ships ten miles upriver, for the reasons he had given earlier. Instead he told the Japanese that all British ships at or above Hankow would be advised to paint their canvas awnings with distinctive red, white and blue sections so that they could be identified from the air. This seems to have been effective for although there were many air raids on Hankow during the next few days, no bombs fell on British ships or indeed in any of the Special Administrative Districts.

It was a different story at Changsha where the gunboat *Sandpiper* was stationed. October 24th was a clear day. A number of Chinese junks were at anchor about fifty yards from *Sandpiper*'s starboard side with a ferry boat 30 yards ahead. There were no military junks on the Siang-Kiang and there were no signs of Chinese soldiers. The Japanese authorities had requested that *Sandpiper* be distinguished by the same markings displayed by the gunboats at Hankow. Distinctive blue, white and red bands completely covered the ship from bow to funnel (blue forward) and a large Union Jack had been spread from the funnel to the end of the superstructure.

About 08.30 hrs a Japanese aircraft flew up and down the river at a height of about 1,000 feet, followed half an hour later by six heavy bombers at 3,000 feet. Bombs dropped on and around *Sandpiper*. Two cabins and other parts of her superstructure were wrecked and many holes made by flying splinters. Fortunately *Sandpiper* suffered no casualties, but the ferry boat was blown up by a direct hit. Lieutenant-Commander H. E. H. Nicholls had no doubt that his ship was the primary target of this raid, but although the Japanese Government later expressed deep regret, they maintained that their pilots had attacked Chinese troop-carrying junks and had been unaware of *Sandpiper*'s presence.

Earlier that morning Admiral Holt had taken a telephone call from Dr Wu, the Mayor of Hankow, who said that he was just leaving. He commended the city and the safety of foreigners to Admiral Holt's keeping. Next morning Chiang Kai-Shek left Hankow by air for Chungking, and a Chinese Government spokesman announced officially that the city would not be defended by the Chinese Army. As the American Rear-Admiral Le Breton was in the International Hospital with a broken arm, it now seemed that most of the burden of organizing the demilitarization of the neutral zone would fall upon Rear-Admiral Holt and his staff. It was important that no Chinese soldier should fire on the Japanese from this zone. Nothing should be destroyed and there should be no rioting, not just for the sake of protecting individual foreign properties, but so that the Japanese should not be given any excuse for forcibly ejecting foreigners from this area.

Quickly the small forces were despatched to their allotted positions. Admiral Holt's headquarters were established in the buildings of the Asiatic Petroleum Company, while Lieutenant-Commander Tait was in the British Consulate, sending out the three platoons of Force RF to patrol the streets and guard the gates. They were accompanied by armed sections from *Peterel* and *Mantis* (moored alongside *Laestrygon*) and by members of the special police. There were also Chinese police in SAD3, the only ones remaining in Hankow. SAD2 was guarded by special police and an armed landing party from the American flagship, the gunboat *Luzon*. She had originally been berthed alongside *Laestrygon*, but her presence had caused mutual radio interference with the British gunboats. She was now secured to another hulk and her landing party accommodated in the American YMCA. Naturally enough, the French defended their own concession, three hundred troops and seamen being dug in with barbed-wire defences and machine-gun posts. They also had the largest warship at Hankow, the 2,000-ton sloop *Admiral Charner*, as well as the gunboat *Francis-Garnier*. SAD1 was guarded by the gunboats *Gnat* and *Tern*. They sent ashore armed sections who co-operated with the volunteer police in patrolling the streets and manning all the gates except one. This was in the charge of 25 Italian naval men and was the important Bund Gate which led directly from the old Japanese Concession. As this area was now in Chinese hands, it was a likely danger spot if the Japanese launched an attack. American and British installations downriver were watched over by the American gunboat *Guam*.

As foreigners living outside the neutralized zone moved into it, so Lieutenant-Commander H. N. A. Richardson, then attached to *Peterel*, set about organizing the removal of demolition charges. The Chinese had prepared about 500 buildings for destruction and most were quite obviously booby-trapped, as wires could be seen leading down into the basements. Other houses were not so clearly mined, and small parties from Force RF had to enter every suspected building. Wires were cut or otherwise rendered safe and a considerable amount of explosive removed. In one case it was found that a junk alongside The Bund was packed full of explosives. The fuse was made safe and the boat taken out into deep water where all the explosives could be thrown overboard. It was just as well that all the work was completed in time, as explosions began in the city outside the neutral

Above: A Japanese Army folding assault boat, Canton, October 1938.
  [*Vice-Adm Sir Patrick Bayly*

Left: Cicala's officers watching an air raid on Canton.
  [*Vice-Adm Sir Patrick Bayly*

Top: A Petty Officers' Course at Kowloon. [*H. G. C. Brice*

Above: A Naval funeral at Hong Kong. *Tamar* in the background. [*H. G. C. Brice*

Left: A Kawanishi Type 91 seaplane taking off at Tsingtao. *Ashigara* in the background. [*H. E. J. Regler*

Top: A rare photograph of *Scorpion* wearing the flag of Rear-Admiral Holt, Shanghai, 19th May 1939.
　　　　　[*Don E. Gammon via A. & J. Pavia*

Above: MTB9 off Hong Kong in 1939.
　　　　　[*Vice-Adm Sir Patrick Bayly*

Right: Like other gunboats, *Scarab* was flatbottomed and so needed no shores to support her sides in drydock at Shanghai. Her three rudders can be seen, but her two propellers are hidden in half-tunnels under her bottom. The square structure above the stern contains the seamen's heads. The Union Jack and the red, white and blue neutrality markings are just visible on her awning.
　　　　　[*Lt J. Evans*

Kia Wo and *Hsin Chang Wo* burnt out at Ichang after the air raid of 6th August 1939. *Gannet* is berthed ahead of them. [*Lt Cdr J. A. McClure*

The view from *Falcon* during an air raid on Chungking. Note *Wanliu*'s Union Jack. [*Lt Cdr J. A. McClure*

A close up of *Falcon* at Chungking. Her motor sampan is clearly visible. [*Lt Cdr J. A. McClure*]

Falcon's half-crew at Kweiyang on 25th January 1940. [*Lt Cdr J. A. McClure*

The fire-engine at Wei-Hai-Wei. [*Cdr H. R. Rycroft*

Durban leaving Singapore on patrol in 1940. She has anti-splinter padding around her bridge and after control position, and a degaussing cable along the top of her hull. [*Vice-Adm Sir Patrick Bayly*]

The Royal Navy Canteen on Liukungtao Island, Wei-Hai-Wei, in summer. [*H. G. C. Brice*

The Royal Navy Canteen on Liukungtao Island, Wei-Hai-Wei, in winter. [*H. E. J. Regler*

The Capture of Canton and the Defence of Hankow

zone during the afternoon of October 25th. Fires were started but were prevented from spreading by heavy rain which fell during the night.

Meanwhile all the Chinese soldiers remaining in the area were being rounded up by the street patrols and gate sentries and taken to the gates. Those who were fearful of Japanese reprisal and wanted to stay in the neutral zone were disarmed. The rifle section from *Mantis* and *Peterel* scoured the foreshore, searching every dugout, junk and sampan in case any Chinese soldier should try to hide amongst the hundreds of refugees sheltering in their little floating homes. A few were found and disarmed, and by 17.30 hrs on October 25th the area was considered to be neutralized, a message to this effect being passed to the Japanese.

That night all the seamen, troops and police shivered in the pouring rain, watching and waiting. Next day the Japanese would arrive. If they felt confident and were not upset, then they would approach the neutral zone with goodwill. If they felt over-confident, displaying arrogance towards the defeated and neutral, then the smallest action, the most inoffensive remark, would be seized upon as a reason for destroying all foreign property and killing all foreigners within the city of Hankow. Over in the old Japanese Concession rioting Chinese made the most of the absence of law and order, shops being looted and fires started. In the neutralized zone, the night passed quietly but uncomfortably.

About 08.00 hrs the next morning, October 26th, Lieutenant-Commander E. Neville in *Gnat*, was informed that two strange craft were approaching his gunboat, apparently some sort of barge driven by a huge aeroplane propeller. They turned out to be Japanese landing craft specially designed for use in shallow waters. The Japanese Navy officers were the forerunners of the main force and it was their duty to make contact with the foreign authorities. They told Lieutenant-Commander Neville that big ships would be arriving that same afternoon. They knew all about the safety zone and stated that Japanese Army troops had also received strict orders not to enter any neutralized area. However, they would not reach Hankow for a day or so and in the meantime the Japanese Navy would be responsible for taking over the city. Having delivered this message, the two landing craft went about and retired downriver.

Although a number of Japanese aircraft flew over the city, nothing further happened until 13.15 hrs when a force of ships was sighted coming upriver, and from then on Japanese vessels arrived throughout the rest of the day. First came eight landing craft, followed an hour later by torpedo boats fitted as minesweepers with their sweeps out. Then came a veritable armada of landing craft, motor boats, motor fishing vessels, to two anti-submarine netlayers (also streaming paravanes), two minelayers, twelve transports and storeships, some river gunboats, more torpedo boats and innumerable small river craft. One of the torpedo boats peppered a small junk with machine-gun fire about two miles downstream, but apart from this there was only an occasional shot.

While everyone's attention was concentrated on the river, Admiral Holt received news from the Italians on duty that a column of Japanese troops had arrived at the Bund Gate, separating SAD1 from the old Japanese Concession – the Japanese Army had arrived at least twenty-four hours ahead of schedule. Admiral Holt sent Captain L. S. Saunders, his chief staff officer, to talk to them, but he met the column halfway through SAD1. The Japanese soldiers had already entered what was supposed to be part of the safe area. Father Jacquinot, a Roman Catholic priest who was generally recognized for his refugee work at Shanghai and elsewhere, was trying to persuade the Japanese to respect the neutral zones. It was soon obvious that few of them, if any, had any knowledge of the refugee areas, but they were very tired after their long forced march and they allowed Father Jacquinot and Captain Saunders to lead them out of SAD1.

Rear-Admiral Kondo then contacted Rear-Admiral Holt to reassure him about the Japanese intention to respect the neutral zone. He had naturally expected Royal Navy landing parties in SAD3, the old British Concession, but it had not been made clear to him that SAD1, the old German Concession, was also part of the demilitarized area. They had not expected to meet foreigners there. As a compromise Admiral Holt agreed to withdraw the *Gnat* and *Tern* landing parties. They had accomplished their duty in protecting foreign life and property from looters during the temporary breakdown of law and order, and no useful purpose would now be served by their remaining on shore. *Tern* later returned to the *Laestrygon* hulk to help with the increased W/T traffic, but *Gnat* remained alongside the Hogee pontoon. If it were unoccupied the Japanese would probably be tempted to use it as a landing stage for their men and equipment. The Japanese Army did in fact use two Butterfield and Swire floating wharves until this irregularity was pointed out to them. *Gnat* also kept in touch with British firms trying to reopen their business premises in SAD1.

Once the Japanese had occupied SAD1 their soldiers tried to get through the next series of gates into SAD2 and SAD3, and the French had similar problems in their concession. Usually the Japanese could be dissuaded from entering after the existence and purpose of the refugee zones had been explained to them, but one large force could not be deterred and insisted on marching through SAD3. Foreign personnel were determined not to be provoked into attacking the Japanese, and the column was allowed to pass through.

So far the Japanese capture of Hankow had been without serious disagreement between them and the foreign nationals. It soon seemed as though their control over the city was strong enough to prevent Chinese gangs looting and killing, while the Japanese themselves gave every indication that they intended to respect foreign property. By the evening of October 26th a party of Japanese military police had begun marking all buildings owned by foreigners to the effect that they were out of bounds to all Japanese soldiers. That same evening the

United States Navy withdrew all their shore parties while the Royal Navy armed patrols exchanged their rifles and steel helmets for batons and caps. The next morning, however, Japanese soldiers told Admiral Holt and the British Consul-General that they only had enough gendarmerie to police The Bund, where they were soon going to start unloading. They requested that the Royal Navy, special police and Chinese police should continue patrolling SAD3, and the British authorities agreed. The Japanese placed sentries on The Bund and The Bund Gates, but the Royal Navy parties relieved from there found plenty to do as firefighters.

Several fires had broken out in Hankow, one very close to the edge of SAD3. *Peterel* and *Mantis* sent sections along to help the Chinese fire brigade, but very little could be done because the city's water supply had failed the previous night. The bluejackets concentrated on saving everything movable and then tried to clear fire-breaks around the blazing shops and shanties. They also had to control the crowds of Chinese milling about in the vicinity. Eventually it seemed that the fire was under control, but several hours later it blazed up again and threatened to spread through the refugee zone. By now the Special Administrative District fire-engines were pumping water all the way from the river, but although the pressure was low the fire was eventually extinguished.

About forty Japanese transports had now arrived and they continued unloading during the whole of October 27th. Most stores, equipment and personnel came ashore on The Bund or across the river at Wuchang, none of it over British property except the Butterfield and Swire pontoons already mentioned. On October 28th the Japanese military police calculated that they would have enough men to take over control of SAD3 the next day. Although Admiral Holt and the British Consul-General agreed, they were concerned lest the Japanese be given a last-minute excuse for violent action. Accordingly the Chinese police were ordered to hand in all their rifles, sidearms and ammunition to be stored in the *Laestrygon* hulk. The unfortunate Chinese police were now defenceless and only too well aware of the fate of many of their compatriots who fell into Japanese hands. They became very nervous and panicky, and begged protection from the British authorities. They were therefore allowed to seek refuge aboard the British river ships *Woosung* and *Pao-Hua*.

At 11.00 hrs on October 29th Force RF and two sections of US ratings paraded in full equipment outside Admiral Holt's headquarters in the Asiatic Petroleum Company's offices. A column of Japanese troops which included a small body of military police, also in full equipment and with machine-guns on donkeys and mules, then arrived and lined up facing the British and American sailors. There was not a lot to be said, especially in the pouring rain, and Admiral Holt merely turned over to a Japanese colonel 'the safety of foreigners and their peace of mind'. Royal Navy sentries were then relieved by Japanese sentries, and a system of passes and identification armbands came into force.

So the Japanese captured Hankow. They had shown at Nanking what they could be like if so disposed and at Hankow they had presented a totally different face. It might be very galling for a British naval man to submit passes to the new Japanese occupiers, but for the Royal Navy it was immaterial whether the Chinese or the Japanese controlled Hankow. Their job had been to protect neutral British property without taking sides. Because there were no incidents, there were no headlines, but it was a job well done just the same.

However, the Japanese immediately seized the opportunity to enforce their superior power. The day after the handing-over ceremony the chief petty officer and a leading seaman from the gunboat *Gnat* were stopped and searched by Japanese sentries. Admiral Holt made a formal protest about this and about the humiliating demand that all 'English pigs' should bow to Japanese sentries. On the whole, this order, which was promulgated throughout China, caused more difficulty with American personnel who were sometimes accompanied by their wives in areas occupied by Japanese. Tempers flared when their womenfolk were searched, assaulted and their faces slapped. Their husbands came to their defence and the Japanese immediately proclaimed that Western colonialists were once again trampling on the rights and dignities of an Asiatic people. Any apology later proffered by the Japanese authorities was usually accompanied by a variety of further insults.

8
The Pearl River Blockade

The authorities at Hong Kong had taken note of the effects of air raids on nearby Chinese targets – air raids that one day might be directed against the colony itself. 50,000 sandbags were purchased to deal with incendiary bombs and all Chinese of British citizenship willing to help were invited to enrol in an emergency force. Combined exercises were held and the civil defence organizations gained experience in dealing with the hordes of refugees streaming across the border. Sir Geoffrey Northcote and the Governor of Macao held discussions about these and other mutual problems early in November 1938, *Falmouth* taking Sir Geoffrey and Lady Northcote across to the Portuguese colony.

The most serious problem was the closure of the Pearl River delta to foreign shipping, resulting in the trapping of several British merchant ships upriver. Even worse was the detention of the gunboats *Robin* and *Cicala* at Canton. The Japanese authorities refused to give them permission to move in spite of Sir Robert Craigie's efforts in Tokyo. But at last *Robin* was allowed to move upriver to Wuchow, where she was to collect a convoy of small ships to be escorted through the gorges to Kongmoon. *Cicala* got under way, making directly through the delta channels to Kongmoon to protect British lives and property there. Four miles beyond Canton she was stopped again by Rear-Admiral Sukigara in Minesweeper No 18 who informed Lieutenant-Commander D. J. Pack-Beresford that the Pearl River delta was completely closed to all traffic. *Cicala's* captain referred the matter to Hong Kong and informed the Japanese that no official notification of closure had been received. Japanese officers then came on board the gunboat and politely put forward the reasons outlined by the Japanese Ministry of Marine why *Cicala* should not proceed.

'1. Canton Delta area is an area of active operations including minesweeping, attacks on minelaying junks, motor torpedo boats and on land forces now in progress, in such an area movement of third Power ships are liable to lead to interference with operations and subsequently to incidents.

2. Japanese Navy have no desire to limit movements of third Power warships in area where there are no military operations in progress. On completion of operations Japanese will recognize movements of third Power warships in this area.

3. It is thought that if all goes well area should be free for this purpose about

November 10. Japanese will then want to know details of areas in which third Power warships propose to operate, their courses and methods of keeping in touch with Japanese naval authorities. Japanese authorities require previous information on these matters.'

The trouble was that Japanese authorities were usually 'busy' or 'indisposed.'

Cicala consulted her headquarters again and was told not to do anything which might provoke an incident. After some time No 18 went upriver, but not before Minesweeper No 17 had arrived to keep close watch on the British gunboat. At one stage Lieutenant-Commander Pack-Beresford decided to move to another anchorage about fifty yards away, but the Japanese interpreted this navigational adjustment as a sign that *Cicala* was 'going to make the war'. There was great activity on board No 17 and as it was obvious that they were clearing for action, Lieutenant P. U. Bayly was quickly sent across to the Japanese vessel to explain the move.

On November 2nd No 17 up-anchored and departed without further ado. Left on her own, *Cicala* also got underway and prepared for action just in case any Japanese ship or shore battery opened fire. They passed a number of Japanese vessels and for a while were shadowed by an aircraft. There were many signs of fighting but the only firing came from a Japanese soldier in his underwear, taking potshots at a flock of domestic ducks paddling about in a creek. When *Cicala* arrived at Kongmoon she helped *Robin* escort her convoy out of the delta and then both gunboats returned to their customary station at Canton.

Vice-Admiral Sir Percy Noble made a special journey to Canton in *Seamew* to see for himself what conditions were like in the Pearl River area. He listened to the reports from *Robin*'s and *Cicala*'s commanding officers and then returned to Hong Kong in *Cicala*, arriving back on November 15th. Two days later the Japanese South China Area Commander-in-Chief, Vice-Admiral Shiozawa, came to Hong Kong in his flagship, the cruiser *Myoko*. He first paid an informal call on the Governor, a visit that was not returned – by mutual arrangement. The Japanese Admiral was then entertained to lunch in *Falmouth* and Admiral Noble put Britain's case for reopening the Pearl River Delta to merchant shipping. Admiral Shiozawa explained that the Japanese authorities were willing to reopen the Pearl River for traffic and trade at the earliest moment, but he could not say when that moment would be. He did allow food, clothing and medical supplies to be sent to Chinese refugees in the Canton area. The 3,204–ton steamer *Wuchang* subsequently carried out this errand of mercy – under Japanese escort. But the movement of a massive backlog of mail destined for Canton and other parts of China was prohibited and had to remain in the Hong Kong General Post Office.

After he had left in *Myoko*, Vice-Admiral Shiozawa issued the following communiqué: 'In response to the invitation which Vice-Admiral Sir Percy Noble extended to me previously with a view to promoting the relations between the

Navies of Great Britain and Japan, I have visited the Crown Colony today after the military operations in the Canton area have come to a conclusion. Availing myself of the opportunity, I have exchanged views with the British authorities in a frank manner'. There was no reference to the possible reopening of the Pearl River to neutral merchantmen.

Nor did any other Japanese authority mention reopening the commercial harbour of Tsingtao inside Kiaochow Bay. The entrance had been completely clear since the beginning of August but British ships were still not allowed to enter and berth alongside the wharves. Any loading or unloading that was permitted had to be into lighters alongside. This was a time-wasting inconvenience in summer and the approach of winter added danger to the situation. During severe gales vessels were compelled to remain outside sheltered waters in the exposed anchorage of Tsingtao Bay, unable to communicate with the shore. Yet only nine out of twenty-three berths were occupied at the time, and some of those were reserved for Japanese shipping lines. The Dairen Kisen Kaisha, Nisshin Kisen Kaisha and Osaka Shosen Kaisha, all ran regular commercial sailings to Tsingtao with no pretence of carrying military supplies. This was a deliberate trading monopoly, similar to the one being built up on the Yangtse and faithfully reported by the ever-present, solitary gunboats.

In the month of November alone, thirty-four cases of Japanese vessels trading at Nanking, Wuhu, Kiukiang, and elsewhere were reported. Details of the import cargoes showed that they comprised many articles which could not be described as 'military necessities'. Numerous advertisements at Wuhu demonstrated beyond all doubt that Japanese goods for trading purposes were reaching that city. The Mitsui Bussan Kaisha, for example, advertised cotton piece-goods, shirtings and sheetings, sugar and canned goods, while the number of firms displaying advertisements showed that the volume of trade was considerable. Export cargoes included wheat, rice, feathers and iron-ore. This amount of business and the names of ships involved, proved that these goods were not being carried as subsidiary cargoes when the transports had room to spare. It was contrary to the Japanese Government's assurance that all vessels trading on the Yangtse were engaged as military transports, while their statement that the Yangtse must remain closed owing to military operations, mines and the removal of navigation marks was challenged by Admiral Holt. He had recently come downriver to join his new flagship *Scorpion*, *Bee* having earlier made her last voyage to Shanghai. (Already she was being prepared for disposal and eventual scrapping in March 1939.) After consultation with the commanding officers of British, French and American gunboats, Admiral Holt could see no reason why the Yangtse should not be opened to foreign steamer trade between the sea and Wuhu. The stretch above Wuhu would be equally accessible once the river started to rise.

But the monopoly remained, augmented by some Japanese officials and by petty insults such as refusing a weekly invitation to play golf. During the observance of the Two Minutes' Silence on Armistice Day at Shanghai, Japanese artillery fired off a number of rounds. It was believed that this particular irritation may have been retaliation for intelligence work being done by Fleet Air Arm officers who often climbed a tall tower in the French Concession to watch and note Japanese aircraft on Hungjao Airfield just outside the Settlement. Yet in spite of the growing mutual friction, there were occasions when British and Japanese still helped each other as when a leading-stoker from *Peterel* suffered a compound fracture of the leg while competing in sports at Hankow in November. Local medical facilities were poor and his prospects looked bleak until the Japanese military authorities suggested that they fly him to Shanghai. Their offer was accepted and six hours later the injured man was leaving Shanghai in a steamer bound for Hong Kong. He was taken to the Royal Navy Hospital and was soon recovering.

Fortunately no casualties resulted from the explosion which shook Hankow on December 10th. Everybody wondered what was happening this time, but there was no need for alarm. All the demolition charges left behind by the Chinese had been piled up into a big heap by the Japanese who then set fire to it. Not surprisingly it blew up. Occasionally suspicious objects were reported floating downstream and it was feared that the Chinese were sowing mines. Infernal machines are certainly no respecters of neutrality and the British gunboats had to take various precautions to guard against them. For example, *Cockchafer's* crew fixed five bamboo poles on her bows which were facing upstream while she was anchored at Kiukiang. One pole projected straight ahead and two were angled outwards each side of the stern. A series of bamboo poles and ropes then joined them together, thus forming a semicircle which just brushed the surface of the water. It was hoped that this home-made boom defence system would divert floating mines either side of the ship but no mines were actually encountered so they never found out if it really were proof against lethal objects.

There were more problems at Hankow right at the end of 1938. About 17.00 hrs on New Year's Eve, Mr Dupree came on board the gunboat *Cricket*. He was Consul-General and Chairman of SAD3 and had come to ask Commander H. T. Armstrong for advice and help. At noon, Mr. Cameron, the Secretary of SAD3 had just finished his morning's work and was going to lunch when two hundred Special Chinese Police burst into the building and hustled him back into his office. They demanded an extra bonus on their discharge pay and tried to force him to sign a promissory note. When he refused he was threatened with hanging and a noose was dangled in front of his face. It was not until four hours later that he had been able to persuade a loyal policeman to smuggle a note to Mr Dupree. This had been the the first news that anyone had had of his plight and Mr. Dupree had immediately turned to the Royal Navy for assistance.

The problem was how to get Mr Cameron out uninjured, and without giving the Japanese who controlled the rest of Hankow, an excuse to intervene in the affairs of SAD3. Mr Dupree set off towards Mr Cameron's office accompanied by Chief Petty Officer Walker and three ratings. They were unarmed but carried entrenching-tool handles under their clothes.

They forced their way through the excited mob easily enough, but once they reached the office they were made prisoners as well. They got as close to the windows as they could, ready to drop into the street if such drastic action proved necessary. Chief Petty Officer Walker lit a cigarette and so did the ratings. The sight of these naval men and the two officials quietly smoking and quite unconcerned by two hundred mutineers seemed to have a soothing effect on the mob. Gradually they calmed down until the last clamorous voices fell silent. Mr Dupree started to speak and instantly there was uproar again. This called for another cigarette and the damping-down process began again. So riot and peace alternated. In each period of calm, Mr Dupree or Mr Cameron managed to explain some particular point before bedlam broke out again. Gradually by verbal persuasion and by a little gentle 'leaning-on' first the office, then the floor, and then the building was cleared. By the time a landing party arrived at 18.30 hrs the riot was over, quelled by two officials, one chief petty officer and three ratings.

So 1938 came to an end. At Hong Kong, Christmas parties with plenty of big eats were held in *Birmingham*, *Eagle*, the Cheero-Club, the Soldiers' and Sailors' Club, the Sailors' Home, the Missions to Seamen and the China Fleet Club. Three hundred guests attended the annual Royal Navy Ball. There were of course plenty of games, for sport was always very important on the China Station. When the cruiser *Kent* had to leave port suddenly, she left behind her representatives in the boxing finals so that they would not miss their bouts. They justified this privilege by carrying off the championship, but the victory was marred by the death of an able seaman from *Dainty* who suffered a fractured skull during the welterweight semi-finals. He was given a full naval funeral and the cortège assembled on the quay alongside the base ship *Tamar*; the coffin, covered with a Union Jack, on its gun carriage drawn by men from *Dainty*; the firing party from *Dainty*; the elaborate floral tributes from the Commander-in-Chief, Officers and Men of the China Fleet, his Messmates, the Captains, Officers and Men of *Dainty*, *Kent* and *Delight*, and the Chiefs' and Petty Officers' Mess in *Dainty*. Led by *Kent*'s Royal Marine Band the little procession moved away, out through the dockyard gates, past the watching Chinese and up the hill towards the cemetery in Happy Valley.

9
The Deterrent

In spite of their attempts to monopolize the wealth and resources of China, the Japanese were not doing so well financially. Not only were the Chinese boycotting Japanese goods in certain areas, but the whole campaign in China was costing far more than was being realized from the profits of Chinese trade. The Japanese intended to solve this problem by undertaking further military operations and by increasing pressure on China's foreign friends.

The Japanese authorities were now demanding advance notice of all British ship and aircraft movements within the operational areas of Japanese forces. They tried to gain control of Shanghai and other international concessions, which they claimed were being used for anti-Japanese activities, and wanted the establishment of a new puppet bank at Shanghai before they would consider opening the Yangtse to merchant ships of other nations. In the meantime they continued to discriminate against British merchants, directly by the organization of a system of trade permits, and indirectly by intimidating Chinese dockers and by a host of excuses and petty insults. At the same time they allowed their own ships to trade at the very ports they declared to be dangerous.

It became obvious to the British Government that appeasement would never satisfy Japanese desires, in spite of the apparent success of such a policy at certain stages of Britain's dealings with Hitler. The Japanese ban on British ships in Chinese waters, coupled with a series of irritating, insulting and damaging incidents would almost certainly result in the expulsion of Britain from the Far East unless the trend of Japanese aggression were stayed. The difficult problem was how to halt this aggression without provoking a major war at a time when Britain's military resources were being deployed to meet an enemy nearer home.

One way was to bolster Chinese resistance. The Yangtse was closed to Western ships, the Hong Kong-Canton route was cut after the occupation of the latter city and soon all other seaborne traffic was halted by Japanese blockade or seizure of ports. However, trade was still carried on via French Indo-China and the Burma Road, but the Chinese were just not getting all the supplies they needed and felt they deserved. They traded with anyone who promised to meet their demands and even the Germans continued to sell weapons to Chiang Kai-Shek, until the Japanese complained that this was putting too much strain on the Axis partnership. The world marvelled at China's infinite capacity for suffering and fighting.

The Deterrent

There did exist the possibility of Anglo-American joint action against Japan, as the United States was aware of the growing danger and maintained naval forces in the Pacific and the Far East. However, certain political lobbies in America almost seemed to consider Japanese aggression less unpleasant than English imperialism. Such people felt that military action against Japan in co-operation with the United Kingdom was purely for Britain's selfish interests – pulling English chestnuts out of the fire like America had had to do in 1917. Nevertheless, although the United States continued to trade with Japan, she also sent an increasing amount of military and economic aid to China, while British and American warships worked together during moments of crisis. Blood was still thicker than water. (This expression has summarized Anglo-American co-operation since 1859 during an attack by British and French naval forces on the Chinese-held Taku Forts. Although technically neutral, the American Commodore Tattnall ordered some of his sailors to help tow several boat-loads of Royal Marines to the assistance of their comrades under fire. He explained his decision with the phrase 'Blood is thicker than water'.) The British Government also considered co-operation with other foreign countries in an attempt to restrain Japan, but their importance in Chinese affairs varied greatly according to their own strength, their interest in the Far East and their attitude towards Japanese fascism.

The British people either did not know about these moves or did not understand the techniques and principles of international law and diplomacy in peacetime. As far as they could see, the Japanese were the aggressors and should be stopped – but without actually going to war. For in spite of their vocal dislike of Japanese atrocities and demands for a boycott of Japanese goods, the British public had no particular wish to get involved in a major war between two yellow races, or even to protect the selfish interests of a few British traders on the far side of the globe. In any case, the League of Nations had expressed its disapproval of Japan's actions and it was assumed that world opinion would soon force the Japanese to halt their aggression and disgorge their plunder without further bloodshed. In the meantime all possible aid should be sent to China, while if British warships were attacked to open fire immediately and worry about legal consequences later.

The British Government was aware of these pugnacious views. They were also aware of the ideals of the Society of the Black Dragon, the aims of the Tanaka Memorial and their obvious results in Japanese affairs. A military clique was attaining absolute power at home, while abroad Japan was bent on the mastery of the Far East. So far the League of Nations had been powerless, but few authorities accorded Japan a very high standard of military effectiveness. It was therefore hoped that Japanese militarism could be deterred by a display of naval might and it was suggested that a powerful squadron be sent to the Far East, a scheme which had first been proposed by Admiral Jellicoe in 1919–20 after a tour of the Dominions. Anticipating Japanese hostility at some future date, he suggested that a large fleet and air force be based at Singapore. However the plan was abandoned after the Washington Naval Treaty, although the Singapore naval base was later built ready to receive a fleet if ever one were sent. This would only be done if a war with Japan did break out. Then such a fleet would be able to stay any Japanese advance until even larger air, sea and land reinforcements arrived from England. The main line of the Japanese advance would probably be towards the rich natural resources of the East Indies, leaving their flank open to attack by American forces based at Hawaii and in the Philippines. The Japanese would have to protect this flank and retain some forces in their home waters against the ever-present enigma of Communist Russia. As the Japanese Navy, like any other, would always have some ships undergoing refit or repair, three or four British ships should be sufficient to deal with any escorted invasion convoy in the Western Pacific and the waters off South-East Asia. The R-class battleships would be suitable for this task as they were about the same age as Japanese capital ships. From time to time some people suggested that the ships be despatched to the Far East before war actually broke out. Not only would they gain experience in operating from Singapore and be on the spot ready for any emergency, they would also act as a deterrent and prevent a war actually starting. The debates, arguments and staff exercises went on, but no fleet was sent.

Early in 1939, the plan was revived by the Foreign Office in a memorandum to the Admiralty. They considered that the argument that the entire battle fleet should be held in European waters ready to defeat a European enemy and thus gain mastery of the world's seas, was no longer valid. We now had a serious potential enemy far away and it could only be defeated by a British fleet in that area. If it were really true that we did not have enough capital ships to station a battle fleet permanently in the Far East as well as in Europe, then we should give up the pretence of trying to defend indefensible colonies and interests, and withdraw entirely from the Far East. But the Admiralty was proposing to scrap the five R-class battleships in the near future. They might just as well be sent to Singapore where they would be no older than all but two of the threatening Japanese battleships. The Foreign Office had looked at comparative tables of the navies' capital ships and considered that the scheme was quite practicable.

Royal Navy	**Completed**	*Royal Oak*	1916
Barham	1915	*Royal Sovereign*	1916
Queen Elizabeth (refitting)	1915	*Renown* (refitting)	1916
Warspite	1915	*Repulse*	1916
Malaya	1916	*Ramillies*	1917
Valiant (refitting)	1916	*Hood*	1920
Resolution	1916	*Nelson*	1927
Revenge	1916	*Rodney*	1927

The Deterrent

Hostile in Europe (Germany)		**Friendly in Europe** (France)	**Completed**
	Completed		
Schlesien	1908	*Courbet*	1913
Schleswig Holstein	1908	*Paris*	1914
Deutschland	1933	*Bretagne*	1915
Admiral Scheer	1934	*Lorraine*	1916
Admiral Graf Spee	1936	*Provence*	1916
		Dunkerque	1937
Hostile in Europe (Italy)			
	Completed		
San Giorgio	1910		
Guilo Cesare	1914	**Friendly in Far East** (USA)	**Completed**
Caio Duilio	1915		
Conte Di Cavour	1915	*Arkansas*	1912
Andrea Doria	1916	*New York*	1914
		Texas	1914
Hostile in Far East (Japan)	**Completed**	*Arizona*	1916
		Nevada	1916
Kongo	1913	*Oklahoma*	1916
Hiei (demilitarised)	1914	*Pennsylvania*	1916
Fuso	1915	*Mississippi*	1917
Haruna	1915	*New Mexico*	1918
Kirishima	1915	*Idaho*	1919
Ise	1917	*Tennessee*	1920
Yamashiro	1917	*California*	1921
Hyuga	1918	*Maryland*	1921
Nagato (refitting)	1920	*Colorado*	1923
Mutsu (refitting)	1921	*West Virginia*	1923

The Royal Navy could work with France in containing Italy in the Mediterranean and with America in withstanding Japanese expansion in the Pacific, and still retain ships in Home waters to watch Germany.

There would be serious disadvantages in waiting until an emergency arose before sending a battle fleet to the Far East. A war or sudden crisis in Europe provoked or inspired by Germany or Italy, might prevent the despatch of the ships or might result in their recall after they had left. Would the Italians allow such a fleet to pass through the Mediterranean unmolested? Suppose the Suez Canal were blocked? It would then take very much longer for the battle fleet to sail round the Cape route. Would Singapore be able to hold out until the ships arrived? In any case, the battle fleet was supposed to act as a striking force dealing with Japanese convoys as far from Singapore and as near Japan as possible. What would happen if Singapore were under siege when the battle fleet arrived needing replenishment, refit and acclimatisation ? The Foreign Office agreed that Singapore was supposed to be able to hold out against any eventuality for a considerable period, but they wondered what the battle fleet was supposed to do if the Japanese did capture Singapore. Where would the ships go? The Foreign Office was of the opinion that stationing a battle fleet at Singapore would give dockyard personnel experience in maintaining capital ships and would create some impression on the Japanese, who were probably susceptible to the very manœuvres of power politics and gunboat diplomacy that they themselves so often employed.

The Admiralty considered the logic of this document, but they were still not happy about the creation of a Far East battle fleet. In March 1939 they outlined their reasons for deciding that ships could not be sent before the end of 1940 or the beginning of 1941 when the new battleships would begin to complete. Even with these extra ships they did not think that Great Britain could deal with the combined fleets of Germany, Italy and Japan. It would probably never be possible to build and maintain the huge navy that would be required for such a task. Even if it were possible, most ships would still have to be kept in Home waters close to the training depots, manning ports and refitting bases. There would certainly not be enough cruisers, destroyers, auxiliaries and aircraft carriers to screen, escort, supply and cover capital ships in the North Sea, the Mediterranean and the Far East. It was all very well for the Foreign Office to explain that ships were needed to back up foreign policy: it would help if the Foreign Office could reduce the number of our enemies. In the meantime we must cut our cloth according to our limited pocket. Unless the situation changed radically, the Admiralty would retain the bulk of the Royal Navy in European and Mediterranean waters, sending ships to the Far East if an emergency arose. However, they did agree to reconsider the matter later while the Government of Australia had already been unofficially informed that at least one capital ship would be stationed in the Far East by 1942.

From time to time the matter was raised and talked over again. It was suggested that a battle squadron escort the Duke and Duchess of Kent on their Australian visit in the autumn of 1939, thus reinforcing the Far East ships without deliberately provoking the Japanese. On another occasion Mr Chamberlain informed the House of Commons that circumstances might force Great Britain to send a fleet to Asiatic waters, but the Axis powers dismissed such proposed movements as empty threats and the Singapore base remained unused.

10
The Hopeful Year

But all these diplomatic and political problems were far removed from the cabarets, weddings, parades, billiards, sports fixtures, funerals, boxing matches, receptions, departures, arrivals, promotions, soccer matches, prize givings, Bisley meetings, presentations, honeymoons, skittles and dinners that still filled everyday life at Hong Kong. Certainly many people believed that 1939 dawned hopefully, now that the dark days of Munich were over. Even Old China Hands were beginning to accept Japanese conquest, although still wondering when normal trade would be resumed.

At Hong Kong Vice-Admiral Sir Percy Noble reviewed three battalions of bluejackets and one battalion of Royal Marines from *Kent, Birmingham, Cardiff, Medway, Eagle* and the 8th Destroyer Flotilla, led by Captain Brind and Commander J. P. de W. Kitcat, both from *Birmingham* and both on horseback. The Navy won both the rugby match against the Army and the yacht race against the Royal Hong Kong Yacht Club. Commodore and Mrs Dicken entertained Sir Geoffrey and Lady Northcote aboard *Tamar*, while *Kent*'s ship's company held a very successful New Year's Ball at the Peninsular Hotel. The flagship and *Falmouth* then sailed for routine visits to Manila and Saigon. A survey of the sloop *Cornflower* showed that she was not in very good condition and it was announced that she would soon have to be scrapped. The Governor, in a speech at the Hong Kong Royal Naval Volunteer Force Dinner, said that he would review the financial situation in two months' time. He hoped that the force would be able to make use of a general duties vessel such as a tug, which could be used for supplying lighthouses and for rescue work during typhoons as well as for RNR training. Even an ARP demonstration ended on an optimistic note when the officer in charge explained that only three out of ten incendiary bombs ever exploded. There was therefore little danger and they could be easily extinguished with sand and water.

Patriotic morale was boosted by the annual St George's Society Ball while Burns' Night performed a similar service for the Scots in Hong Kong. Lady Northcote launched the 10,000-ton Glen Line steamship *Breconshire* at Taikoo Dockyard, with the aid of loud cheers and firecrackers – a fitting portent for the ship that was destined to see so much action in the Mediterranean. *Seamew* took Mr Byrne of the Canton Consulate to Macao on an official visit, preceding a much more formal occasion when Sir Percy and Lady Noble travelled in *Falmouth* to the Portuguese colony. Later the Commander-in-Chief went on to Bangkok and Singapore where he presided over the annual combined exercises. While he was away another visit was paid to Macao, this time by Major-General A. E. Grasett in the gunboat *Moth*. Reliefs destined for the Upper Yangtse gunboats faced a much more complicated journey. First they took passage in the steamer *Yochow* to Haiphong where they joined a French naval surgeon and his party of ratings. They went on by train to Kunming and then by road to Chungking where *Falcon* was stationed. The men assigned to *Gannet* had to go downriver to Ichang in the ss. *Wantung*. The ratings who had been relieved had an even more uncomfortable journey as their trucks were stranded on a shingle bank in the middle of the Yangtse when the river suddenly rose.

But these travelling problems were merely inconveniences. Behind the façade of peace and order, Royal Navy warships were persevering in difficult, hazardous work which rarely received attention. They were increasingly involved in disputes with the Japanese, who always seemed ready to impress any vessel into their fleet, no matter how insignificant. In January the destroyer *Thanet* chased a Japanese armed trawler which had seized a fishing junk registered in Hong Kong. The owner, Li-San, and his family of six had been forced to abandon their little boat which was towed away by the trawler. *Thanet* picked up the Chinese and then recovered the junk, which had been cut adrift by the Japanese.

Birmingham was at Wei-Hai-Wei during January, acting as guardship for the North China area in rotation with other cruisers and sloops. The monotony of this duty was relieved by football, concerts and amateur dramatics, and it was also possible to go skating on a small pond – a pastime that ended abruptly when the crisp, frosty weather finished and the ice and snow melted. On January 27th, *Birmingham* was ordered to proceed to Tsingtao at high speed as a British ship there had been arrested by the Japanese for trading up the Hwang Ho, or Yellow River. The Japanese had also taken reprisals against the Chinese coolies alleged to have been loading the ship. *Birmingham* cleared for action and arrived at Tsingtao at 09.00 hrs on January 29th. A midshipman and an armed guard were immediately sent on board the arrested ship, the 1,339-ton ss *St Vincent De Paul*, built in 1919 and owned by a Hong Kong firm.

The ship's master explained that he had been about five miles off the Yellow River estuary when intercepted by two Japanese destroyers and a Chinese customs cruiser under the local control of the Japanese. *St Vincent De Paul* stopped and was boarded by the customs officer who ordered the ship to proceed under escort to Tsingtao. He protested but eventually bowed to superior force and sailed for Tsingtao accompanied by the other ships. They arrived at Tsingtao only half an hour before *Birmingham* came on the scene. *St Vincent De Paul* had not even had time to hoist the quarantine flag and her captain declared that he had

The Hopeful Year

no intention of doing so as he did not consider that he was making a proper call in the port.

Captain Brind and the local British Consul-General then went on board *Ashigara*, flagship of the Japanese 5th Cruiser Squadron. She had represented Japan at King George VI's Coronation Review at Spithead in 1937, but this time the atmosphere was different. Captain Brind demanded that *St Vincent De Paul* be released. There was no reason to suppose that she had been acting illegally and in any case it seemed likely that she had been outside territorial waters. The Japanese had no right to arrest British ships on the high seas. The argument went on for hours. Throughout it no senior Japanese officer was present and without him his juniors refused to make any decision. In the words of one of them: 'Ah yes. I will tell the C-in-C but it is so sad. He is ashore and I don't know where to find him.' Although the officers involved could speak English, all letters and messages were written in Japanese, unaccompanied by a translation. Eventually, through the time-wasting and frustration, the point at issue was made clear: *St Vincent De Paul* had earlier visited a port not on her clearance papers.

This was something to go on. The armed guard was left on board *St Vincent De Paul* and the Consul-General went off to see the Chinese Commissioner of Customs. This latter official examined the ship's papers, and explained that she did not have clearance to trade in the Yellow River, but this was a mere formality and could be obtained easily at Shanghai. It was no excuse for arresting *St Vincent De Paul*, he had no responsibility for the arrest and did not wish to detain the vessel. This interview had begun at 20.30 hrs. When it was over the British representatives returned to *Ashigara* and told the Japanese that *St Vincent De Paul* was going to sail the next morning at 08.00 hrs whether they agreed or not.

Half an hour before the time set for her departure a party of Chinese customs officials tried to board the merchant ship, but were turned away by the armed guard at the foot of the gangway and referred to *Birmingham*. Meanwhile a Japanese officer had presented himself aboard the British cruiser but he had no new facts or proposals, and it was obvious that he was stalling for time. Punctually at 08.00 hrs all the characters in the drama got under way. *Ashigara* trained her ten 8-inch guns on *Birmingham*, who cleared for action and returned the compliment with her 6-inch armament, placing herself between her charge and the Japanese cruiser and customs vessel. It was a tense moment. Captain Brind was not going to open fire first, but nobody knew the state of mind aboard *Ashigara*. The Japanese had lost face in full view of the population of Tsingtao, and might open fire in desperate humiliation, and at a range of less than a mile there would be little left of *Birmingham* to reply. In this manner *St Vincent De Paul* was escorted out and on her way.

When *Birmingham* later returned to Wei-Hai-Wei, Captain Brind found that *Ashigara* had arrived before him. The Japanese were not pleased at being balked. *Birmingham*'s navigating officer paid a courtesy call on the Japanese officers and found them still 'in a spittle of rage'. Although diplomatic circles were perturbed about the legality of such an action, the Admiralty considered that Captain Brind had done well and made a complimentary signal to him. The Japanese sent the destroyer *Hatsushimo* to lay a minefield off Tsingtao.

It was about this time that an operation originally begun several months earlier was successfully completed. At the beginning of 1939, *Aphis* (later relieved by *Ladybird*) and the American gunboat *Oahu* had arrived at Kiukiang when it became known that anti-guerrilla operations had cut off a large number of British, American and other nationals at Kuling. Situated up in the mountains, twenty miles from the Yangtse, Kuling was highly regarded as a haven from the muggy heat of the summer valleys. It was laid out as a large estate of many holiday bungalows, each with a long garden. There were also hospitals and hotels, but it was so remote and hilly that the only approach was by a winding road so steep that it was cut into steps. Coolies were the only form of transportation.

The Chinese Army had built a pillbox right beside the missionary hospital and because of this the Japanese refused to recognize Kuling as an agreed neutral zone. They also refused to allow foreigners to be evacuated, as this would involve passing through their front line. Japanese staff officers explained their point of view at a conference held in Kiukiang on the evening of February 11th when they met Lieutenant-Commander R. S. Stafford from *Ladybird* and Lieutenant-Commander Jeffs from *Oahu*. After further consultations the Japanese agreed to allow the evacuation of the foreigners, but responsibility for organizing the move must fall upon the Royal Navy and United States Navy. On February 18th, the two commanding officers set off from Kiukiang by road. About 09.20 hrs they passed the last Japanese outposts. Leaving behind their vehicles and Japanese escort, they began the long climb.

They toiled upwards alone for almost two hours. Occasionally they were fired at by some unseen sniper and sometimes they clambered over barbed-wire entanglements or across a ravine where a bridge had been blown. Once or twice they spotted, and avoided, booby traps placed on the path. About 11.00 hrs they passed through the Chinese front line and a Chinese guerrilla snatched away Lieutenant-Commander Stafford's sweater which he was carrying on his arm. Soon afterwards the two officers met British and American representatives and also a selection of Chinese civil and military authorities. By 17.00 hrs all the foreign residents had assembled in the Fairy Glen Hotel. About a hundred were ready to go, but a few invalids at the sanatorium were not fit enough for the hazardous and difficult journey. They would be left behind in the care of local missionaries in a safe neutral zone. There was also the question of money, as the Chinese coolies demanded extra pay for this particular trip. Once the conference had ended, General Yung, the local Chinese commander, gave a dinner-party at the hotel.

Early next day the two captains set off back to Kiukiang. They passed through

The Hopeful Year

both firing lines and met Major Kishinami of the Japanese Army. They handed him a list of the people to be evacuated and also a map showing the exact limit of the proposed safety zone at Kuling. After leaving instructions aboard their gunboats for obtaining the coolies' money, they returned to Kuling before dark. They rested for a day and then went down the steps and paths to Kiukiang again on February 21st. Major Kishinami had checked and approved the list of evacuees and had also agreed to respect the neutral zone around the sanatorium. Carrying the money for the coolies, the two officers retraced their weary way back up to Kuling with the glad news that the evacuation could take place the next day. There was only one snag. When the column was ready to move off it was found that there were a number of Chinese amahs or children's nurses who were not on the list. They had to be left behind, but apart from this the journey was completed without incident. After a meal in some ruined houses in Kiukiang, they went aboard the old transport *Naruto Maru* and were taken downriver.

Meanwhile, other gunboats were still patrolling up and down the Lower Yangtse and the West River. Japanese permission had to be obtained before making these journeys, and even then the move could only be carried out in convoy under the escort of several Japanese destroyers. When the old coalburning Italian gunboat *Ermanno Carlotto* was in company, convoy speed on the Yangtse was of farcical sluggishness. No river pilots had been available for a long time so the gunboat captains were paid a few pence per mile pilotage money. The gunboats visited missions and godowns where trade was still allowed. They carried civilian passengers on important journeys. They towed barges full of raw silk cocoons down to Shanghai, thus preventing unemployment in the foreign-owned mills. Usually they anchored for the night and were often overtaken by swollen corpses which floated grotesquely downriver more quickly than the gunboats' speed over the ground. Their hands were often tied behind their backs and they were usually headless – Chinese victims of Japanese executioners. The stinking things were so distended that the gunboat crews hated fending them off with oars and boathooks lest they burst.

The gunboat captains argued with the Japanese authorities over their attitude to British property. They found that although the Japanese openly banned trade by vessels of other nations, they were secretly conniving at blockade-breaking, provided they could collect 65 per cent of all tolls collected on the river. (Guerrillas were taking the other 35 per cent). In some places they learned that the Japanese were even prepared to act as agents for British companies – in return for a major share of the profit from such trade and a dominant voice in local company policy. The gunboats also investigated the state of the river and charted new channels hitherto unknown except to local junk crews. When it flooded excessively they cut corners across drowned paddy fields. If they did touch bottom they let the current swing them clear, went astern, or laid out an anchor and kedged themselves off. They were only moving slowly if going against the current and the bottom was usually soft so that damage was rarely done and they just continued their journey – it was all part of the job.

Many of the gunboats refuelled at Wuhu where an oil barge had been stationed for that purpose. The Americans who ran the local mission hospital found it increasingly difficult to get on with the Japanese authorities, so they were always pleased to see the British gunboats. The Japanese had decreed that no Chinese should own silver; all transactions had to be conducted in Japanese-printed paper money. This was not accepted at Shanghai, so the missionaries sent their silver dollars downriver in the gunboats who purchased supplies for the hospitals.

All this time the gunboats were on their own away from their fellows and sisterships. They never met another gunboat of the Royal Navy except when being relieved and there was very little to do in off-duty hours. Apart from a nearby tennis court, Wuhu had no entertainment to offer British sailors given shore liberty and an empty godown was therefore turned into a naval canteen. A stage was built and concerts improvised, while a fresh consignment of beer was always among the stores of every gunboat calling at Wuhu. So too were chickens and ducks and once a piglet which was specially fattened up for Christmas. In fact someone joining a gunboat remarked that it looked like a cross between a medieval transport, a Mississippi showboat and the original Ark.

Each mess had one coalburning stove for winter use. It was only effective if all the hatches and scuttles were closed, but then the mess ran the risk of being suffocated. In summer-time the heat brought out rats and bugs which were not kept at bay even by the highest standards of cleanliness – and no ships were smarter than the Royal Navy's river gunboats with their enamel gloss paint, buff-yellow funnels, white sides, green waterline, gleaming brasswork and holystoned snow-white decks. The only alternative to discomfort below was to sleep on camp beds on the upper decks. The sleepers awoke covered in dew, but this was mere inconvenience compared with the thousands of small slug-like creatures deposited everywhere by the morning mist. Drinking water was another problem. The evaporators rarely worked properly and a bucketful of Yangtse river water had to be settled with alum before it could be used for washing.

The oil barge at Wuhu was due for a routine docking for cleaning and painting in February. The normal procedure was for an Asiatic Petroleum Company tug to come and tow the barge down to Shanghai, but this time the Japanese refused to allow the tug to come upriver. They also demanded that they be allowed to inspect the barge as they did not think it needed a refit. This was refused and the gunboat *Scarab* despatched from Nanking to Wuhu. The barge was secured alongside and taken to Woosung where the tug *Ah Ming* took over. After being refitted the barge was later towed back to Wuhu by *Cockchafer* who also delivered seven goats to the missionary hospital and orphanage at Chinkiang.

The Hopeful Year

Scarab's own return voyage upriver was not without incident. About 10.00 hrs on February 22nd, when the gunboat was passing Beaver Island, three Japanese destroyers came racing downstream at 20 knots, far above the recommended maximum speed. Their wash rocked every ship and boat on the river and completely capsized one Chinese junk. Its masts stuck in the mud at the bottom of the river, with its keel above the surface. Two men, a woman, two children (aged about seven and five years) and a six months old baby were left floundering in the water. They were all saved by *Scarab*'s motor sampan and brought back. Shivering from shock and cold they were warmed up, dried out and given a good meal, some old clothes and 26 dollars, the proceeds of a quick whip-round. Petty Officer Ah Ching, *Scarab*'s senior Chinese hand, was not happy. He reminded his captain of the Chinese tradition that a person rescued from drowning becomes the property of the rescuer – for always. It looked as though *Scarab* would be stuck with six Chinese civilians for the rest of her days. Ah Ching was completely taken aback when Lieutenant-Commander H. F. Robertson-Aikman accordingly ordered the family to be put in the sampan and thrown back into the river. The sampan was brought up close alongside and the Chinese got in. At a suitable spot they were forced into the river. The water was ankle-deep and they paddled ashore. So six lives were saved and the ancient traditions of China preserved.

Hitler's occupation of Czechoslovakia on March 15th made it clear to the British Government that war with Germany was now most probable. The ships of the China Fleet were therefore issued with their war stations. For example, *Birmingham* would be expected to patrol the Pacific, searching for German commerce raiders and blockade runners. *Birmingham* was undergoing refit in March when these top secret instructions arrived, so her officers made use of their time to examine the possibility of lone warships, such as enemy raiders, using uninhabited atolls with no communications facilities to rendezvous with oilers and supply ships. There were also discussions with French staff officers aboard their flagship *Lamotte-Picquet* which called at Hong Kong during this period.

No war plans conference in the Far East could ignore the Japanese threat no matter how great the danger from Germany. Nor could advances in Japanese technology be dismissed without adequate investigation. *Birmingham* had just completed her refit and was exercising off Hong Kong when she was ordered to proceed to Amoy where Captain Brind was to obtain as many good, clear photographs as possible of the Japanese ships. The crew were told that Admiralty Intelligence was very interested in VHF radio which was then in its infancy, so they had to take careful note of any odd-looking aerials. A powerful Japanese force was now anchored at Amoy. The battleships *Kirishima, Ise, Hyuga, Nagato, Mutsu, Fuso* and *Kongo*, the cruisers *Chokai, Natori, Tatsuta, Tenryu, Nachi, Suzuya, Myoko* and *Katori*, the minelayers *Tsubame* and *Kanome*, the destroyers *Shimakaze, Shiokaze* and *Nadakaze* had all been reported in the area.

Many Japanese warships had never been seen before, let alone photographed, so some sort of record of their armament and silhouettes would prove invaluable even if no peculiar aerials were visible.

Birmingham crept along the coast and approached the harbour unseen. Every member of the crew who owned a camera was on deck. So too was anyone with a claim to artistic ability, ready with pencil and sketch book, their activities being co-ordinated by officers so that each ship would be faithfully recorded. At 08.00 hrs *Birmingham* came round and proceeded up harbour. There were four lines of Japanese warships, all with their armament, fire control and aerials uncovered. *Birmingham* passed between the first two columns, her crew sketching and snapping, and then turned and passed between the other two lines although by now the Japanese were rushing about, trying to cover all their secret equipment with tarpaulins. By 11.00 hrs *Birmingham* was returning to Hong Kong, her crew feeling that they had won a small victory over the Japanese. They were even more proud when the photographs were received by the Admiralty who made a signal expressing their appreciation.

It all seemed rather a big fuss over quite a trivial matter, but then, at that time, *Birmingham*'s ship's company had not heard of anything called radar. British Intelligence were pleased that the Japanese seemed equally ignorant. Reports and photographs from other sources apparently confirmed this impression.

Interpreting the Munich Agreement as a sign of Britain's permanent weakness, the Japanese lost no opportunity to discriminate and humiliate. At Hankow, two British sailors from *Peterel* were ordered to dismount from a rickshaw by a Japanese sentry. When they refused he began hitting them and they were arrested by a group of soldiers who came on the scene. Lieutenant-Commander E. B. Carnduff secured their release, but the Japanese announced that two drunken sailors had been beating up a rickshaw coolie and had then set about a Japanese sentry who went to his aid. They were released after their commander had apologized. (However, Japanese violence was not always directed against foreigners. A British gunboat at Hankow in March reported that they had seen a Japanese naval officer remonstrate with a party of four drunken Japanese sailors. He slapped the face of one of them, whereupon all four grabbed him and held him upside down, banging his head on the road until they killed him.)

In spite of British insistence that the Royal Navy would investigate any British merchantman suspected of carrying contraband, there was a whole series of incidents as 1939 progressed. On 5th April the 2,333-ton *Sagres* was loading Government salt at Chuan Bay, forty miles from Swatow, when she was interrupted by a Japanese warship. The destroyer *Thracian* was sent round from Swatow where she had been standing by to assist British citizens during the Japanese attack on the Chinese garrison. Although *Thracian*'s crew went to

The Hopeful Year

action stations, they arrived too late to prevent a Japanese boarding party taking over *Sagres*. The merchant ship was escorted by the Japanese to the Pescadores Islands with *Thracian* following, but no Royal Navy officer was allowed to board the ship. The Japanese authorities stated that they wanted to verify the ownership of the ss *Sagres* as she was owned by the Chinese-named Kin Hong Steamship Co. but registered in the British port of Hong Kong. Her crew were later released but *Sagres* was still detained and part of her cargo confiscated. From then on Royal Navy guards were placed aboard all British ships trading between Hong Kong, Hainan, Swatow, Amoy and Foochow.

The advantages of this move were immediately apparent when the 2,455-ton *Seistan* was boarded at Amoy. She was not seized as the naval guard on board would not allow the Japanese to examine the ship's papers. But farther north the river steamer *Tung Wo*, owned by the Jardine, Matheson Company was detained by a Japanese destroyer in the Yangtse Estuary whilst on passage from Nantung with five hundred pigs for Shanghai market. She was ordered to unload her cargo, but her master radioed for help and the new gunboat *Scorpion* arrived, wearing the flag of Rear-Admiral Holt. Captain Saunders went on board *Tung Wo* and offered to provide an armed guard on board as well as *Scorpion*'s close escort. However the master decided to unload as the Japanese threatened to cut off the heads of the Company's Chinese agents ashore.

The outcome of such incidents seemed to indicate that the Japanese were prepared to back down when confronted by a show of force. Reports from the Royal Navy officers involved no doubt influenced the Foreign Office in their belief that Japanese aggression on a continental scale might be deterred by a British battle-fleet in the Far East. The most impressive display of combined naval power was seen at Amoy in May. On the 13th the destroyers *Scout* and *Edsall* (an American ship) were lying off the little island of Kulangsu, where the International Settlement was situated, when two hundred Japanese troops were landed to arrest the assassins of Hung Li-Son. He had been the puppet Chinese President of the Kulangsu Chamber of Commerce although some sources referred to him as a head lighterman who been shot by a rival merchant. The Japanese seized on this murder as a pretext for searching foreign residences and carrying off many of the ten thousand Chinese refugees for further interrogation. In the face of a large Japanese fleet, the two destroyers could do nothing, but they were soon joined by *Birmingham* (wearing the C-in-C's flag), *Dorsetshire, Duncan, Defender*, the uss *Marblehead, Bulmer* and *Asheville* and the French cruisers *Emile Bertin* and *Lamotte-Picquet*.

The Japanese Consul-General presented the following demands to the Kulangsu Council:

1 Appointment of a Japanese Chief of Police, Chairman and Secretary of the Council.

2 Japanese to have a permanent majority on the Council.
3 Japanese to control the Settlement's police force.
4 Formosans to be appointed to the Council.
5 Co-operation with the Japanese Police.

The Council naturally refused these demands which would have turned the International Settlement into a Japanese colony. All day, conferences were held aboard *Birmingham* to arrive at a suitable compromise. At last the Japanese reduced their forces ashore to forty-two men, but as they showed no sign of withdrawing these, the British, American and French admirals each landed a party of forty-two naval personnel themselves. The Japanese immediately tried to increase their landing party by putting reinforcements ashore during the night, then suddenly withdrew all their forces, leaving only a handful of men to guard their consulate.

Having been forced to lose face, the Japanese were determined not to give up their attempt to occupy the International Settlement at Kulangsu. They insisted that ships could only trade in the area if they held a permit from the appropriate Japanese authorities. These permits were rarely given, thus establishing an effective blockade which soon created food shortages in the Settlement. Sir Archibald Clark Kerr arrived at Kulangsu on May 26th, having travelled from Hong Kong in the cruiser *Cornwall*. Together with Admiral Sir Percy Noble, he delivered protests to the Japanese regarding the blockade and the stopping of British merchant ships on the high seas. He particularly referred to the P. & O. liner *Ranpura* which had been boarded by a party of Japanese after their warships had fired blank shots. They announced their intention of examining the ship's papers to establish her identity but they were interrupted by the destroyer *Duchess* forty minutes later. The French and German liners *Aramis* and *Sauerland* were also stopped.

The Ambassador and Commander-in-Chief later left for Shanghai in *Birmingham*. Admiral Noble subsequently took *Kent* to Singapore where he presided over the Anglo-French Defence Conference which considered the threat of Japanese expansion. They decided that the Singapore and Malayan garrisons should be increased and more combined exercises held when the expected reinforcements arrived in August.

Hainan had been invaded in February, Kulangsu was under virtual siege and it seemed possible that Foochow would be the next Japanese objective. It was therefore decided to evacuate ninety-three British and American civilians from Sharp Peak, a little island at the mouth of the Min River. They left in *Duchess* and the USS *Asheville*, while the new gunboat *Grasshopper* took thirty-six bluejackets up the Min River to protect the British Consulate at Foochow. Although the river had been officially blocked by the Chinese since 1937, warships could still use it, but merchant ships had to stay below the boom and unload their cargo into Chinese barges which then went upriver. The British freighter *Haitan* was so engaged on June 2nd, when some Japanese soldiers opened fire with a machine-gun on the coolies working on the lighters alongside. The destroyer *Diamond* sent across an armed guard and the attacks stopped, but started again as soon as the sentries were withdrawn. *Haitan*'s master tried for four days to land his cargo, and then gave up and took it back to Hong Kong.

11
The Wuhu Beer Incident

In such situations, Japanese allegations or counter-charges were swiftly propagated, skilfully directed and always seemed successful in putting foreigners in the wrong. The Wuhu Beer Incident certainly proved the impossibility of out-arguing the Japanese authorities.

During May the gunboat *Scarab* had gone into dock at Shanghai for a routine ten-day refit. Her ship's company took advantage of this break to fire off their annual rifle and pistol practices and on May 4th they watched a demonstration of street fighting put on by the Shanghai Volunteer Corps. Five days later Deputy Commissioner Fairbairn showed the crew something of the workings of the Shanghai Police and also expounded on his pet theory about the use of the knife in hand-to-hand combat. When the refit was complete *Scarab* took on board 146 cases of beer for the Royal Navy Canteen at Wuhu and then proceeded to Woosung where she met *Sui Wo* and *Wuhu*. All three ships arrived at Wuhu about midday on May 30th. *Scarab* immediately went alongside a pontoon belonging to Butterfield and Swire so that the cases of beer could be unloaded, taken up the brow, across The Bund and into the canteen compound. Fortunately all this was British property and there was no need for a long rigmarole about Japanese landing passes. A gang of coolies arrived and began unloading the beer.

As the leading coolies stepped on to The Bund from the pontoon gangway, they were stopped by a Japanese sentry. He was unable to speak English, but Lieutenant-Commander Robertson-Aikman at last made him comprehend that he wanted to see somebody in authority. Half-an-hour later two Japanese officers and an interpreter arrived. They announced that they had received instructions to keep *Wuhu* and *Sui Wo* under surveillance to make sure nothing was landed from either of them, but in future nothing was to be landed from any ship – including *Scarab*. It was pointed out that these cases of beer were not merchandise as such. They were for consumption in the Royal Navy Canteen and there was no question of their sale to the Chinese. In any case, Great Britain had a right of way from the pontoon to the canteen. The Japanese insisted that there was no right of way across The Bund. They would not even let a British officer visit the Japanese Consul because he did not have a valid pass.

Scarab sailed back to Nanking with all the cases of beer on board again. After reporting to Rear-Admiral Holt, Lieutenant-Commander Robertson-Aikman

The Wuhu Beer Incident

was told on June 5th that in future all gunboats must hand a list of the numbers and contents of cases for the canteen to the Japanese military authorities. However, the Japanese agreed to instruct their local people to allow this particular consignment of beer to be landed forthwith. The next day *Scarab* took two crates to Wuhu, but these were destined for the Asiatic Petroleum Company who made arrangements for their reception. It was not until June 11th that the next chapter in the beer saga began, but the intervening period was filled with a succession of minor events which all contributed to the bizarre kaleidoscope of this incident.

Japanese sentries with rifles and fixed bayonets had been posted to prevent people going ashore from *Scarab* without a pass. Sometimes it was possible to distract them and sometimes they seemed to be satisfied with any piece of paper. If Lieutenant-Commander Robertson-Aikman took his little dog ashore for an evening walk, or if an officer put a flower in his button-hole, he would be greeted with 'Pretty-pretty' from the sentry and there was no demand for a pass. It was different when a certain Sergeant Kaneda was on duty. He could not be distracted and would allow no one to visit even the canteen without a pass. After dark it was quite disconcerting when walking towards the canteen to be blinded by a dazzling light and to feel the point of a bayonet pass through thin tropical uniform and just rest on one's skin.

One night Lieutenant-Commander Robertson-Aikman was awakened by a commotion on deck which soon reached the door of his cabin. Opening it he found several senior Japanese officers had rushed on board before the duty watch could stop them. They intended no offence but were merely making a courtesy call at two o'clock in the morning. In their own words: 'Sergeant Kaneda, he is drunk. We know this.' The connection between this fact and the visit was not obvious, so they went on, 'Ah, but he is drunk and asleep. Therefore he will not know we are here. He is Kempetai. His job is not only to watch you but to watch us also'. So at two o'clock in the morning, bottles were opened and formal toasts, that gradually became more convivial, were drunk.

Several nights later it was decided to move *Scarab* out into midstream as a typhoon was forecast. Admittedly the ship would be in no danger so far from the sea, but the wind would probably blow hard and there was no point in having the ship damaged by grinding against the pontoon. The crew singled up and were about to slip when a party of Japanese soldiers came dashing on to the pontoon. 'You go to make the war', they shouted, apparently thinking that *Scarab* was moving away to get a clear field of fire for her guns. In spite of explanations about the approach of bad weather and the obvious fact that *Scarab*'s awnings were still rigged and the guns shrouded, they still regarded the move with suspicion. They remained watching until *Scarab* anchored without having fired anything.

The weather was not as bad as had been feared, but again their night's sleep was disturbed. Awakened by a terrific crash they raced on deck to find two junks drifting past either side while hordes of Chinese leapt on to the gunboat. Their first thought was that one of His Britannic Majesty's warships was being pirated. Somebody was brandishing a revolver and everyone was shouting. Then, quite quickly, the whole situation was made clear. A large Chinese junk had come drifting down the fast-flowing Yangtse with no lights lit and the helmsman asleep. Broadside on, she crashed into *Scarab*'s sharp stem with such a force that she split in two, each half scraping past *Scarab* before sinking. An entire Chinese family had been living aboard the junk. Awakened by the collision, parents, grandparents, children, babies, relatives, in-laws and friends threw themselves onto the only safe place in sight – *Scarab*. All were saved and taken ashore next day when the gunboat resecured alongside the pontoon.

About 11.00 hrs on June 11th, coolies came on board and began unloading. Again they were stopped at the end of the pontoon gangway and this time the Japanese soldiers ostentatiously loaded their rifles ready for firing. Again the same two Japanese officers and an interpreter arrived, but they had received no instructions to allow beer to be landed. They refused to accept a list of the contents of the cases because they were only interested in permits issued by the Japanese authorities in Shanghai. Lieutenant-Commander Robertson-Aikman asked to speak to higher officers, but they all refused to come down to The Bund. This brought the day's proceedings to an end and those cases which had got as far as The Bund were taken back on to the pontoon. One of the cases was opened, but the Japanese refused to drink believing that it was not beer, but some sort of English trick.

On the 12th Lieutenant-Commander Robertson-Aikman went to see the Japanese Consul who said that he knew nothing about instructions from Shanghai to allow stores to be landed. He made several telephone calls but nobody had heard anything. He explained that the delay might have arisen because this particular consignment had left Shanghai on May 28th, before the Japanese authorities had ordered that all goods must have approval prior to unloading.

The next day a Royal Navy signal was received aboard *Scarab* stating that the Japanese in Shanghai had given permission for the cases of beer to be unloaded immediately at Wuhu. Shortly afterwards the gunboat *Tern* arrived with the British Consul on board. The ship was also carrying a consignment of material for repairing a Butterfield and Swire godown. To the astonishment of *Scarab*'s captain these items were allowed to be landed without interference. The Japanese did not even ask for a pass or a list and the British Consul explained that arrangements had already been made for this consignment to be landed. He agreed that there should be no objection to landing the cases of beer the next day, thus allowing plenty of time for the permissive signal to get to Wuhu from Shanghai. At last the great day dawned. At 08.30 hrs on June 14th, coolies came aboard and began unloading 146 cases of beer. The crates were placed on little barrows and trundled down the gangplank, across the pontoon and up the bridge leading to

The Wuhu Beer Incident

The Bund. Here they were stopped by the Japanese sentry who refused even to accept the list of stores. Everything had to wait until Japanese officers arrived. Half-an-hour passed and nothing happened, although five more sentries reinforced their comrade on The Bund. Soon after 09.00 hrs the British Consul got tired of waiting. The coolies were not too happy at working in the face of Japanese threats so it was decided that the ratings from *Scarab* should unload the cases. They were busy painting ship and were therefore already wearing overalls. They promptly took over the barrows and began pushing them across The Bund, ignoring the threats and gestures of the Japanese sentries.

They actually managed to get two cases of beer into the canteen, but then the Japanese soldiers lined up across the entrance. They worked the bolts of their rifles and threatened to shoot the British Consul, Lieutenant-Commander Robertson-Aikman and the Royal Navy ratings standing by the canteen door. More and more Japanese soldiers arrived on the scene, all shouting and waving firearms. They also brought up a heavy machine-gun on a wheeled trolley.

This was too much. Lieutenant-Commander Robertson-Aikman ordered his crew to leave the cases exactly where they were – there was no point in British lives being lost over a few pints of beer. However, militant threats and insults demanded an answer, so he called across to his executive officer to break out a light-machine-gun and cover the Japanese. An armed section of ratings was also fallen in on board *Scarab*. Meanwhile the British Consul was persuading the Japanese to allow the remaining 144 cases of beer to be stacked on The Bund against the wall of the canteen. The other two cases were to stay in the canteen.

This agreement was endorsed by the two Japanese officers and the interpreter who had originally met *Scarab* on May 30th and had been present at almost every altercation ever since. They were soon joined by the Japanese Consul who took his British counterpart off to telephone Nanking. The Japanese authorities there at long last agreed to allow the beer to be landed. A Major Akagi would be sent from Nanking to implement this decision. *Scarab*'s machine-gun was then dismounted and the armed section fell out, but feeling was still high. The British Consul was staying ashore, but Lieutenant-Commander Robertson-Aikman was prevented from seeing him by the Japanese sentries. They proved so trigger-happy that they then fired at some Chinese women in a sampan for no apparent reason other than to relieve their feelings.

At 10.00 hrs on the 15th, four cars drew up on The Bund at the head of the bridge leading to the pontoon. Twelve Japanese officials got out and were met by the British Consul and Lieutenant-Commander Robertson-Aikman. The conference was held aboard *Scarab*.

Major Akagi apologized for the actions and high-handed attitudes of the local authorities at Wuhu. There would have been no difficulty about landing the stores if only a list had been produced. He was informed that a list had been handed to, and refused by, two Japanese officers and an interpreter who were pointed out to Major Akagi, but they declared that they had never seen the list before and in any case had not been on the wharf at the times and dates stated. Major Akagi smoothed over Lieutenant-Commander Robertson-Aikman's puzzlement and anger. He asked for the list, read it, declared it to be in order and said that the landing of stores could now begin. However, just to save face – the self-respect of the Wuhu authorities – he suggested that the cases of beer be transferred back to the pontoon. This would correct any unpleasantness that had occurred and a completely fresh start could be made on moving the beer straight from the pontoon across the Japanese-controlled Bund into the Royal Navy Canteen without any fuss. This seemed perfectly reasonable and the British Consul agreed. Soon coolies were trundling the cases back onto the pontoon. The conference moved on to more general conversation until it became apparent that the coolies had stopped working – all 146 cases were now stacked on the pontoon. The coolies were waiting for the order to take them back up the bridge and straight into the canteen.

The British Consul pointed out to Major Akagi that all was now ready for him to give the word and a fresh start would be made. Major Akagi immediately refused to allow any British stores to cross the Japanese Bund and said that he had never given permission for this. All cases on the pontoon must be loaded aboard *Scarab* and be taken away because the Royal Navy did not need to drink so much beer.

There were arguments and discussions, claims and debates – all to no avail. The Japanese refused to allow the beer to be taken into the canteen. The British Consul refused to move the beer from the pontoon until he had consulted the Embassy. Lieutenant-Commander Robertson-Aikman refused to leave until the beer was in the canteen. This was something the Japanese seized on:

'You do not have enough food.'

'We will live on ship's biscuit as in the days of Nelson,' was the reply. 'You have no women,' declared the Japanese. 'Your sailors will not stay because they have no women at Wuhu.' They were assured that the Royal Navy would stay. It was the Japanese's turn to be amazed. They just did not understand and were even invited to search *Scarab* and look for women on board.

This was just getting nowhere and the conference had reached an impasse. The British Consul decided to return to Nanking. He therefore went across to *Tern* and that gunboat left. The Japanese officials departed and soon *Scarab* was left alone with 146 cases of beer on the pontoon and Japanese sentries barring the way to The Bund. Presently *Scarab* also sailed away from Wuhu. The 146 cases of beer remained on the pontoon.

They may still be there today.

12
The Blockade of Tientsin

For a while the fighting-fronts in China remained relatively static. The Japanese Navy intensified its blockade, the Army was engaged in clearing occupied areas of guerrillas and the air forces were bombing communications, cities, ports and villages. This much was visible. What was not so obvious was the division in the Japanese Government over the possibility of a full alliance with Germany. Some Japanese did not think that Britain was quite as effete as the Munich Agreement seemed to indicate, while in July the USA told Japan that their commercial treaty would be allowed to expire, thus cutting off the sale of war material to Japan. Completely unknown was the Nomonhan Incident which began at the end of May – Japanese and Russian troops were fighting over territory on the borders of Manchukuo and Outer Mongolia. Japan had enough outright enemies without upsetting possible foes by linking herself closely with the aggressions of Nazi Germany. Yet the China War had to go on. One more landing, one more thrust – and Chiang Kai-Shek might surrender. Next on the list was Swatow.

On June 21st two Japanese aircraft carriers, five destroyers, two troop transports and two armed trawlers arrived off the port. The destroyers *Thanet* and *Pillsbury*, charged with the protection of British and American lives and property, refused to be overawed by such a large force. They did recall their landing parties but were soon reinforced by the destroyer *Scout* and the two American ships *Asheville* and *Pope*. The situation was serious enough to warrant Admiral Sir Percy Noble's personal inspection, taking passage in *Falmouth* with *Thracian* as escort. One of the Japanese carriers chose the arrival of the British warships as a suitable time to fly off a striking force against Chinese troops near the port. The attack was carried out very close to British ships in the harbour so *Falmouth*'s and *Thracian*'s guns' crews closed up, but no incident developed. The Japanese assault went according to plan and they had soon advanced to and seized their objective, Chaoan. British merchant ships continued to ply to and from Swatow, being escorted through the danger zone by Royal Navy destroyers. On one occasion a merchantman was forced to remain outside, so a British warship ferried in her mail and passengers.

More serious events were taking place very much farther north at Tientsin. The Chinese had attempted to send $30,000-worth of silver from their bank deposits in the Foreign Concessions to Shanghai, but the ss *Siang Wo* had been boarded by armed Japanese who arrested four Chinese crew-members and confiscated the silver. The Japanese then demanded that the British and French authorities hand over the rest of the Chinese silver reserves still lodged in the concessions. They also demanded control over the British Concession's telephone system and all foreign wireless stations which they claimed were being used as part of China's military telecommunications network. Matters were brought to a head in April 1939, when four Chinese terrorists suspected of murdering a Japanese puppet official were arrested in the British Concession. The Japanese demanded the extradition of these men and increased pressure on the local British authorities culminating in a blockade of the British Concession from June 14th onwards. They surrounded the perimeter of the Concession with an electrified barbed-wire fence and announced that the only merchant ships allowed up the Hai Ho river to Tientsin (over thirty miles from the sea), would be those bearing an official permit from the Japanese military authorities. Such permits would seldom be granted.

Falmouth brought Major-General Grasett in to inspect the troops there and the sloops *Grimsby* and *Lowestoft* also stood by to render assistance. General Grasett had to continue his tour of inspection so *Sandwich* was ordered north from Wei-Hai-Wei to relieve *Falmouth*. En route, *Sandwich* called at Chefoo where a Japanese armed merchant ship was anchored. She cleared for action and trained her guns on *Sandwich* as she approached the breakwater. The British ship reciprocated and anchored without incident. Soon afterwards, much to Commander H. T. T. Bayliss' surprise, the Japanese captain came on board and the two commanding officers exchanged courtesy calls. The Japanese captain was a pleasant man whose previous appointment had been as executive officer of a battleship. When Commander Bayliss asked which he preferred, he replied: 'There is a saying in Japan that it is better to be the head of a hen than the back of a cow'.

Sandwich was a welcome sight for the British residents at Tientsin although Commander Bayliss suspected that his little sloop would not have been able to do much if the Japanese had assaulted the Concession. For most of the time he was worried lest his ship be trapped up the Hai Ho. The Japanese had suspended dredging operations – all part of their blockade programme – and the navigable channel through the sandbar at the mouth of the river was rapidly silting up. *Sandwich* was called upon to undertake several tasks – right from her arrival, arrangements were made for the British Concession Telegraph Department to continue working from the ship. Then on July 24th she moved to the Asiatic Petroleum Company's wharf about twenty-five miles down from Tientsin. British installations there had been extensively damaged by Chinese demonstrators apparently led by Japanese agitators dressed in Chinese clothes. Commander Bayliss hoped that the mere presence of *Sandwich* would protect British property, but the Chinese rioters could not be dissuaded by anything less than a show of

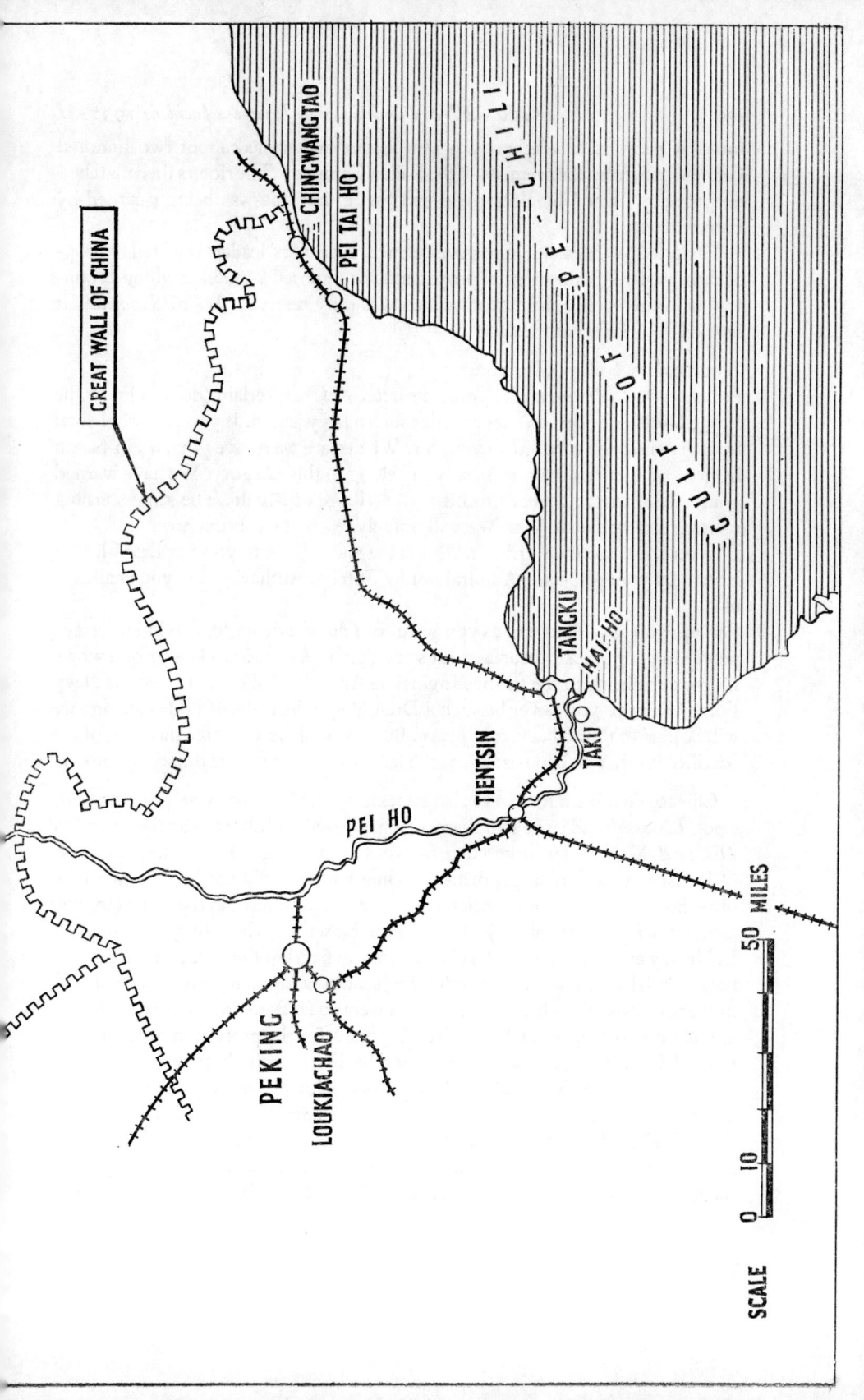

force. A party of bluejackets was sent ashore and turned about two hundred Chinese back from the premises of the Kailan Company. The rioters then marched on property owned by Butterfield and Swire, but this was being guarded by French troops.

Thwarted by this solid, impassive defence, the rioters' leaders resorted to propaganda warfare. Some oriental propagandist composed a blood-curdling prophecy of future events and threats which was duly received aboard *Sandwich*. It seemed quite funny at the time.

'Your kindest Sailor of Britain.
Perhaps you don't know why you came here. Mr Chamberlain (do you know, he Prime Minister of Britain) never order such a navy action. If you are only brutal barbarian no need of word to you, Sir. We declare we derive you Anglo-Saxon from Asia. We are very sorry that you belong to this category. We have warned your friend here to go back to his native village of Britain. The same warning message still be also to you. We will politely teach you for first greet.
Do you know sacrifice Armada. This is the name given to you Far East Fleet of Britain by your respected Admiral not by Foreign Authority. Do you challenge us?
Perhaps you can kill us free as you want. But do you do it glory to kill disarmed people in your unjust reason as your same deed in Arabia? God never be a word. Do you challenge to the furious Invincible Armada of World of Japanese Navy Force? Perhaps you never be such a Dunglike foolish boy. If you challenge we will be glad to throw back your grave. But you shall be know the meaning of the Sacrifice Fleet. You had best know the fish of the China Sea is thirsty for blood.'

Chinese demonstrators were also attacking British property at Tsingtao. The sloop *Lowestoft* had to be sent there, being relieved on July 12th by the destroyer *Diamond*. Mobs threw stones and fireworks, smashing the doors and windows of British-owned buildings. British landing parties could not be everywhere at once, but the Japanese authorities made no attempt to restrain the rioters in their areas – their military guards just looked on. However, when Rear-Admiral A. J. L. Murray arrived in the 5th Cruiser Squadron flagship *Cornwall*, he was given a most cordial welcome. Not only did the Japanese admiral regretfully disapprove of the activities of the Japanese Army, he went so far as to order a party of Japanese marines to be stationed with fixed bayonets for the protection of the British Consul-General. Japanese attitudes could be disconcertingly erratic.

Meanwhile near-famine at the British Concession at Tientsin had been exacerbated by floods, with the attendant risk of epidemics, but still the Japanese did not relent. British civilians were assaulted and a British seaman from the ss *Harmatris* was detained for a time when he arrived at Tientsin from Tangku for medical treatment. Japanese naval authorities at Chefoo confiscated a house

The Blockade of Tientsin

belonging to a Mr Gardner, while Chinese shops in Pei-Tai-Ho displayed notices asking British subjects not to enter as they would not be served. In Peking a prize of $50 was offered for the best anti-British song. At Tientsin the Japanese paid 30 cents an hour to Chinese coolies to attend anti-British lectures. Although this sum was worth about 1np., it was good pay for coolies who frequently lived on 15 cents a day. Some Royal Navy officers wondered whether the Chinese workers could be won over if European traders paid a higher wage, but they were told such economic matters were apparently not their business.

It was not until the British Government agreed to hand the four detainees over to a local Chinese puppet court on the grounds that they were murderers rather than political extremists that the Japanese lifted their blockade of Tientsin. They immediately began to allow supplies into and refugees out of the British Concession. They even helped to rescue people marooned by the floods.

The gunboat *Ladybird* was spending most of the summer at Chinchipu, a small trading centre about five miles below Kiukiang. The Yangtse had been mined by Chinese guerrillas – so the Japanese said they were not allowing any vessels past this point. Ships under Japanese control were allowed upriver and this was the only source of stores and mail. Every so often *Ladybird*'s postman had to make the five-mile trip to the Japanese flagship *Akitsu Maru* to collect the mail. The journey was done in an Asiatic Petroleum Company's motor boat and even on that short passage they would often be stopped twice by Japanese patrol craft. Every time the Chinese crew of civilians were beaten up and the Royal Navy personnel had to look on helplessly. The Japanese quartermaster at *Akitsu Maru*'s gangway always drew his revolver and levelled it at *Ladybird*'s postman. This humiliation had to be borne. No excuse could be given to the Japanese for justifying their possible aggression. If a minor incident escalated into war the Royal Navy had insufficient strength up the Yangtse and probably not enough in the whole of the Orient to withstand Japan.

The China Fleet was being stretched to the limit to cover every possible danger point and the signs of war were multiplying. More ARP exercises were carried out at Hong Kong, sirens were installed and new blackout restrictions imposed. Firefighting and medical services practised their emergency drills and there were fresh orders for sandbags, the total figure running into millions. Every British subject was to be registered and had to notify the Police Department of any change of address. The Compulsory Service Bill required all able-bodied British subjects to undergo medical examination prior to joining the defence units as reservists. The health authorities redoubled their efforts against meningitis and cholera brought in by the Chinese refugees, the inoculation centres working tirelessly; there were enough problems in Hong Kong without an epidemic as well.

Routine business acquired a new importance as urgent messages and personnel were hurried from one problem-ridden treaty-port to another. *Tarantula* linked

Hong Kong with the Consulate at Canton, making the journey twice a month. Her twelve passengers, who included six nuns, found one trip a little longer than usual when the gunboat ran aground and had to be towed off by her sistership *Cicala*, while the civilians were taken on to Hong Kong by MTB. Taikoo Dockyard found that the gunboat had only suffered minor damage. The destroyer *Duncan* was also having her troubles, having collided with a battle-practice target while on gunnery exercises off Wei-Hai-Wei. Although the damage was only slight she had to return to Hong Kong on July 19th for drydocking. Battle-practice targets featured in *Birmingham*'s life as well during this period. On July 30th the cruiser left Wei-Hai-Wei escorting a target towed by *St Breock*. The little convoy was bound for Hong Kong, but off Amoy *Birmingham* parted company and anchored off Amoy for most of August.

By now Chiang Kai-Shek's capital of Chungking had suffered so many air raids that it had become known as 'the most bombed city in the world'. The Japanese enjoyed complete air superiority and their bombing was undisturbed – mere target practice. *Falcon* was still there acting as a floating radio station for the British Embassy. Although moored at Lung Men Hao a quarter of a mile opposite the city she was once straddled by bombs. The Americans in the gunboat *Tutuila* thought she had gone but *Falcon* suffered little damage apart from started rivets. *Falcon*'s first consideration was to send ashore fire parties to the areas where British property was threatened by flames roaring up the narrow streets of steps. Then, at a suitable opportunity, she moved to a still, eddyless berth at Tan Chia To, where twenty-five rivets were replaced in the ship's bottom. No drydock facilities were available, so the ship's company had to do the job themselves. A rating inside dangled a weighted line through the rivet hole, while another man in a sampan alongside fished for it with a long bamboo pole with a hook on the end. A bolt was bent onto the end of the line, its shaft pulled through the rivet hole and secured in position with a nut held by the rating inside the ship. It was a task simple in its mechanics, but full of exasperating frustration, communication between those inside and those outside involving plenty of shouting and banging on the hull with hammers.

Gannet too was having her adventures. She spent most of her time at the Asiatic Petroleum Company's Compound on the northern bank a couple of miles below Ichang. There was a soccer-cum-cricket pitch within the compound walls and a small canteen, the beer stocks being occasionally replenished by a sampan which the Japanese sometimes allowed to proceed beyond Hankow. The Asiatic Petroleum Company's Compound was healthier than Ichang itself and had been recognized by the Japanese as a definite neutral zone. Besides *Gannet* there were six British merchant steamers, one floating dock, two tugs and eighteen lighters, each clearly marked with Union Jacks. Details of their intended movements were transmitted to the Japanese in advance, but for the two river steamers *Kia Wo* and

Hsin Chang Wo such a procedure was of academic interest only. *Kia Wo* had not been properly repaired since her grounding a year before and both were laid up in the charge of care and maintenance parties each consisting of two British officers and several Chinese seamen.

The Asiatic Petroleum Company was also *Gannet*'s sole source of oil fuel, which was now so low that main boilers were only flashed up in an emergency. There was just enough diesel oil for electric light in the evenings and for fans, W/T and engine room use during working hours, but everything had to be switched off during the afternoon. Often on a Friday a coalburning Jardine, Matheson tug towed *Gannet* upstream to Ichang. Having encouraged the local population over the weekend and, more important, given her crew a change of scenery, company and recreation, she returned downstream on the Monday morning.

So it was that on the morning of Sunday, August 6th *Gannet* was at Ichang when four light bombers raided the Asiatic Petroleum Company's installation. While the gunboat was raising steam, a Jardine, Matheson tug came alongside, her decks littered with wounded coolies. *Gannet*'s doctor rendered first aid, the coolies were transferred to hospital ashore, and the gunboat made for the Asiatic Petroleum Company's Compound, where several bombs had hit the cricket pitch. Japanese aircraft were still droning around and suddenly one of them dived out of the sun directly at *Gannet*. Its bomb actually passed over the gunboat and hit *Kia Wo*'s stern. The resulting fire quickly spread to *Hsin Chang Wo* and in spite of the Royal Navy's efforts, both steamers were burnt almost to the waterline. *Hsin Chang Wo*'s chief officer was wounded by bomb splinters, while two Chinese seamen were killed and three others injured. The steamship *Kiang Wo* was also attacked, but was not damaged. As soon as the raids were over a Jardine, Matheson tug, under *Gannet*'s protection, set about moving all the neutral ships in the vicinity to the south bank of the Yangtse where it was hoped they would be safer. Rear-Admiral Holt protested to Vice-Admiral Oikawa that the Japanese had previously recognized the original area as neutral and safe for neutral shipping. Admiral Oikawa promised to investigate this most regrettable incident.

That same day the destroyer *Tenedos* arrived back at Hong Kong with a story of disturbances at Swatow. A small crowd of Chinese had started demonstrating in front of the British Consulate and the Foreign Club. An unarmed party of bluejackets was landed from *Tenedos* to guard the Consulate, but they promptly became the target for stones and other missiles. To avoid complications the party withdrew into the Consulate, whereupon the mob began fighting among themselves until dispersed by Japanese soldiers. The Japanese immediately alleged that the Royal Navy detachment had started the disturbance by assaulting several Chinese. They demanded that the sailors should be punished and compensation paid. They also claimed that apologies had been received from the British Consul and the captain of *Tenedos*. In fact, Lieutenant-Commander J. O. B. Milner Barry had expressed regret that any difficulty should ever arise out of the presence of British sailors. This comment had been seized on by the Japanese as a formal apology and distorted into a British admission of guilt.

Then on August 10th the British steamer *Shinai* entered the small harbour of Hsiuhu, north of Amoy. She was about to load a cargo of salt when she was boarded by a party from a Japanese armed trawler. *Shinai*'s master made a signal to the destroyer *Westcott* who arrived and escorted the British freighter out of the harbour.

13
The Hitler War

Birmingham spent most of August at Amoy, her crew continuing their close observation of the Japanese Navy that they had begun at Wei-Hai-Wei. They were always very intrigued by the paradox of Japanese cleanliness at home and comparative filth on board ship. Japanese crews also spent many hours at physical drill, but never went ashore for games or recreation. Their punishment was particularly severe and some British officers felt that it was specially demonstrated for the benefit of any European onlookers. Men under punishment had to do hours of arduous drill, usually until they collapsed. The ratings in charge encouraged the weaker members by jumping on their bare feet or thumping them with rifle butts. It was also common for a prisoner to be lifted up by his arms and legs and then dropped on the steel deck so that he hit his back or his head. This punishment was repeated until the detainee became unconscious.

Naturally the Japanese also watched the British ships in the harbour. *Birmingham* was kept under constant surveillance by an officer with large binoculars who took careful note of every aspect of Royal Navy routine and activity. They also sent boats to row around *Birmingham* with notebooks and cameras only a few yards from the cruiser's side. Unfortunately, this particular duty usually coincided with washing down the deck aboard the British ship, and the Japanese boats were quite often drenched by high pressure hoses which were accidentally swung outboard.

The Japanese could be equally careless, but with more lethal weapons than hoses. On August 18th four officers from *Birmingham* took a sampan to a quiet beach for a swim and a siesta. It was very hot and the officers did not worry when a shot disturbed the heavy peace of the afternoon – there was always a lot of shooting between the Japanese and local Chinese guerrillas. A second shot raised a splash about a yard from the boat. A Japanese rifleman in a patrol vessel about half a mile away had decided to improve his already excellent marksmanship by getting in a spot of target practice on some insignificant Chinese boatman. He did not wait to ascertain whether anyone else was in the boat. The Chinese sampan-man did not wait to argue the matter. He replied to the shots with a string of apparently apt Chinese oaths and took his boat straight back to *Birmingham*. The incident was reported to Captain Brind and a formal protest prepared for communication to the Japanese via the British Consul. Within a couple of days the sailing boat returned to the cruiser with seven bullet holes in her sails. This time Chinese guerrillas had done the shooting. It seemed that nobody liked *Birmingham*.

The protest was never lodged as *Birmingham* received orders to return to Hong Kong. Captain Brind had drawn up a compromise scheme for the international administration of Kulangsu, which had been accepted by all the local authorities, including the Japanese, but their government in Tokyo flatly rejected any proposals. As there was no point in trying to reason with them any more, Captain Brind was ordered to leave, especially as war with Germany was extremely probable. Immediately after her arrival at Hong Kong at the end of August, *Birmingham* embarked a contingent of troops and took them to Singapore at full speed.

The Japanese now began yet another series of mopping-up operations, yet another anti-guerrilla drive. This time it was directed at the areas north-east and south-east of Canton. In this latter phase Japanese troops landed at Paoan and swept along the border of the British New Territories at Hong Kong. The British were warned not to interfere and not to allow Chinese forces to operate from or shelter in British territory. This request was complied with, but the authorities responsible for the defence of Hong Kong took what precautions they could against the possibility of a surprise attack by the Japanese. There might even be some sort of military action resulting from the expected war with Germany. A direct radio-telephone service therefore linked Manila, Hong Kong and Chungking. Extra food, especially large quantities of rice, was ordered from Siam and French Indo-China, and arrangements were made for the voluntary evacuation of British women and children, should such a step become necessary.

Then for no apparent reason the Japanese announced that the minefield below Chinchipu had been cleared and *Ladybird* was able to come down the Yangtse. Off Woosung the gunboat was ordered to 'Commence hostilities against Germany'. There were Japanese warships in sight. What would they do? *Ladybird*'s Lewis guns were manned but the Japanese made no move and *Ladybird* proceeded safely up the Whangpoo to Shanghai. Nobody knew it at the time but the Japanese had just suffered a severe defeat at the hands of the Russian General Zhukov at Nomonhan. The apparent German alliance with the Soviet Union meant that for the time being the Japanese were no friends of Germany.

To Old China Hands, the immediate consequence of the declaration of war on Germany on September 3rd was the calling up of reservists. Most of them joined ships of the Royal Navy based in the Far East while the troopship *Dunera* made a special voyage to Hong Kong to collect reservists and other service personnel. *Falmouth* immediately went into dock to remove the extra accommodation used by the Commander-in-Chief and his staff. The sloop remounted her after 4-inch gun and sailed on her first wartime patrol among the islands of the Dutch East Indies. The destroyer *Thracian* also remounted a 4-inch gun and was fitted with torpedo-tubes and mine rails. She was then employed in laying most of the minefields in the Hong Kong area.

As far as Commander Bayliss in *Sandwich* was concerned the outbreak of war meant that at long last he could get away from Tientsin. If he did not leave soon the sloop might be permanently marooned up the Hai Ho River as the Japanese had still not allowed any dredging and the estuary was almost completely silted up. *Sandwich* received permission to move on the last possible spring tide. She left Tientsin at 07.30 hrs on September 15th and called at Taku before approaching the bar at the mouth of the river. Her engines were stopped and a tug prepared to take her out into the open sea. The water was so shallow that if she tried to get out under her own steam, mud would have been sucked into the condensers, while the rudder could be badly damaged if it touched while moving under power.

As it was *Sandwich* grounded halfway across. Most of her oil fuel had to be pumped into a lighter alongside, but it still took the efforts of five tugs to get her off. Their task was hindered by other craft in the area which kept getting in the way, while a strong wind made the job even more difficult. No sooner had the tugs pulled *Sandwich* clear, than one of the towing lines fouled the sloop's starboard propeller. The ship's diver went down to free the obstruction, but he gashed his hand and was soon suffering from the severe cold, so he had to be brought up. With *St Breock* in attendance *Sandwich* limped to war on her port propeller only.

Most of the seagoing warships on the China Station were employed in patrolling the waters in the Dutch East Indies, focal points of the trade of the Orient. During the early weeks of the war, the carrier *Eagle* and the cruisers *Hobart*, *Birmingham* and *Cornwall*, the depot ship *Medway*, the submarines *Rover*, *Regent*, *Grampus*, *Olympus*, *Odin*, *Parthian* and *Rorqual*, the oiler *Appleleaf* and the sloop *Falmouth* all spent some time in the area. There were weeks of monotonous patrol in hot, damp weather, broken by sub-calibre throw-offs, launching and recovering aircraft, troop convoy escorts and battle exercises – there were always exercises. Occasionally there was excitement when two ships met to refuel, send across fresh bread, exchange mail or swop rumours. Always there were rumours: rumours of pocket battleships just over the horizon; rumours of disguised merchant raiders operating from Japan; rumours of blockade runners putting to sea; rumours of German supply ships lurking in deserted atolls; rumours of Russian submarines manned by German crews; always rumours.

Very rarely was there real drama. On September 6th *Eagle*'s aircraft intercepted the German steamer *Franken*, but the merchantman kept safely inside neutral Dutch territorial waters until she reached Padang. On November 13th, the ss *Sirdhana* ran on to an inadequately advertised minefield off Singapore and was sunk. Usually tense emergencies ended on a note of farce. A British submarine would sight a suspicious-looking merchantman and radio her position and course so that other forces could draw the net tight. Within minutes a British tramp steamer would be radioing for help because she was under attack from a hostile submarine. Somewhere navigation and communications officers would compare positions of submarine and freighter, note they were identical, carry out various intelligence checks – and the action would be called off before somebody got hurt.

It was a similar story farther north with the added disadvantage of bitterly cold weather. *Birmingham*'s patrol off the coasts of China and Japan was typical of life aboard a China Station cruiser at this period in the war. On November 4th she was relieved by the cruiser *Dauntless* in Sunda Strait and arrived at Singapore on the 6th. After a brief conference ashore, and taking on board stores and fuel, *Birmingham* left the next day for Hong Kong, investigating a Japanese whaling convoy en route. Three days in the colony and then the cruiser was at sea again, still heading north.

British intelligence expected the German merchant ships sheltering in Japan to break out at any time. The slightest alteration in their routine was the signal for British warships to move to an intercepting position. Invariably the German captain was only changing anchors or going alongside a different jetty and the excitement soon died down again. Then on November 22nd the submarine *Rainbow* reported a darkened ship leaving Kobe, perhaps *Scharnhorst*, *Elsa Essberger* or *Anneliese Essberger*. *Birmingham* tried to intercept but found no sign of any suspicious vessel. The cruiser turned back, fuelled from the oiler *Francol* and escorted the French liner *André Lebon* to Hong Kong, arriving there on November 28th. During the passage a stoker was lost overboard.

While *Birmingham* was in harbour one of those episodes occurred which showed that for some ships life on the China Station seemed to continue as normal. The river passenger steamer *Wulin* was attacked by pirates in the mouth of the Yangtse during the early hours of December 1st. The British officers and an armed guard composed of White Russian exiles killed one pirate and wounded another before driving off their assailants. One Russian guard and a Chinese sailor were also injured. This happened in waters under Japanese control, but it was the British gunboat *Gnat* who went to *Wulin*'s assistance and escorted her to Woosung.

On December 5th there was another rumour that the German merchant ships were about to break out from their refuge in Japan. All *Birmingham*'s libertymen were recalled and the cruiser sailed for the north again the following day. Off Formosa Captain Brind sounded 'General Quarters' and the exercise was carried out satisfactorily, with the exception of a man who was carrying a message bag clearly marked 'Main W/T Office to Bridge'. He was 'killed' at three separate times on his way to the bridge and although the drill for establishing his death was carried out each time, on only one occasion was the message sent on up to the bridge. Captain Brind pointed out that such an omission could have serious consequences in a real battle. By December 9th *Birmingham* was making for the Kii Channel to investigate a report that the German motor vessel *Burgenland* had left Kobe, but the ship turned out to be a Dutch merchantman. However, *Birming-*

The Hitler War

ham continued to patrol the area in company with the submarine *Pandora* and the armed merchant cruiser *Moreton Bay*. They saw no sign of any German ships and the only thing of Japanese origin to be sighted was the top of Mount Fujiyama, over a hundred miles away.

December 17th was not a lucky day for *Birmingham* when she met *Francol* at the Saddle Islands off Shanghai. The oiler and the cruiser touched when coming —alongside, holing *Birmingham*'s port bow. That evening a greater disaster occurred – the soil-pipe from the seamen's heads cracked. The cruiser's shipwrights effected temporary repairs by 22.30. After investigating a Japanese ship, *Birmingham* spent Christmas Day at sea, her company making the best of their lot. Holy Communion was celebrated and the Royal Christmas cards distributed, followed by a carol service. Streaming paravanes, *Birmingham* arrived at Hong Kong on December 27th and went straight into Taikoo Dockyard. One of the port propellers was exchanged and the damage done in the bump with *Francol* was made good. Other workmen cleaned and painted the ship's bottom, while the crew took on stores and oil fuel. Two days later *Birmingham* left the dock and the ship's company celebrated an official Christmas Day on New Year's Day 1940. When they put to sea again they would be heading for Singapore, the Mediterranean, home leave and the war in Europe.

Many other ships had already gone, for the European war showed no sign of spreading to the Far East. In November the Japanese launched yet another offensive, this time directed against Nanning. The attack cut the road from French-Indo China to Kweilin and provided a suitable base for air strikes against the supply route to Chungking. Nanning was successfully captured and held, but the Japanese were unable to exploit their gains. Their troops marched and countermarched and were ambushed and encircled and withdrawn to Nanning. A similar campaign was being fought north of Canton, with similar sparse results. These operations might be embarrassing to the Chinese war effort, but they did show that the Japanese were not going to divert their attention away from China towards Germany's enemies. Disenchanted by the Non-Aggression Pact between Germany and Soviet Russia, Japan had certainly seemed to quieten her demands. Although no doubt prepared to seize what Far Eastern spoils came her way as a result of the European war, she did not want to risk hostilities with Russia, especially after her recent experiences in Mongolia. Japan made her position quite clear by renouncing the Anti-Comintern Agreement. So the Admiralty were soon able to regard the China Station as a reservoir of efficient ships and trained men.

One division of the 21st Destroyer Flotilla had left Wei-Hai-Wei as long ago as the announcement of the German-Soviet Non-Aggression Pact. The rest of the flotilla had followed in September. *Eagle*, *Cornwall* and *Dorsetshire* formed a raider hunting group in the Bay of Bengal and soon the China Station submarines were also heading westwards. *Kent* was ordered to reinforce the Home Fleet while the sloops were needed to escort East Coast convoys in the North Sea. However the China Station was not to be completely denuded of seagoing warships.

The cruiser *Liverpool* was transferred from the Indian Ocean to relieve *Birmingham* being joined by the old cruisers *Danae*, *Durban* and *Dauntless* and by three armed merchant cruisers. They were mainly employed on patrols north of Hong Kong and availed themselves of the colony's dockyard facilities to carry out refitting in readiness for wartime action.

The redeployment of Britain's armed forces due to the exigencies of the war in Europe, also went some way to meet the Japanese suggestion that all ships and men belonging to the belligerents be withdrawn from Chinese waters. They announced that they did not want to get involved as a result of some clash between Britain, France and Germany. Yet the Japanese were still not satisfied, being particularly irritated by the presence of the battalion at Tientsin (which moved to Egypt at the beginning of 1940) and the gunboats. Still, even these vessels, almost permanent features of the Chinese landscape, were under Admiralty consideration. There was now virtually no riverine trade within China which they could protect, nor could they hope to put up more than a token defence if the Japanese did start a full-scale war. So it was decided that most should be withdrawn as soon as possible to Singapore where they could be converted to minesweepers or anti-submarine vessels. *Aphis*, *Cockchafer*, *Cricket*, *Gnat*, *Ladybird* and *Scarab*, destined for the Mediterranean and the Persian Gulf, would have their hulls shored up internally and battened down. Nobody would be allowed below during their passage across the Indian Ocean. *Tarantula*, *Scorpion*, *Dragonfly* and *Grasshopper* got as far as the East Indies, while *Mantis*, now very old and decrepit indeed, was sent to the shipbreakers at Shanghai.

The three gunboats on the Upper River were even more of a problem. *Sandpiper*, *Gannet* and *Falcon* were still stationed at Changsha, Ichang and Chungking respectively. Although outside the zone of Japanese occupation, all three cities were subjected to prolonged air raids. Even if commerce along the Yangtse had been proceeding without these interruptions the three gunboats would have had little to do. Their original role had been the protection of British property and trade against Chinese rioters and pirates. Now China and Britain were friends against a hostile Japan, and there were no riots. *Falcon* provided a radio link for the British Embassy at Chungking, but this facility was not required at Ichang or Changsha. There were also extra maintenance and mooring problems at the other two cities. So it was decided that *Sandpiper* (who had completed her last refit in June 1937) should be laid up at Changsha. Her crew was withdrawn via a perilous overland route to the sea at Ningpo, part of the journey being completed in passenger-carrying wheelbarrows. *Gannet* was ordered to leave Ichang and move upriver to Chungking where she would be decommissioned. Two half-crews from her and *Falcon* (the men who had been longest in China) would be withdrawn and the rest accommodated in *Falcon*, who would remain in commission.

On December 19th, 1939 the German liner *Columbus* was scuttled off Cape Hatteras in the Atlantic, a distant event which resulted in yet another incident between Japan and Britain. Some of the *Columbus* survivors were reservists and technicians, important members of the German war effort. They made their way across neutral America and took ship to Honolulu. There they boarded the Nippon Yusen Kaisha liner *Asama Maru* bound for Yokohama, whence they would cross to Korea and travel back to Germany via the Trans-Siberia Railway Their intended journey was known to British Intelligence. On 21st January they were nearing the end of their Pacific voyage, being thirty-five miles off Nozaki, a town in the Chiba Prefecture. Fujiyama was already in sight, but they were still outside territorial waters when stopped by the cruiser *Liverpool* in bitterly cold weather. Twenty-one Germans were taken off the liner and put in the cruiser's cells and cable locker. The *Liverpool*'s crew noted with some satisfaction that the most arrogant Nazi became the most seasick when they passed through a storm en route to Hong Kong.

The Japanese were furious and said that the interception was a personal affront to the Emperor because it had taken place within sight of the Sacred Mountain. But it had been outside territorial waters, everything had been conducted in accordance with international law and Japan's rights as a neutral had not been infringed. As reprisal they stopped and searched the British steamer *Wing Sang* off Foochow, but she was not carrying contraband destined for the Chinese and could not be detained. Presently, however, the British Ambassador in Tokyo, Sir Robert Craigie, came to an agreement with the Japanese Government. Of the Germans taken off *Asama Maru*, nine were definitely civilians who were not on their way to join the German armed forces. They were later returned to *Asama Maru* herself outside Yokohama on February 29th. For their part, the Japanese promised to refuse passage in their ships to German reservists and technicians. They expressed the hope that the British Government would avoid taking action in intercepting non-contraband goods or civilian passengers bound for Germany, when in Japanese waters. In a further reply the British Government stated that they had no wish to offend Japan, but they would continue to exercise their rights as a belligerent. The Royal Navy would carry out its duty in preventing war material from reaching Vladivostock, whence it might find its way overland to Germany. The British authorities maintained that the Sea of Japan and the wide straits leading into it did not constitute Japanese territorial waters, but were legally regarded as the high seas.

This exchange of Notes tended to conceal from the general public the fact that both sides were diplomatically satisfied, while Britain had really won a bloodless victory. Although some Germans were smuggled through, on the whole the Japanese kept their promise and the Royal Navy was relieved of the necessity of maintaining a force of cruisers in the Pacific. From the Japanese point of view, the agreement served as a reminder to Hitler that they did not approve of his alliance with Soviet Russia.

Meanwhile preparations had been going ahead for the withdrawal of the two half-crews from *Falcon* and *Gannet* at Chungking. Four officers and fifty ratings would travel by road to Kunming and then over the Yunnan Railway into French Indo-China. This was the plan, although they had to carry enough provisions to live on independently along the road to Kunming, and then right through Burma, in case Japanese bombing had completely cut the Yunnan Railway. These provisions were in addition to a quantity of naval stores that had to be returned to Hong Kong for various reasons. The Asiatic Petroleum Company's installation about nine miles below Chungking ran a well-maintained fleet of trucks and ten vehicles were hired from them, together with experienced Chinese drivers. Officers and men were not to wear visible uniforms, so padded Chinese gowns and jackets, balaclavas and insubstantial coarse-haired boots were bought and issued. They were to prove quite adequate, even in the cold weather of the mountains. Plenty of travel and identity documents for personnel, stores, baggage and lorries were provided by the Consul-General, but were never required once on the road.

Because overnight accommodation was scarce on the road journey, two convoys of five lorries each were formed. One truck, loaded with stores and baggage, carried the commanding officer and one petty officer with the rest of the half-party travelling in the remaining four. Lashed-up hammocks were used to form a fairly warm and comfortable nest in the back of the trucks. Commander A. F. St. G. Orpen's convoy with *Gannet*'s half-crew left on the morning of January 22nd. Lieutenant J. A. McClure followed with *Falcon*'s half-crew next day. Both mornings were cold and wet. Despite their official anonymity each lorry of the second convoy bore, in chalk, the proud slogan '*Falcon*'s Mystery Tour'.

As the road ran through magnificent mountains at a height of 3000–6000 feet, there was a good deal of ice. This, combined with steep gradients, narrow width, unmetalled surface, hairpin bends, sheer precipices and numerous wrecks, was not very soothing to the nerves. Still, the drivers were skilful and each day's journey ended before dark. At each night's stop, the commanding officer called on the local military authorities and his request for guards for the lorries was always granted. Conversations were conducted in a mixture of Mandarin Chinese and French, but there was never any lack of understanding. They slept in local inns, most of which (except for the one in the beautiful city of Kutsing) were primitive, dirty and infested with rats who seemed to spend the night jumping on top of the sleepers. The hairy boots afforded some protection against these and other vermin, while boiling water was always available. Unlimited quantities of eggs and cooked chicken could be bought at very low prices. The rum ration at the end of the day was a boon and so too was a stiff whisky before the early morning starts.

In spite of the discomforts the journey was enjoyable and full of interest. They were held up for two hours at one icebound pass and there was one minor accident in which a seaman broke his nose, but otherwise everything went according to plan. They arrived at Kunming in the afternoons of January 28th and 29th respectively, in warm sunny weather. The British Consul-General had arranged accommodation in excellent French hotels and the small British community lavished hospitality on them during their stay. The trucks were emptied and filled with naval stores destined for *Falcon* back at Chungking while the travellers' stores and baggage were loaded into a railway wagon.

The French had built, and were operating the steam-hauled, single-track Yunnan Railway which ran between Kunming, Lao Kai, Hanoi and Haiphong. The northern half dropped from the Yunnan Plateau through the mountains to the flatter, jungle country to the south. On the mountainous stretch there were one hundred and seventy-two tunnels and one hundred and seven major bridges, the most spectacular being the Butterfly Bridge (two inverted cantilevers spanning a gorge with a tunnel at each end) and the Lace Bridge (a tall and graceful lattice structure with a tunnel at the northern end). The journey to the Chinese Indo-China frontier promised superb views. It also promised trouble. Japanese bombing had destroyed one bridge, but a shuttle service was operating either side of the damaged section.

Coaches had been reserved on a train which left Kunming at 08.00 hrs on January 31st and that evening they reached the wrecked bridge. It was still under repair, so all the passengers and their gear had to be transferred to another train waiting on the far side. Next day they crossed the Lace Bridge about 14.30 hrs and just beyond waited in a loopline at Paochai Station for a northbound train to pass. Immediately after it had gone by, they heard the familiar drone of Japanese bombers. Everyone jumped out and threw themselves down on the embankment while two waves of twenty-seven bombers made unopposed attacks on the Lace Bridge from about 5,000 feet.

Although the gorge below was pitted with craters, the Lace Bridge was undamaged, while the northbound train had taken cover in the short tunnel. This was its undoing. Bombs had burst in the tunnel mouth at each end and their blast had totally shattered the heavy wooden carriages. The tunnel was pitch dark and full of choking dust and smoke, from which came the cries of the injured. There were some torches but most of the rescue work had to be done by feel and sound. The heavier baulks of timber could not be dislodged and protruding limbs which felt cold when touched were left. Others, dangling, had to be snipped off by the doctors before their owners could be moved. In the engine was the grisly sight of the driver and fireman roasting against the firebox where they had been hurled. After three hours the sailors and local Chinese had extricated about a hundred casualties and had carried them to the southbound train. This was less than half the number known to be on the train and did not include any of the French passengers. The train arrived at Lao Kai about 00.30 hrs. The casualties were taken to the French hospital, the two Royal Navy doctors helping there for the rest of the night.

Next evening their train reached Gai Lam Junction near Hanoi where they were met by the Director of the Railway and the ADC to the Governor of Tongking. A special rail car was laid on for the last lap to Haiphong where a heroes' welcome awaited them. A fleet of bicyclettes-pousse-pousse (trishaws) whisked them to the docks and the local British community raised a fund to give everyone a night ashore before sailing in the ss *Yu Sang*. Butterfield and Swire provided a free quart of beer a day for each man during the three-day passage to Hong Kong. Presently they boarded a P & O liner, bound for the United Kingdom; their China adventures were over.

The gunboat *Scarab* had also been instructed to leave the Yangtse at the end of 1939, but these orders were rescinded because of the danger from winter storms in the open sea. She therefore stayed at Shanghai and sailed for Hong Kong in the spring of 1940. The perils of the sea would still have to be faced and the Germans would make life very hazardous, but as the coastline of the Yangtse Estuary disappeared astern, her commanding officer was content that for the next few days at least, he would not have to worry about sandbanks and sampans, junks and Japanese permits. Gradually he became aware of a growing commotion on the foc'sle. The Chinese crew-members kept pointing ahead and making a great deal of fuss about something, so Petty Officer Ah Ching was called up to the bridge for an explanation. He pointed to a line in the water far ahead and replied 'The crew believe we will fall over the edge of the world'.

Lieutenant-Commander Robertson-Aikman realized what had caused this fear. For hundreds of square miles beyond the estuary, the China Sea is muddied by the silt brought down by the Yangtse. By some trick of the currents there is an abrupt contrast between the khaki water of the Yangtse Estuary and the blue of the salt-water sea. Some of the Chinese crew-members had spent twenty years in the service of the Royal Navy – and had never seen the sea. *Scarab*'s captain explained the situation, but the Chinese remained unconvinced. As the gunboat approached the dividing line, they hung on to stanchions and ladders, ready for the everlasting drop they knew must come. *Scarab* came up to the line and passed over on to the clear water. The Chinese opened their eyes. They had not fallen. The water held the ship up even though it was clear. There was no mud or silt in it. It was as clear as water out of a tap. Therefore it must be drinking water. The next commotion came when they decided to try it out and found that it was not drinking water.

In May 1940 the Japanese in Central China recommenced their drive on Ichang, *Falcon* calling there before they occupied the city. Returning upriver she spent most of the summer at Tan Chia To where *Gannet* lay empty and lifeless. They checked her condition and put in some time at the local tennis courts before proceeding the last few miles to *Falcon*'s usual berth at the Butterfield and Swire pontoon opposite Chungking. There she remained, unharmed by continuous Japanese bombing which was directed more towards the part of Chungking overlooking the Kialing River. Their life was enlivened by two incidents: once they entertained Sir Stafford Cripps during a stopover on his journey through China and Russia and once *Falcon* hid a Gaullist seaman from the Vichy French gunboat *Balny*. There was also a rather memorable cricket match. With only two runs to go *Falcon*'s First Lieutenant responded to his partner's 'Come on!' and was run out. The watching Chinese, already baffled by this strange British ceremony, were amazed to see one phlegmatic Englishman chasing his fellow-countryman, waving a cricket bat and threatening all sorts of dire fates.

Life was even quieter for those warships patrolling from Hong Kong. Once *Durban* went to help the salvage vessel *Marie Moller*, who had been hit by a shell off Haimen and then arrested by the Japanese for alleged gunrunning. *Durban*'s captain could speak Japanese and sent across Lieutenant Bayly bearing a letter written in Japanese. They were so pleased that anyone could converse in their language that they expressed their regrets, explained that the shell had been fired at some junks in the harbour and released the merchantman next day. Captain J. A. S. Eccles later admitted that it was the only time he had found his interpreter's course to be of any value.

By now the China Squadron was virtually an Indian Ocean or East Indies force—a fact that was recognized when Admiral Noble moved his flag to Singapore. The cruisers operating from there, *Emerald*, *Enterprise*, (both of the East Indies Fleet) *Danae*, *Durban* and *Dauntless* spent most of their time patrolling the trade routes searching for raiders or waiting to intercept blockade runners. The US Pacific Fleet had been formed and was based at Hawaii, but the British warships saw more of the French Indo-China Squadron. Their two cruisers, four sloops and a submarine helped search for German raiders reported to be operating in the Indian and Pacific Oceans. This assistance ended when France fell. Vice-Admiral Jean Decroux, a Vichy sympathiser, opposed the Gaullist Governor of Indo-China (General Georges Catroux) and refused to take his squadron to Singapore. However, Admiral Noble and Admiral Decroux agreed to refrain from undertaking warlike activities against each other on the China Station. No French merchantman which might be employed as an armed merchant cruiser was to go to Japan and in return the Royal Navy promised that no French merchantman would be stopped except for the purpose of flag verification. There were also reciprocal agreements on bunkering facilities in Malaya, Hong Kong and Indo-China together with a mutual agreement to abstain from anti-British and anti-Vichy propaganda.

The possibility of a German invasion of the British Isles and the Italian entry into the war necessitated even more withdrawals of troops and ships from the Far East. British forces were now so weak that they dared not run the slightest risk of offending the Japanese whose ambitions and admiration of the Germans had taken on a new lease of life. The United Kingdom therefore 'eased off' on the conversations being held with the Dutch Navy, lest they give the appearance of preparing concerted action against Japan. Then in July, in response to fresh pressure from the Japanese, Britain agreed to close the Burma Road 'pending negotiations for a wider settlement between Japan and China'. And in August, the Japanese threat appeared so dangerous, and Britain so beleaguered, that the Chiefs of Staff suggested to the Prime Minister, Winston Churchill, that if Japan decided to eliminate all British interests in China (including Hong Kong itself), we should submit without going to war.

On August 7th Admiral Decroux became Governor of Indo-China, thus establishing Vichy rule there. Speaking through this government, the Germans insisted that no ships could leave Vichy territory without their permission. As retaliation three French ships were held at Hong Kong until British merchantmen detained in Indo-Chinese ports were released. This period of strain did not last long and in September normal trade was resumed between Hong Kong and Indo-China. Of course, all foreign ships were liable to be intercepted by the Japanese if suspected of smuggling contraband to the Chinese, or if they did not hold the correct papers.

Vice-Admiral Sir Geoffrey Layton had hoisted his flag at Singapore as Commander-in-Chief, China Station, on 12th September. For the rest of 1940 he was concerned with investigating reports of German raiders in the Indian and Pacific Oceans, but his chief preoccupation remained the Japanese threat. On September 22nd the Japanese 2nd China Expeditionary Fleet landed troops at Haiphong and occupied the province of Tongking. In theory this was carried out by agreement with Vichy, but some Frenchmen put up a certain amount of resistance. The immediate result was the reimposition of a trade embargo between Indo-China and Hong Kong. This was relaxed later and commerce allowed between Saigon and Hong Kong, provided that all goods were transhipped at Kwangchow. It was inconvenient but both parties needed that trade.

The next Japanese step was a direct challenge to Britain. Although so many warships had been withdrawn from the Far East, the Royal Navy was taking a much longer-term view. In 1939 the cinema on the island of Liukungtao at Wei-

The Hitler War

Hai-Wei had been dismantled and taken to Singapore in the depot ship *Medway* for reinstallation at the Naval Base Canteen there. The other Royal Navy buildings on Liukungtao, normally used as a sanatorium, canteen and recreational centre, were now empty, but remained in the charge of a care and maintenance party. The old Chinese dockyard was already in Japanese hands. The British property was in fact leased from the Chinese Government, the lease being due to expire on September 30th, 1940. Negotiations were conducted with Chiang Kai-Shek's Government at Chungking and on October 1st the lease was renewed for a further ten years. Unfortunately, the Japanese-controlled puppet government of China at Nanking refused to recognize either Chiang Kai-Shek or his agreements. The same day as the renewal came into force, the Japanese announced that British interests had terminated there on September 30th and they were taking over the whole island for reasons of military necessity. Sixty Chinese sailors and Japanese marines were therefore landed on Liukungtao from the cruiser *Iwate* and the British property occupied. Faced with this impossible situation, the British Government announced that all Royal Navy personnel and stores would be removed forthwith from Liukungtao.

Her ports seized, those few still open blockaded, her rivers blocked, her roads cut, her railways destroyed, her cities occupied or in ruins, China still fought on. Her government had made many protests about the closure of the Burma Road and on October 18th, when Britain was in a slightly stronger position at home, it was reopened. Some of the first travellers out of China, were a small group of *Falcon*'s crew returning home via Lashio. In the reverse direction went stores and arms, many now from America, as China had appealed to the USA for aid. Alliances were being re-forged on the other side, too, with the announcement of the Mutual Assistance Pact between Japan, Germany and Italy.

14
The Deterrent is Despatched

At the beginning of 1941, it was hoped that Hong Kong might be reinforced, but later the British Government reluctantly decided that the colony must be considered expendable. Mr Churchill even considered withdrawing those few troops that were still there, but it was pointed out that such a move would be noticeable and dangerous. They must hold Hong Kong for as long as possible, but it could never be regarded as more than an outpost – its defence having no real bearing on the final outcome of the war. Its true fate would be decided at the post-war conference table.

China was having even greater difficulties. At long last the precarious United Front between Chiang Kai-Shek and Mao Tse-Tung had broken down. In many areas, especially in the northern and central provinces, bitter three-cornered fights between Nationalists, Communists and Japanese were raging. The Japanese Army took as little part in this as possible, letting the two warring factions spill each other's blood. The Japanese then undertook a whole new series of amphibious operations, making further cuts in Chiang Kai-Shek's regional supply lines right round the coast from Peihai to Ningpo. They also occupied Saigon and part of southern French Indo-China, following up this success by infiltrating Siam – a strategic threat to Malaya, Burma and the East Indies. Unknown to outsiders the Japanese Army had already begun jungle training, while the Japanese Navy was preparing for their attack on Pearl Harbor. Their rear was safeguarded by the Japanese-Soviet Neutrality Pact and by Germany's assault on Russia.

The Powers endangered by the worsening situation now took steps to defend themselves, beginning with a number of international and inter-service discussions. They stressed the importance of air power and the desirability of a united front for the preservation of the East Indies. Hong Kong would be abandoned and China must also be expended. However, lease-lend to Chiang Kai-Shek was stepped up via Rangoon, the Irrawaddy, Mandalay, the Burma Railway and the Burma Road to Lashio, Kunming and Chungking. All these bottlenecks caused huge stockpiles to be built up at Rangoon and the opportunities for pilfering and 'sidetracking' multiplied. It has been estimated that two-thirds of the supplies despatched never reached Chungking. Most of what did arrive was used by Chiang Kai-Shek to bribe warlords, although the scale of this corruption was either unknown or not admitted at the time.

The Deterrent is Despatched

More directly, the USA, the United Kingdom and the Netherlands froze all Japanese assets. Now Japan could not obtain raw materials from abroad, especially petroleum and must now inevitably stop dead within two years unless she went to war to seize the natural resources she needed or unless she obtained them by diplomatic means. To this end, discussions were opened with the United States, but attempts at friendlier relations failed. Simply, America demanded the withdrawal of all Japanese forces from China. Japan refused this and demanded recognition of her 'New Order in East Asia'. The result was an impasse and a growing Japanese belief that America was the chief enemy that must be eliminated.

Britain, however, was still not to be discounted. The outbreak of war in 1939, the threat of invasion in 1940 and Axis expansion in the Mediterranean had lent strength to the Admiralty's insistence that the bulk of the Royal Navy be retained in European waters. The creation of the Far Eastern Fleet had been postponed repeatedly until the question was raised again on 25th August 1941, about the time forecast by the Admiralty for sending at least one capital ship to Singapore. On that date, Mr Churchill (now Prime Minister after holding the office of First Lord of the Admiralty) sent a memorandum to the First Sea Lord. He suggested that the time was now ripe for the despatch of a small squadron of the Royal Navy's best ships to the Indian Ocean before Japanese aggression actually took place.

Admiral of the Fleet, Sir Dudley Pound, replied that by April 1942 a task force formed around the capital ships *Nelson*, *Rodney* and *Renown* and the carriers *Hermes* and *Ark Royal* would be operating from Ceylon, while the four surviving R-class battleships would be available for covering troop convoys in the Indian Ocean. The Prime Minister did not consider that this plan was entirely satisfactory. It would be necessary to have fast capital ships operating from Singapore to deal with any modern Japanese battleships acting as commerce raiders. In spite of protests from the First Sea Lord and the Commander-in-Chief Home Fleet (Admiral Sir John Tovey) that the new King George V-class battleships were needed in European waters to watch the German battleship *Tirpitz*, it was decided that *Prince of Wales* should be sent to Singapore to join the lighter forces already east of Suez.

Prince of Wales would be accompanied by the battlecruiser *Repulse*, this latter ship being relieved later by her modernized sister *Renown*. The carrier *Indomitable* should have provided air cover, but she had been temporarily disabled while working up in the West Indies. *Prince of Wales* sailed without her, but with an escort of two destroyers, *Electra* and *Express*. *Repulse* had already left England escorting a convoy to the Indian Ocean, where she met *Prince of Wales* and her destroyers. They were also joined by the destroyers *Encounter* and *Jupiter* from the Mediterranean.

While this force was bound for the Far East, the most threatening Japanese moves and speeches heightened the belief that they would attack South East Asia only. There was a counter-suggestion that Japan might first strike Russia, already weakened by Germany's invasion but a Japanese onslaught eastwards across the Pacific was not considered. However, in the tense situation it was desirable that all noncombatants should be encouraged to leave. Even the neutral French left Indo-China in special evacuation convoys to Madagascar. (They also sailed the ss *Francis L. D.* to Casablanca with 6,700 tons of rubber. She was officially bound for Kure, but the cargo was apparently destined for Germany.) British wives and children were voluntarily evacuated from Shanghai and Hong Kong in phases – although not all left – and were taken to Australia, the Philippines and Burma. A China Station destroyer usually provided an escort on such journeys. The gunboat *Seamew* was also allowed to leave Canton in September 1941, and departed for the Persian Gulf, being escorted as far as Jesselton by the destroyer *Thracian*.

This last ship was one of the few Royal Navy vessels still left in Chinese waters. There were two other old destroyers, *Thanet* and *Scout*, the four gunboats *Moth*, *Tern*, *Robin* and *Cicala*, a handful of harbour craft, the immovable *Tamar* and the 2nd MTB Flotilla. This group of fast boats continually carried out practice high-speed attacks on each other day and night, risking – and experiencing – collisions in the darkness. But they all persisted, preparing and ready to play active roles in the defence of Hong Kong.

Opinion in the colony was divided on the possibility of Japanese attack. Some uninformed people, lulled into false security by over-confident propaganda, still believed that the inefficient and myopic Japanese would never take on both Britain and America, especially since the arrival of Canadian reinforcements at Hong Kong. Others, who had seen the Japanese in action and noted the gradual escalation of Japanese aggression from personal insults to global strategy, remarked on the Japanese warships ceaselessly watching Hong Kong from just outside the 3-mile limit. *Thracian*, when not minelaying, had frequently shadowed Japanese convoys and had brought back full details of their composition and direction. Her reports, plus interception of radio traffic, showed that the Japanese were now building up their forces in Siam and Indo-China. South East Asia was definitely the target. In that case the United States Asiatic Fleet (two cruisers, thirteen destroyers, seventeen submarines and twenty-four seaplanes) would strike at the Japanese expeditions against the Philippines and Hong Kong. The Americans would then leave their base in the Philippines and retire to Singapore – a move they did not relish. There they would join three D-class cruisers and the Dutch warships (three cruisers, six destroyers and eleven submarines). They would be expected to hold out for eighty days, by which time the British Eastern Fleet would have arrived, the China Station would be officially disbanded and Admiral Layton would go home. The only problem was a big question. 'What

The Deterrent is Despatched

constituted a Japanese act of war directly harmful to all the Allies?' No one could answer.

Meanwhile the Allied forces in the Indian Ocean were being built up and on December 2nd the Eastern Fleet arrived at Singapore. Admiral Sir Tom Phillips had left his flagship at Colombo and flown on ahead to Singapore and Manila for conversations with Admiral Hart, Commander-in-Chief of the American Asiatic Fleet. By now British, American, Dutch and Free French naval forces had eleven battleships in the Pacific and Far East compared with ten Japanese capital ships. There were thirty-six Allied cruisers, a hundred destroyers and sixty-nine submarines, while the Japanese had thirty-six cruisers, one hundred and thirteen destroyers and sixty-three submarines. There were however only three Allied aircraft- and seaplane-carriers, compared with sixteen Japanese – the only disparity, which perhaps seemed of lesser consequence at the time.

If Admiral Phillips' squadron had been able to show the flag on a series of peaceful cruises in the waters of the Far East, it would no doubt have impressed friendly and neutral Asiatics, and might perhaps have acted as a deterrent to Japanese ambition. Certainly the Japanese considered that the Royal Navy still exercised a profound influence on the Oriental mind and much of their anti-British propaganda was directed towards belittling British warships. It would not look very good if the British built up a battlefleet in the Far East as big as Japan's. However, unknown to any except the ships' companies, the material condition of the newly-arrived squadron was not really of the high standard it should have been. A defect in *Jupiter*'s fuel tanks caused her to list ten degrees when full of oil, while *Encounter*'s hull had been damaged by some previous grounding or strain. Both these destroyers had to be taken into dockyard hands as soon as they arrived at Singapore. *Express* and *Electra* were relatively modern destroyers, but had been hard worked since the beginning of the war, while *Repulse* was a veteran of the First World War. *Prince of Wales* had been completed in May 1941 but she had spent so much time on special missions or in dock under repair that it had seriously interfered with her working up to full efficiency.

Yet this squadron was only intended to be the first instalment of a well-balanced fleet comprising seven capital ships, one carrier, ten cruisers and twenty-four destroyers – the final goal of planning that had begun early in 1939 and proposed even long before that. These ships, operating from Singapore and in distant co-operation with the United States Navy at Pearl Harbor, were intended to be the main defences of their own base, rather than the guns of the fortress itself. But the Japanese were not waiting until the British Far Eastern Fleet had been assembled. Western realists were convinced that it was only a matter of time before the Japanese struck somewhere. No one possibly imagined that they would strike at all their objectives simultaneously.

15
The End of an Era

For many months now *Peterel* had been at Shanghai acting as a floating radio-station for the British Consulate ashore. The breech blocks had long been removed from her 3-inch guns and her sole armament was now two Lewis guns.

Soon after 04.00 hrs on December 8th 1941 a Japanese demand for surrender was rejected by Lieutenant S. Polkinghorn, who had just received news of a Japanese attack on Pearl Harbor. As the Japanese launch moved away, the cruiser *Idzumo*, a destroyer, a gunboat and various shore batteries opened a furious fire on the British ship. Her crew immediately set about burning confidential books in the furnaces and completed their preparations for scuttling the ship. On deck the Lewis guns fired back at the aggressors. Hit many times at point blank range, she caught fire, the demolition charges blew up and *Peterel* sank beneath the foul waters of the Whangpoo.

The Rising Sun was approaching its zenith. When it set, there would indeed be a new order in Asia.

The Appendices

These list the ships under the command of the Flag Officer, China Station; they do not include vessels from other commands passing through the China Station, nor do they include East Indies warships based at Singapore at the same time as those of the China Station. They do include a large number of lightly armed converted merchant vessels which were specially commissioned for the European War. Of only limited value, they were officially on the strength of the China Station, but never moved far from the waters around Singapore. Indeed, after 1939, even the fleet units of the China Station spent more time patrolling the East Indies and Indian Ocean than the coasts of China.

I The Royal Navy on the China Station. July 1937 - August 1939

5TH CRUISER SQUADRON
Cumberland (launched 1926; displacement 10,000 tons; armament 8–8in, 6–4in, 4–3pdr, 4–2pdr, 4–MG, 8–Lewis MG, 3 Walruses of No 715 Squadron; left September 1938).
Danae (1918; 4,850 tons; 6–6in, 3–4in, 4–3pdr, 2–2pdr, 2–MG, 8–Lewis MG, 12–TT; left October 1937).
Capetown (1919; 4,290 tons; 5–6in, 2–3in, 2–3pdr, 2–2pdr, 2–MG, 8–Lewis MG, 8–TT; left April 1938).
Suffolk (as *Cumberland*; left April 1939).
Dorsetshire (1929; 9,900 tons; 8–8in, 4–4in, 4–3pdr, 16 smaller, 8–TT, 1 Walrus; arrived October 1937).
Birmingham (1936; 9,100 tons; 12–6in, 8–4in, 4–3pdr, 16 smaller, 6–TT, 3 Walruses; arrived March 1938).
Kent (1926; 9,850 tons; 8–8in, 8–4in, 4–3pdr, 1 Walrus; arrived August 1938).

Cardiff (1917; 4,290 tons; 5–6in, 2–3in, 2–3pdr, 8–TT; arrived September 1938; left May 1939).
Cornwall (1926; 10,000 tons; 8–8in, 8–4in, 4–3pdr, 16 smaller, 2 Walruses; arrived April 1939).

8TH DESTROYER FLOTILLA
Duncan (1932; 1,400 tons; 4–4.7in, 1–3in, 6 smaller, 8–TT).
Delight (1932; 1,375 tons; armament as *Duncan*).
Diamond (as *Delight*).
Diana (as *Delight*).
Duchess (as *Delight*).
Decoy (as *Delight*).
Dainty (as *Delight*).
Daring (as *Delight*).
Defender (as *Delight*).

4TH SUBMARINE FLOTILLA
Medway (depot ship; 1928; 15,000 tons; 6–4in, 4–3pdr, 8 smaller).
Westcott (destroyer; 1918; 4–4in, 2–2pdr, 1–MG, 4–Lewis MG, 6–TT).
Osiris (1928; 1,475/2,030 tons; 1–4in,

2–MG, 8–TT; left August 1937).
Oswald (as *Osiris*).
Odin (as *Osiris*).
Olympus (as *Osiris*).
Orpheus (as *Osiris*).
Otus (as *Osiris*).
Pandora (1929; 1,475/2,040 tons; armament as *Osiris*).
Parthian (as *Pandora*).
Perseus (as *Pandora*).
Phoenix (as *Pandora*).
Proteus (as *Pandora*).
Rainbow (1930; 1,472/2,015 tons; armament as *Osiris*).
Regent (as *Rainbow*).
Regulus (as *Rainbow*).
Rover (as *Rainbow*).
Rorqual (1936; 1,520/2,157 tons; 1–4in, 2–MG, 6–TT; arrived August 1937).
Grampus (as *Rorqual*; arrived August 1937).
ESCORT VESSELS
Folkestone (1930; 1,045 tons; 2–4in, 2–3pdr).
Sandwich (1928; rest as *Folkestone*).
Falmouth (1932; 1,060 tons; 1–4in, 4–3pdr).
Grimsby (1933; 990 tons; 2–4·7in, 1–3in, 4–3pdr, 10–MG; left July 1939).
Lowestoft (1934; rest as *Grimsby*).
Bideford (1931; 1,105 tons; 2–4in, 4–3pdr; arrived June 1939).
YANGTSE GUNBOATS
Bee (1916; 625 tons; 2–3in, 2–3pdr; scrapped March 1939).
Aphis (1915; 625 tons; 2–6in, 1–3in, 10 smaller).
Cockchafer (as *Aphis*).
Cricket (as *Aphis*).
Gnat (as *Aphis*).
Ladybird (as *Aphis*).
Mantis (as *Aphis*).
Scarab (as *Aphis*).
Falcon (1931; 372 tons; 1–3·7in howitzer, 2–6pdr, 10–MG).

Gannet (1927; 310 tons; 2–3in).
Peterel (as *Gannet*).
Sandpiper (1933; 185 tons; 1–3·7in howitzer, 9 smaller).
Tern (1927; 262 tons; 2–3in, 8–MG).
Scorpion (1937; 700 tons; 2–4in, 1–3·7in howitzer, 2–3pdr, 10 smaller; arrived November 1938).
Dragonfly (1938; 585 tons; 2–4in, 1–3·7in howitzer, 8–MG; arrived June 1939).
Grasshopper (1939; rest as *Dragonfly*; arrived June 1939).
WEST RIVER GUNBOATS
Tarantula (1915; 625 tons; 1–6in, 1–3in, 2–3pdr).
Cicala (as *Aphis*).
Moth (as *Aphis*).
Seamew (as *Tern*).
Robin (1934; 226 tons; 1–3·7 howitzer, 9 smaller).
HONG KONG LOCAL DEFENCE DESTROYERS
Thracian (1920; 905 tons; 2–4in, 1–2pdr, 1–MG, 4–Lewis MG).
Tenedos (1918; rest as *Thracian*; arrived March 1938).
Thanet (as *Tenedos*; arrived June 1938).
Scout (as *Tenedos*; arrived December 1938).
2ND MOTOR TORPEDO-BOAT FLOTILLA (HONG KONG)
MTB7 (1937; 18 tons; 8–Lewis MG, 2 torpedoes; arrived October 1938).
MTB8 (as *MTB7*; arrived September 1938).
MTB9 (as *MTB7*; arrived October 1938).
MTB10 (as *MTB7*; arrived October 1938).
MTB11 (as *MTB7*; arrived October 1938).
MTB12 (as *MTB7*; arrived October 1938).
HONG KONG LOCAL DEFENCE AND HARBOUR CRAFT, ETC
Aldgate (mooring vessel; 1934; 290 tons).

Alliance (tug; 1910; 615 tons).
Barnet (boom working trawler; 1919; 583 tons; 1–3in; left end 1938).
C406 (steam pinnace).
C409 (tug named *Sir W. Jervaise*; 200 tons).
Cherub (lighter-cum-tank vessel; 390 tons).
Cornflower (RNVR drill sloop; 1916; 1,175 tons; 2–4in, 4–3pdr).
Moorlake (mooring steamer; 1919; 767 tons).
Poet Chaucer (tug).
Redstart (minelayer; 1938; 498 tons; arrived November 1938).
Tamar (ex-troopship used as base ship; 1873; 4,650 tons; 6–6pdr).
Watergate (as *Aldgate*).
Barlight (boom defence vessel; 1938; 730 tons; 1–3in; arrived early 1939).

2ND MINESWEEPING FLOTILLA
(SINGAPORE RESERVE)

Abingdon (1918; 710 tons; 1–4in, 1–12pdr).
Aberdare (as *Abingdon*).
Bagshot (as *Abingdon*).
Derby (as *Abingdon*).
Fareham (as *Abingdon*).
Stoke (as *Abingdon*).
Harrow (as *Abingdon*).
Widnes (as *Abingdon*).
Huntley (1919; rest as *Abingdon*).

SINGAPORE LOCAL DEFENCE AND HARBOUR CRAFT, ETC

Buffalo (mooring steamer; 1916; 750 tons).
C450 (steam launch).
C451 (lighter).
Dowgate (1935; as *Aldgate*).
Fastnet (boom working trawler; 1919; 639 tons; 1–3in).
Laburnum (1915; as *Cornflower*).
Ludgate (as *Aldgate*).
Ruthenia (oiler used as refuelling jetty; 1900; 12,788 tons).
Terror (monitor used as base ship; 1916; 7,200 tons; 2–15in, 8–4in, 2–3in, 8 smaller, 1 Walrus).
Loch Long (tug; arrived early 1938).
Barricade (as *Barlight*; arrived October 1938).
Barlane (as *Barlight*; arrived early 1939).

OTHER VESSELS

Adventure (minelayer; 1924; 6,740 tons; 4–4·7in, 4–3pdr, 20–MG; left October 1938).
Appleleaf (oiler; 1917; 12,370 tons).
Eagle (aircraft carrier; 1918; 22,600 tons; 9–6in, 4–4in, 4–3pdr, 15 smaller, 18 Swordfish of Nos 813 and 824 Squadrons).
Ebonol (oiler; 1917; 2,392 tons).
Francol (oiler; 1917; 5,620 tons).
Herald (survey ship; 1918; 1–3pdr).
Pearleaf (oiler; 1917, 12,270 tons).
St Breock (tug; 1919; 820 tons).
St Monance (as *St Breock*).
St Just (as *St Breock*; arrived April 1938).

WUHU

C407 (oil barge).

II The Royal Navy on the China Station. September 1939

5TH CRUISER SQUADRON
Dorsetshire
Birmingham
Kent
Cornwall

8TH DESTROYER FLOTILLA
Decoy
Dainty
Daring
Defender

4TH SUBMARINE FLOTILLA
Medway
Westcott
Odin
Olympus

Orpheus
Otus
Pandora
Parthian
Perseus
Phoenix
Proteus
Rainbow
Regent
Regulus
Rover
Rorqual
Grampus

ESCORT VESSELS

Folkestone
Sandwich
Falmouth
Lowestoft
Bideford

YANGTSE GUNBOATS

Scorpion
Aphis
Cockchafer
Cricket
Gnat
Ladybird
Mantis
Scarab
Falcon
Gannet
Peterel
Sandpiper
Tern
Dragonfly
Grasshopper

WEST RIVER GUNBOATS

Tarantula
Cicala
Moth
Seamew
Robin

HONG KONG LOCAL DEFENCE DESTROYERS

Thracian
Tenedos
Thanet

Scout

2ND MOTOR TORPEDO BOAT FLOTILLA
(HONG KONG)

MTB7
MTB8
MTB9
MTB10
MTB11
MTB12
MTB26 (1938; 14 tons; 2–Lewis MG, 2 torpedoes).
MTB27 (as *MTB26*).

HONG KONG LOCAL DEFENCE AND HARBOUR CRAFT, ETC

Aldgate
Alliance
C406
C409
Cherub
Cornflower
Moorlake
Poet Chaucer
Redstart
Tamar
Watergate
Barlight

2ND MINESWEEPING FLOTILLA
(SINGAPORE RESERVE)

Abingdon
Aberdare
Bagshot
Derby
Fareham
Stoke
Harrow
Widnes
Huntley

SINGAPORE LOCAL DEFENCE AND HARBOUR CRAFT, ETC

Buffalo
C450
C451
Dowgate
Fastnet
Laburnum

Ludgate
Ruthenia
Terror
Loch Long
Barricade
Barlane
Raub (auxiliary patrol vessel; 1926; 1,161 tons 1–4 in, 1–Lewis MG).
OTHER VESSELS
Appleleaf
Eagle
Ebonol
Francol
Herald
Pearleaf
St Breock
St Monance
St Just
WUHU
C407

III The Royal Navy on the China Station. October 1939–November 1941

5TH CRUISER SQUADRON
Birmingham (left January 1940).
Kent (left late 1939).
Arawa (AMC; 1922; 14,462 tons; 7–6in, 2–3in; arrived October 1939; left August 1940).
Moreton Bay (AMC; 1921; 14,193 tons; 7–6in, 2–3in; arrived October 1939; left August 1940).
Liverpool (1937; 9,400 tons; 12–6in, 8–4in, 8–2pdr, 8–MG, 6–TT, 2 Walruses of No 714 Flight; arrived November 1939; left April 1940).
Danae (arrived November 1939).
Durban (1919; 4,850 tons; 6–6in, 3–4in, 2–2pdr, 12–TT, arrived November 1939).
Dauntless (1918; rest as *Durban*; arrived November 1939).
Kanimbla (AMC; 1936; 10,985 tons; 6–6in, 2–3in; arrived November 1939; left August 1940).
Manoora (AMC; 1935; 10,856 tons; 8–6in, 2–3 in; arrived March 1940; left April 1940).
Ceres (1917; 4,190 tons; 5–6in, 2–3in, 2–2pdr, 8–TT; arrived April 1940; left May 1940).
Colombo (1918; 4,290 tons; 8–4in, 4–2pdr, 8–MG; arrived April 1940; left May 1940).
Westralia (AMC; 1929; 8,108 tons; 8–6in, 2–3in; arrived April 1940; left May 1940).
4TH SUBMARINE FLOTILLA
Medway (left April 1940).
Westcott (left December 1939).
Pandora (left March 1940).
Perseus (left June 1940).
Proteus (left March 1940).
Rainbow (left June 1940).
Rover (left August 1940).
Rorqual (left April 1940).
Grampus (left April 1940).
ESCORT VESSELS
Falmouth (left April 1940).
GUNBOATS
Scorpion
Aphis (left March 1940).
Cockchafer (left April 1940).
Cricket (left November 1940).
Gnat (left April 1940).
Ladybird (left March 1940).
Mantis (for disposal March 1940).
Scarab
Falcon (laid up March 1941).
Gannet (laid up January 1940).
Peterel
Sandpiper (laid up January 1940).
Tern
Dragonfly
Grasshopper
Tarantula (left December 1940).
Cicala
Moth
Seamew (left September 1941).

Robin

SINGAPORE AND HONG KONG DEFENCE

DESTROYERS

Thracian
Tenedos
Thanet
Scout
Stronghold (1919; rest as *Thracian*; arrived end 1939).

2ND MOTOR TORPEDO BOAT FLOTILLA (HONG KONG)

MTB7
MTB8
MTB9
MTB10
MTB11
MTB12
MTB26
MTB27

HONG KONG AUXILIARY PATROL VESSELS, ETC

Kai Ming (in service August 1941).
Swanley (1924; 5,004 tons; in service August 1941).

HONG KONG AUXILIARY MINESWEEPERS, ETC

Indira (tug; 1918; 637 tons; in service January 1941).
Han Wo (tug; 1919; 248 tons; in service January 1941).
Shun Wo (tug; 1917; 220 tons; in service January 1941).
Minnie Moller (tug; 1909; 377 tons; in service January 1941).
St Sampson (tug; 1919; 451 tons; in service January 1941).
St Aubin (tug; 1918; 468 tons; in service January 1941).
Margaret (1929; 248 tons; in service January 1941).
Poseidon (1914; 696 tons; in service January 1941).
Perla (1903; 346 tons; in service January 1941).

HONG KONG LOCAL DEFENCE AND HARBOUR CRAFT, ETC

Aldgate
Alliance
C406
C409
Cherub (stricken July 1940).
Cornflower
Moorlake
Poet Chaucer
Redstart
Tamar
Watergate
Barlight
Wave (tug-tanker; 1939; 300 tons; in service early 1940?).
Manyeung (auxiliary minelayer; ex-ferry; 1933; 371 tons; in service August 1940).
Chunghsing (accommodation ship for Chinese ratings; 1922; 2,558 tons; in service August 1941).
Way Foong (boom defence tender; in service August 1941).

SINGAPORE AUXILIARY PATROL VESSELS, ETC

Raub
Lipis (1927; 845 tons; in service late 1939).
Tien Kwang (1925; 787 tons; in service May 1940).
Shu Kwang (1924; 788 tons; in service May 1940).
Fuh Wo (1922; 955 tons; in service July 1940).
Li Wo (1938; 707 tons; 1–4in; in service July 1940).
Wo Kwang (tug; 1927; 350 tons; in service July 1940).
Kudat (1914; 1,725 tons; in service 1940).
Larut (1927; 894 tons; in service 1940).
Tung Wo (1914; 1,337 tons; in service 1940).
Vyner Brooke (1928; 1,670 tons; in service 1940).

The Appendices

OK (motor launch; in service January 1941).
Pangkor (1929; 1,250 tons; in service February 1941).
Bulan (1924; 1,048 tons; –Lewis MG; in service late 1939).
Ping Wo (1922; 3,105 tons; in service April 1941).
Giang Bee (1908; 1,646 tons; in service April 1941).
Kelana (300 tons; in service April 1941).
Siang Wo (1926; 2,595 tons; in service April 1941).
Mata Hari (1915; 1,020 tons; 1–Lewis MG; in service late 1939).
Fanling (in service June 1941).
Hungjao (in service June 1941).
Ban Hong Liong (1908; 1,671 tons; in service August 1941).
Kuala (1911; 954 tons; in service August 1941).
Kampar (paddle steamer; 1915; 971 tons; in service August 1941).
Sylvia (motor launch; in service September 1941).
Simit (in service September 1941).
Rhoda (in service September 1941).
Shun An (in service September 1941).
Tenggaroh (yacht).

STRAITS SETTLEMENTS RNVR MOTOR LAUNCHES
Pahlawan (1939; 60 tons; 1–3pdr, 1–Lewis MG; in service February 1941).
Panglima (as *Pahlawan*; in service February 1941).
Pengawal (as *Pahlawan*; in service February 1941).
Penghambat (as *Pahlawan*; in service February 1941).
Pengail (= *Panji?*) (as *Pahlawan*; in service February 1941).
Peningat (as *Pahlawan*; in service March 1941).

2ND MINESWEEPING FLOTILLA (SINGAPORE)
Abingdon (left March 1940).
Aberdare (left February 1941).
Bagshot (left March 1940).
Derby (left March 1940).
Fareham (left March 1940).
Stoke (left March 1940).
Harrow (left March 1941).
Widnes (left February 1940).
Huntley (left February 1940).

21ST MINESWEEPING FLOTILLA (SINGAPORE)
Burnie (1940; 650 tons; 1–4in, 1–20mm, 4–Lewis MG; arrived July 1941).
Gouldburn (as *Burnie*; arrived July 1941).

SINGAPORE AUXILIARY MINESWEEPERS, ETC
Jarak (1927; 208 tons; in service 1941).
Changteh (tug; 1914; 1,244 tons; in service January 1941).
Gemas (1925; 207 tons; in service January 1941).
Huatong (1927; 208 tons; in service January 1941).
Jeram (1927; 210 tons; in service January 1941).
Jerantut (1927; 217 tons; in service January 1941).
Malacca (1927; 211 tons; in service January 1941).
Rahman (1926; 209 tons; in service January 1941).
Sin Aik Lee (1928; 198 tons; in service January 1941).
Tapah (1926; 208 tons; in service January 1941).
Trang (whaler; 205 tons; in service January 1941).
Circe (1912; 778 tons; 1–4in; in service January 1941).
Medusa (1913; 793 tons; in service January 1941).

Banka (1914; 623 tons; in service February 1941).
Scott Harley (1913; 620 tons; in service February 1941).
Klias (1927; 207 tons; in service April 1941).
Prince (in service August 1941).
Vulture (in service August 1941).

SINGAPORE LOCAL DEFENCE AND HARBOUR CRAFT, ETC

Buffalo (mined April 1941).
C450
C451
Dowgate
Fastnet
Laburnum
Ludgate
Ruthenia
Terror (left early 1940).
Loch Long
Barricade
Barlane
Herald
Barrier (as *Barlight*; arrived late 1939).
Endeavour (survey ship employed as depot ship; 1912; 1,280 tons; arrived March 1940).
Kwang Ming (in service August 1940).
Whangpu (depot ship; 1920; 3,204 tons; in service 1940).
Pelandok (depot ship; in service February 1941).
Kung Wo (minelayer; 1921; 4,636 tons; in service March 1941).
Yin Ping (tug; 1914; 191 tons).
Sui Wo (depot ship; 1896; 2,672 tons).

OTHER VESSELS

Appleleaf
Ebonol
Francol
Pearleaf
St Breock
St Monance (left 1940/41).
St Just

St Dominic (as *St Breock*; in service late 1939).

SHANGHAI

Ah Ming (tug; 1931; 93 tons; in service January 1941).

WUHU

C407

IV The Warships of the China Station December 1941 and their Immediate Fate

THE EASTERN FLEET (SINGAPORE)

Prince of Wales (battleship; 1939; 35,000 tons; 10–14in, 16–5·25in, 48–2pdr, 16–20mm, 2 Walruses) sunk by air attack.
Repulse (battlecruiser; 1916; 32,000 tons; 6–15in, 20–4in, 16–2pdr, 8–TT, 2 Walruses) sunk by air attack.
Danae escaped.
Durban escaped.
Dragon (as *Danae*) escaped.
Mauritius (cruiser; 1939; 8,000 tons; 12–6in, 8–4in, 9–2pdr, 8–MG, 6–TT; refitting) escaped.
Kanimbla escaped.
Manoora escaped.
Jupiter (destroyer; 1938; 1,690 tons; 6–4·7in, 4–2pdr, 8–MG, 10–TT) sunk by surface vessels.
Electra (destroyer; 1934; 1,375 tons; 4–4·7in, 8–MG, 8–TT) sunk by surface vessels.
Encounter (as *Electra*) sunk by surface vessels
Express (as *Electra*) escaped.
Tenedos sunk by air attack.
Vampire (destroyer; 1917; 1,090 tons; 4–4in, 1–2pdr, 6–TT) sunk by air attack.
Vendetta (as *Vampire*) escaped.
Isis (destroyer; 1936; 4–4in, 8–MG, 10–TT; refitting) escaped.
Rover (refitting) escaped.
Anking (base ship; 1925; 3,472 tons) sunk by surface vessels.

The Appendices

Appleleaf escaped.
Ebonol scuttled.
Francol sunk by surface vessels.
Pearleaf escaped.

SINGAPORE LOCAL DEFENCE

Stronghold sunk by surface vessels.
Scorpion sunk by surface vessels.
Dragonfly sunk by air attack.
Grasshopper sunk by air attack.
HDML1062 (harbour defence motor launch; 50 tons; 1–1pdr, 4–Lewis MG) sunk by surface vessels.
HDML1063 (as *HDML1062*) sunk by surface vessels.
ML310 (motor launch; 73 tons; 1–3pdr, 2–Lewis MG) lost off Singapore.
ML311 (as *ML310*) sunk by surface vessels.
MMS51 (motor minesweeper; 165 tons; 2–Lewis MG) sunk by surface vessels.

SINGAPORE AUXILIARY PATROL VESSELS, ETC

Raub sunk by air attack.
Lipis lost off Singapore.
Fuh Wo lost off Singapore.
Li Wo sunk by surface vessels.
Wo Kwang lost off Singapore.
Kudat sunk by air attack.
Larut sunk by air attack.
Tung Wo lost off Singapore.
Vyner Brooke sunk by air attack.
OK fate unknown.
Pangkor escaped.
Bulan escaped.
Ping Wo escaped.
Giang Bee lost off Singapore.
Kelana bombed and scuttled.
Siang Wo sunk by air attack.
Mata Hari captured.
Fanling fate unknown.
Hungjao fate unknown.
Ban Hong Liong escaped.
Kuala sunk by air attack.
Sylvia fate unknown.
Simit fate unknown.
Rhoda fate unknown.
Shun An fate unknown.
Tenggaroh lost off Singapore.
Seekingjas (motor launch) fate unknown.

STRAITS SETTLEMENT RNVR MOTOR LAUNCHES

Pahlawan escaped.
Panglima escaped.
Pengawal escaped.
Penghambat lost off Singapore.
Pengail/Panji? escaped.
Peningat lost off Singapore

21ST MINESWEEPING FLOTILLA (SINGAPORE)

Burnie escaped.
Gouldburn escaped.
Bendigo (1941; rest as *Burnie*) escaped.
Maryborough (as *Burnie*) escaped.

SINGAPORE AUXILIARY MINESWEEPERS, ETC

Jarak scuttled.
Changteh sunk by air attack.
Gemas damaged, then scuttled.
Huatong sunk by air attack.
Jeram captured at Singapore.
Jerantut scuttled.
Malacca scuttled.
Rahman lost at Batavia.
Sin Aik Lee lost off Singapore.
Tapah lost off Singapore.
Trang scuttled.
Circe escaped.
Medusa escaped.
Banka lost off Malaya.
Scott Harley lost in the Indian Ocean.
Klias scuttled.
Prince fate unknown.
Vulture fate unknown.
Springdale (deperming vessel; 1937; 1,597 tons) escaped.

SINGAPORE HARBOUR CRAFT, ETC

C450 fate unknown.
C451 fate unknown.
Dowgate scuttled.
Fastnet abandoned at Batavia.

Laburnum lost at Singapore.
Ludgate scuttled.
Ruthenia scuttled.
Loch Long fate unknown.
Barricade escaped.
Barlane escaped.
Herald scuttled.
Barrier escaped.
Endeavour escaped.
Whang Pu escaped.
Pelandok fate unknown.
Kung Wo sunk by air attack.
Yin Ping sunk by surface vessels.
St Breock sunk by air attack.
St Just scuttled.
Sui Wo lost at Singapore.
Chuting (tug; 1921; 207 tons) fate unknown.
Wuchang (depot ship; 1914; 3,204 tons) escaped.

VESSELS UNDER CONSTRUCTION OR CONVERSION AT SINGAPORE

HDML1096 (as *HDML1062*) lost incomplete.
HDML1187 (as *HDML1062*) lost on stocks.
HDML1168 (as *HDML1062*) lost on stocks.
HDML1169 (as *HDML1062*) lost on stocks.
HDML1170 (as *HDML1062*) lost on stocks.
HDML1213 (as *HDML1062*) existence uncertain.
HDML1214 (as *HDML1062*) existence uncertain.
HDML1215 (as *HDML1062*) existence uncertain.
HDML1216 (as *HDML1062*) existence uncertain.
HDML1217 (as *HDML1062*) existence uncertain.
HDML1218 (as *HDML1062*) existence uncertain.
HDML1219 (as *HDML1062*) existence uncertain.
HDML1220 (as *HDML1062*) existence uncertain.
Lantaka (tug; 300 tons) lost on stocks.
M7 (minelayer; 346 tons) lost on stocks.
ML362 (as *ML310*) lost on stocks.
ML363 (as *ML310*) lost on stocks.
ML364 (as *ML310*) lost on stocks.
ML365 (as *ML310*) lost on stocks.
ML372 (as *ML310*) lost on stocks.
ML373 (as *ML310*) lost on stocks.
ML374 (as *ML310*) lost on stocks.
ML375 (as *ML310*) lost on stocks.
ML388 (as *ML310*) destroyed on stocks.
ML389 (as *ML310*) destroyed on stocks.
ML432 (as *ML310*) destroyed on stocks.
ML433 (as *ML310*) destroyed on stocks.
MMS52 (as *MMS51*) blown up on stocks.
MMS93 (as *MMS51*) destroyed on stocks.
MMS94 (as *MMS51*) destroyed on stocks.
MMS125 (as *MMS51*) destroyed on stocks.
MMS126 (as *MMS51*) destroyed on stocks.
MMS127 (as *MMS51*) destroyed on stocks.
MMS166 (as *MMS51*) destroyed on stocks.
Moorwind (mooring vessel; 1,000 tons) lost on stocks.
Rhu (minelayer; 1940; 254 tons) lost fitting out.

TRENGGANU LOCAL DEFENCE
Tien Kwang lost off Singapore.
Shu Kwang sunk by air attack.

PENANG LOCAL DEFENCE
Kampar sunk by air attack.

The Appendices

HONG KONG LOCAL DEFENCE
Thracian wrecked and scuttled.
Thanet sunk by surface vessels.
Scout escaped.
Tern scuttled.
Cicala sunk by air attack.
Moth scuttled.
Robin scuttled.

2ND MOTOR TORPEDO BOAT FLOTILLA (HONG KONG)
MTB7 damaged and scuttled.
MTB8 sunk by air attack.
MTB9 scuttled.
MTB10 scuttled.
MTB11 scuttled.
MTB12 sunk by surface vessels.
MTB26 sunk by surface vessels.
MTB27 scuttled.

HONG KONG AUXILIARY PATROL VESSELS, ETC
Kai Ming fate unknown.
Swanley fate unknown.

HONG KONG AUXILIARY MINESWEEPERS, ETC
Indira sunk by air attack.
Han Wo fate unknown.
Shun Wo fate unknown.
Minnie Moller lost off Hong Kong.
St Sampson escaped.
St Aubin escaped.
Margaret fate unknown.
Poseidon fate unknown.
Perla fate unknown.

HONG KONG HARBOUR CRAFT, ETC
Aldgate scuttled.
Alliance lost at Hong Kong.
C406 fate unknown.
C409 fate unknown.
Cornflower sunk by air attack.
Moorlake escaped?
Poet Chaucer fate unknown.
Redstart scuttled.
Tamar scuttled.
Watergate scuttled.
Barlight scuttled.
Wave escaped?
Manyeung fate unknown.
Chunghsing fate unknown.
Way Foong fate unknown.

VESSELS UNDER CONSTRUCTION OR CONVERSION AT HONG KONG
Grinder (as *Lantaka*) captured on stocks.
Lantan (minesweeper; 672 tons) captured on stocks.
Lyemun (as *Lantan*) scuttled soon after launch.
ML376 (as *ML310*) destroyed on stocks.
ML377 (as *ML310*) destroyed on stocks.
ML434 (as *ML310*) destroyed on stocks.
ML435 (as *ML310*) destroyed on stocks.
MMS95 (as *MMS51*) destroyed on stocks.
MMS96 (as *MMS51*) destroyed on stocks.
MMS123 (as *MMS51*) destroyed on stocks.
MMS124 (as *MMS51*) destroyed on stocks.
Moorberry (as *Moorwind*) destroyed on stocks.
Skilful (as *Lantaka*) destroyed on stocks.
Taitam (as *Lantan*) captured on stocks.
Waglan (as *Lantan*) captured on stocks.

SHANGHAI
Mantis captured while awaiting scrapping.
Peterel sunk by surface vessels and shore artillery.
St Dominic lost off Saddle Islands.
Ah Ming fate unknown.
Kwang Ming fate unknown.

CHUNGKING
Falcon transferred to Chinese Navy.
Gannet transferred to Chinese Navy.

CHANGSHA
Sandpiper transferred to Chinese Navy.

WUHU
C407 fate unknown.

Index of Ships

This index does not include the appendices and the list of capital ships on page 109

Adventure, 28, 77–9, 82, 88
Ah Ming, 116
Akashi, 35
Akitsu Maru, 131
Alliance, 88
Amiral Charner, 96
André Lebon, 138
An Lee, 43
Annaliese Essberger, 138
Aphis, 29, 51, 86, 114, 140
Appleleaf, 89, 137
Aramis, 120
Ark Royal, 149
Asama Maru, 43–4, 141
Asheville, 119–20, 127
Ashigara, 113
Ataka, 61–2
Augusta, 37, 40–1, 60, 63

Balny, 145
Barker, 45
Barnet, 28
Bee, 29, 56, 59–62, 83, 88–90, 103
Birmingham, 58, 76–8, 82, 88–90, 105, 111–13, 117–20, 132, 135–40
Breconshire, 111
Bremerhaven, 84
Bruce, 53
Bulmer, 119
Burgenland, 138

Capetown, 29, 34, 46–50, 63–5, 71–2, 77
Cardiff, 111
Chengyang, 56–7
Chenonceaux, 88
Chiang Hsing, 82
Chitral, 29
Chokai, 117
Christine Moller, 84
Cicala, 29, 33–4, 48, 82, 101–2, 132, 150
Cockchafer, 29, 47, 77, 91, 104, 116, 140
Columbus, 141

Comorin, 69
Conte Verde, 43
Cornflower, 28, 43, 69, 111
Cornwall, 120, 130, 137–9
Cricket, 29, 45, 56–60, 63, 69, 75–6, 90, 104, 140
Cumberland, 29, 34–43, 51–4, 69–70, 78, 88–90

Dainty, 29, 105
Danae, 29–31, 34–41, 52, 140, 145
Daring, 29, 78
Dauntless, 138–40, 145
Decoy, 29, 54, 78, 87
Defender, 29, 42–3, 78, 119
Delight, 29, 34–5, 40–1, 45, 78, 105
Diamond, 29, 43, 78, 121, 130
Diana, 29, 50, 81
Don Pedro, 79
Dorsetshire, 29, 66–7, 78–9, 82, 89, 119, 139
Dragonfly, 140
Duchess, 29, 36, 40–3, 52, 73, 78, 120
Duncan, 29, 36, 41, 78, 89, 119, 132
Dunera, 136
Durban, 140, 145

Eagle, 28, 54, 65, 78–9, 82, 105, 111, 137–9
Edsall, 119
Electra, 149–51
Elsa Essberger, 138
Emerald, 145
Émile Bertin, 119
Empress of Asia, 40
Empress of Canada, 40
Encounter, 149–50
Enterprise, 77, 145
Ermanno Carlotto, 115
Express, 149–50

Falcon, 28, 93, 112, 132, 140–7
Falmouth, 29, 36–7, 40–3, 70, 79, 101–2, 111–12, 127–8, 136–7
Fausang, 50
Folkestone, 29, 53, 57, 63, 66, 78, 90

Foo Shing, 12
Francis-Garnier, 96
Francis, L. D., 150
Francol, 51, 138–9
Franken, 137
Fuh Wo, 33
Fuso, 117
Fuso Maru, 35

Gannet, 28, 33, 88, 93, 112, 132–3, 140–2
Gnat, 29, 64, 82, 96–8, 100, 138–40
Grampus, 78, 137
Grasshopper, 120, 140
Grimsby, 29, 34–5, 87, 128
Guam, 196

Haian, 80
Hai Cheng, 80
Hai Kong, 84
Haitan, 120–1
Hansa, 84–6
Harmatris, 130
Haruna Maru, 73
Hatsushimo, 114
Herald, 28
Hermes, 149
Hobart, 137
Hozu, 161–2
Hsin Chang Wo, 133
Hupeh, 84
Hyuga, 117

Idzumo, 12, 36–7, 41, 152
Indomitable, 149
Ise, 117
Iwate, 147

Jupiter, 149–51

Kaga, 92
Kaiser-i-Hind, 69
Kaitangata, 51
Kamoi, 54
Kanome, 117
Kasasagi, 61–2, 65
Katori, 117
Kent, 88–90, 105, 111, 120, 140
Kiang Wo, 133
Kia Wo, 50, 88, 132–3
Kirishima, 117
Kongo, 117
Kuma, 79, 89
Kung Wo, 63
Kut Wo, 47, 93

Ladybird, 29, 56–63, 114, 131, 135, 140
Laestrygon, 49, 93, 96–9
Lamotte-Picquet, 117–19
Liverpool, 140–1
Loong Wo, 82
Lowestoft, 29, 41, 73–5, 128–30
Luzon, 130

Mantis, 29, 80, 97–9, 140
Marblehead, 119
Marian Moller, 73
Marie Moller, 145
Maron, 36, 40
Medway, 28, 40, 111, 137, 147
Mei An, 61
Mei Ping, 61
Mei Shia, 61
Minesweeper No 17, 101–2
Minesweeper No 18, 102
Monocacy, 77
Moorlake, 77
Moreton Bay, 139
Moth, 29, 92, 112, 150
Mutsu, 117
Myoko, 69, 89, 102, 117

Nachi, 117
Nadakaze, 117
Nagato, 117
Nanning, 51
Naruto Maru, 115
Natori, 117
Nelson, 149
Notoro, 54

Oahu, 62–3, 80, 114
Odin, 27, 78, 137
Olympus, 27, 137
Ootori, 61–2
Orpheus, 27
Osiris, 27
Oswald, 27
Otus, 27, 78

Panay, 58–65
Pandora, 27, 139
Pao-Hua, 99
Parthian, 28, 40, 78, 137
Patroclus, 40
Perseus, 28, 78
Peterel, 28, 93, 96–9, 104, 118, 152
Phoenix, 28, 78
Pillsbury, 127
Poochi, 53

Index of Ships

Pope, 127
President Hoover, 43
Prince of Wales, 149–51
Proteus, 28

Raimondo Montecuccoli, 89
Rainbow, 28, 78, 138
Rajputana, 40
Ranchi, 52
Ranpura, 120
Regent, 28, 137
Regulus, 28
Renown, 149
Repulse, 149–51
Robin, 29, 101–2, 150
Rodney, 149
Rorqual, 78, 137
Rosalie Moller, 45
Rover, 28, 137
Ryujo Maru, 35

Sagres, 118–19
St Breock, 28, 43, 52, 78, 132, 137
St Vincent De Paul, 112–13
Sandpiper, 29, 45, 79–80, 95, 140
Sandro Sandri, 85
Sandwich, 29, 35, 45, 67–72, 128–30, 136–7
Saucy, 85
Sauerland, 120
Scarab, 29, 56–62, 80, 84–9, 116–17, 122–6, 140, 144
Scharnhorst, 138
Scorpion, 103, 119, 140
Scout, 119, 127, 150
Seamew, 29, 102, 111, 150
Seistan, 119
Shasi, 93
Shengking, 40
Shimakaze, 117
Shinai, 134
Shinsu Maru, 35
Shiokaze, 117
Shu Kwang, 58
Shun Wo, 85
Siangtan, 93

Siang Wo, 127
Sirdhana, 137
Suffolk, 29, 36, 39, 43–4, 51, 66–7, 70, 76–8, 82, 89
Sui-An, 55
Sui Wo, 58, 122
Suzuya, 117

Takasaki, 35
Taksang, 53
Talamba, 43
Tamar, 28, 52, 105, 111, 150
Tarantula, 29, 82, 92, 131, 140
Tatsuta, 117
Tatung, 57
Tenedos, 133–4
Tenryu, 117
Tern, 28, 93, 96–8, 124–6, 150
Thanet, 88, 112, 127, 150
Thracian, 29, 35, 44, 51–2, 118–19, 127, 136, 150
Tin Sang, 33
Tirpitz, 149
Tseang Tah, 58
Tsubame, 117
Tsurugizaki, 35
Tuck Wo, 56–7
Tung Wo, 75–6, 85–6, 119
Tutuila, 132

Victoria, 85–6

Wantung, 56, 60, 63, 112
Westcott, 28, 31, 43–4, 51, 78, 134
Whangpu, 58
Wing Sang, 141
Woosung, 50, 64, 99
Wuchang, 102
Wuhu, 122
Wulin, 82, 138

Yamakaze, 86
Yochow, 67, 112
Yolande, 71–2
Yu Sang, 144

RENEWALS 458-4574